FINANCIAL
FREEDOM

FINANCIAL FREEDOM

*A 7-Stage Plan to Outsmart the Future and
Fulfil Your Retirement Dreams*

Bernice Cohen

ORION BUSINESS
BOOKS

Previous books by the author:

The Cultural Science of Man (3 volumes)
The Edge of Chaos
The Armchair Investor
The Money Maze

Copyright © 1999 by Bernice Cohen

All rights reserved

The right of Bernice Cohen to be identified as the author of
this work has been asserted by her in accordance with
the Copyright, Designs and Patents Act 1988.

This edition first published in Great Britain in 1999 by
Orion Business
An imprint of The Orion Publishing Group Ltd
Orion House, 5 Upper St Martin's Lane, London WC2H 9EA

A CIP catalogue record for this book
is available from the British Library.

ISBN 0-75282-098-2

Filmset by Selwood Systems, Midsomer Norton
Printed and bound in Great Britain by
Butler & Tanner Ltd, Frome and London

To my wonderful mother –
just ninety-two years young
and always smiling

Contents

THE PATH TO FINANCIAL FREEDOM

STAGE 1
STEP INTO
RETIREMENT: AVOID
DRIFTING

STAGE 2
PUT YOUR HOUSE
IN ORDER

STAGE 3
BUILD AN INCOME
TO RELY ON

STAGE 4
CREATE A LUMP
SUM FOR CAPITAL

STAGE 5
PREPARE FOR LIFE –
LONG OR SHORT

STAGE 6
PASS DOWN YOUR
NEST EGGS

STAGE 7
TACKLE THE DETAIL

WELCOME TO THE WORLD OF FINANCIAL FREEDOM!

INTRODUCTION

Retirement Should Work For You

*'I don't have time to get out the charts and show you
how the world works'*

Jim Rogers to CNBC-TV's *Square Box* host, Mark Haines

When I set out to write *Financial Freedom*, I wondered how it would differ from my previous books on personal finance. Was there anything new to say without repeating the same topics again?

As I wrote in *The Money Maze*, everyone climbs an investment staircase, from age ten years to sixty plus. Changing circumstances and different phases of family life place differing demands on one's **income** and savings, even though we all have similar financial goals: everyone hopes to achieve a secure and rising income together with a **capital** sum of money (terms highlighted in bold are defined in the glossary at the end of the book) large enough to allow for major luxury items or to pay for emergency events. These key objectives are the main foundations for designing your personal financial pyramid. For retirement planning, your pyramid consists of three major building blocks; owning your own home, building your **pension** as a secure replacement income and creating a lump sum of capital.

Within these universal aims, I believe long-term planning for retirement is a special task. Surprisingly, it is relevant to everyone; for people in their twenties, with a whole working life before them, to those in their thirties, coping with the demands of a growing family. For people in their forties approaching a career peak, active planning for a sound retirement makes even more sense, although it is still years away, while sensible planning really becomes important for those in their fifties as the children leave home and working life is nearing an end.

Extended Retirements

In future, achieving a long, happy retirement may not be a straight-forward process. Whatever your current situation, it is bound to involve money. Your retirement might last thirty or more years, possibly longer than an average working life, so it is vital to address the main issues. Avoid simply drifting into a period which can be the most exciting, but challenging time of your life.

Since retirement will probably occupy a large slice of your future life, it makes good sense to give yourself plenty of time to plan. The more time you allow, the better the final result can be. Even if you are so close to retirement that there is little time left for planning, by following the seven logical Stages outlined here, you can achieve measurable improvements in your prospects. Then, your financial assets will start working constructively for you once you are no longer working for them.

When you follow a planning path, step by step, you gain the confidence which comes from knowing you are working systematically towards your goals. You will gain that advantage by using *Financial Freedom* to guide you one step at a time, through the seven key Stages of effective retirement financial planning. Together, the seven Stages form the basis of your personal retirement blueprint; to help you prepare your own master plan and put you in continuous control of your finances. The purpose of *Financial Freedom* is to guide you along the paths professionals use if they manage your financial affairs. Learning these skills will help you to behave more like a professional financial adviser. When you have a collection of valuable assets, savings and investments, whether you realise it or not, you have become a fund manager, in charge of your own portfolio funds. You may hope to delegate this responsibility, but ultimately, the success or failure of managing your portfolio rests with you. It is clearly important to know how to manage it properly so it will serve you well throughout retirement.

'I have a lot of energy – I think I could work till I'm 100. No one is going to dictate to me when I'm going to retire. It's my call.'
Maria Fiorini Ramirez, President,
Maria Fiorini Ramirez Capital, Inc

A Growing Army of Retirees

By 2006 an estimated third of the UK population will be over fifty. When this detail came to light during research for one of the television programmes for Channel 4, *Mrs Cohen's Money*, it evoked a personal thought: in 2006 my mother would celebrate her hundredth birthday.

I still have a vivid memory of a steady trickle of over-eighties turning up to collect their weekly pensions at the local post office during a filming session for another of those television programmes. While chatting with some of them, it was clear that many live a hand-to-mouth existence on their state pension, perhaps topped up by housing benefit or income support. They had

'What the poor lack is money.'
Old Chinese saying

2

an air of sad resignation towards the state which has so obviously failed their expectations of a comprehensive welfare system. After decades of promises by politicians that the state would care for people 'from the cradle to the grave' for millions of today's pensioners, the reality is a bitter disappointment.

The Ageing Revolution

Small numbers of people lived into their seventies or beyond in earlier centuries, but the twentieth century is unique. Today it is the many, not the few, who can confidently expect to enjoy a ripe old age, as the retirement life span for millions has grown by an unprecedented amount and can now extend to forty years. At the standard retirement age of sixty-five, a man in good health can still anticipate many productive years.

Longevity acquires a new dimension for citizens of wealthy industrialised nations, like Britain, America and Western Europe, born in this century. Just think, when a centenarian of today was born around the year 1899 a motor car was a rare and incredible curiosity; there were no aeroplanes, computers, radios, televisions or cinemas; electricity was still a recent novelty, so no one had electric kettles, fridge freezers, washing machines or central heating systems: even the humble plastic bag had not yet been invented.

When the welfare state was first introduced between 1946 and 1948, today's sixty-year-old was hardly into adolescence while any one of the 8,000 centenarians would have been approaching fifty – precisely the age at which serious retirement planning should already be producing positive results.

How many of today's centenarians have enjoyed all the potential advantages such a prolonged retirement can offer? As the numbers of centenarians rise this is not a rhetorical question. By 2020, there will be about 30,000 centenarians. Sadly, however, some of them could be among today's disillusioned eighty-year-olds, struggling on a dwindling state pension.

Don't worry about how the future will turn out; it is out of your control. Think about what you're going to do now to get where you want to be in your future

Increasing longevity has resulted from extensive improvements in healthcare and better nutrition, reducing death tolls in childhood and middle age so more people live out a full life span. The bible describes a human life as three score years and ten, but improving living conditions mean a full life span now stretches to four score years or more. The 1998 *Social Trends* annual report forecast the numbers of over sixty-fives would reach 12 million by 2021, up from 9.3 million in 1996. By 2008, they will outnumber the under-sixteens for the first time.

If you retire after forty working years, anticipating a further twenty to thirty years ahead, will this be an exhilarating opportunity for a life of ease, comfort and financial security, or a daunting prospect where time is the only thing in plentiful supply? Poverty is a miserable constraint, curtailing your enjoyment of all the liberating freedoms additional time allows. Lack of money makes empty time drag and a lengthy retirement will then fall far short of your long-treasured aspirations.

Two Phases of Retirement

Increasing longevity highlights the idea of the 'young old' and the 'old old', separating people in their sixties and seventies from the over-eighties. Most of the 'young old' are fit and actively able, while more of the over-eighties are frail, debilitated or dependent on family, neighbours or the state for support.

Many of today's 'old old' probably never imagined that they would reach such a ripe age. Perhaps they would have paid more attention to planning if they had realised how lengthy their retirements would be. We must be forewarned by their experience and recognise the possibility that embarking upon retirement, probably during our sixties could be a long, eventful journey. We must plan thoughtfully if we want to ensure it is also a deeply enriching and fulfilling journey. This is where *Financial Freedom* begins. It is a seven Stage plan designed to guide you logically through all the important aspects of retirement financial planning. This plan forms the basis of your own retirement master plan.

The Rising Cost of Ageing

Forty years ago, the life expectancy for a man who retired at sixty-five was much lower than today. Moreover many lived little more than another three to five years. If men in their late sixties were calculated to die so soon after leaving full-time work, the state commitment to providing lifetime pensions was reasonably affordable. Had they factored longevity of today's proportions into their equations, the welfare state's founding fathers might have baulked at its formidable costs.

Similar demographic changes affect the whole industrialised world. Within ten years, in Japan, one in three people will be over sixty. For comparison, in Iran in 1998, 75 per cent of the population was below twenty-five. Across western Europe demographic changes similar to those in Japan threaten a financing problem for the continued provision of state pensions. Falling numbers of workers, supporting a larger and increasing retired population create a contribution gap, especially in France and Germany, where the retired draw around two-thirds of average national incomes as state pensions. This highly attractive outcome is not sustainable: in Italy, in 1995, almost 14 per cent of national income (officially termed **Gross Domestic Product**) was paid out as pensions: in Germany, the corresponding figure was 11.1 per cent, but in Britain it was 4.5 per cent, only marginally above the lowest level of 3.6 per cent in Ireland.

The British government introduced two measures to reduce future costs of state-funded pensions. First, they altered the date at which all women who were born after 6 April 1950 can draw their pensions. Women will be treated equally to men, and must reach age sixty-five before they draw a state pension. While this measure only affects around half of future pensioners, the second measure, severing the link between pensions and average earnings affects them all. Pension increases are now tied to the current rate of **inflation**, that is, to rising prices. This was a truly detrimental step for all state pensioners, because in the wider economy, average earnings tend to rise faster than prices. Productivity gains and product improvements from technology, produce economic growth, which ripples out across the whole economy and working people naturally want their pay, and hence their standard of living to rise in **real** terms, that is, after accounting for inflation. Without this lift to average earnings, living standards for some workers would be frozen at a set level which does not reflect further rises for the general population. This is the actual outcome that occurs for everyone whose income or earnings are linked only to inflation.

Since 1981, this is the sorry fate that has befallen the state pension in Britain. Our European partners continue to enjoy excellent levels of state pensions, but British pensioners have been drastically short-changed by the state, although unfortunately, very few understand this outcome. Even before 1981 the UK state pension was comparatively miserly, but since that date its value has shrunk alarmingly. The state pension in 1981 was equivalent to 21 per cent of average earnings (compared to around 60 per cent for French or German state pensions), but by 1998 its value had fallen to a mere 15.4 per cent. On current estimates, it will fall to around 10 per cent or less of average earnings over the next two decades. As a result of this measure, the burden on UK tax-payers has fallen, but the sad truth is, British people are financially naive. They have totally failed to understand the dire consequences of this one (among many) detrimental government action.

'When people cease to complain, they cease to think.'
Napoleon Bonaparte

The 'Haves' and 'Have-nots' Divide
The state pension has drastically declined in **purchasing power**, that is, the amount of goods and services that money will buy. This has created a sad army of around 3 million pensioners who are sinking into relative poverty. The collapse in the real value of the state pension over the past eighteen years has increased the financial plight of millions of elderly folk totally reliant on state pensions, with perhaps some modest supplementary income sources. Alarmingly, as around one half of adults currently have no savings at all, the future for many people approaching old age looks equally bleak. Without a change in attitudes towards personal finance and savings habits, the numbers of seriously poor people will rise remorselessly in Britain.

We might optimistically hope to escape this sorry plight in due course, but it would be foolhardy to be complacent. An NOP survey in 1998 revealed that 36 per cent, or 16 million people, have no regular savings. An additional 4 million save less than £30 a month. In total therefore, about 45 per cent of the population are not making adequate financial provision for their future which surely must include one or two decades in retirement. Among those who save, 27 per cent of adults or 12 million people save over £100 each month.

The £5 billion 'pensions tax' in Labour's 1997 budget means a thirty-year-old needs to pay £20 a month more into his pension plan just to recoup what he lost in that budget

Freedom to Choose

Drastic changes are afoot as politicians try to make ends meet in a cash-strapped welfare state. One popular solution suggests extending working life to seventy or over, so the state has fewer pensionable years to finance. This seems a retrograde step; retirement should be a time for choice. These are the years for rich fulfillment, when we are finally free from the tyranny of work, ready to pursue the hopes and dreams we have harboured throughout our lives. The decision to continue working should be voluntary. After thirty or forty years within a compulsory work environment, it would be better to let people decide their retirement date. Many will want to remain active and in work, but, others, while equally active, will want to branch out into new ventures to make their retirement years productive in ways that were almost impossible during a full working life. However, as in other fields of life, making choices can be expensive, even if you are in command of all the necessary facts to make sensible choices.

Learning Money Skills

The UK population has been poorly served on learning how to manage money. Although successfully handling money is a special skill, it is not part of our school or university curriculum; neither do we learn how to manage the money we earn when we begin our working lives. This is a drastic oversight when you realise that a skilled clerical worker could earn in excess of one million pounds during a forty-year career.

With poor knowledge of money skills, many people arrive at their pre-retirement decade totally ill-equipped to handle large cash sums or plan effectively for future financial security. They have no idea where to start or even what their goals should be. Many simply drift into retirement without recognising the pitfalls that may lie ahead if they have only a small pension and modest savings to rely on.

If you recognise yourself in this description, you are in very good company.

In 1998, a welter of surveys on people's awareness of financial services revealed a lethal mix of apathy and ignorance. Six out of ten people thought that pension payments are tax-free while 28 per cent of unit trust investors thought their fund was guaranteed to outperform deposit accounts. Many people had no idea how savings products worked and six out of ten people did not realise there is a link between the return on an **endowment policy** and the performance of the **stock market**. Even more worrying, most people seemed to have no idea of the various investment options they could use and just under half the people surveyed who did not own any equity-based products were unaware of the existence of **shares** which represent part-ownership in a publicly quoted company listed on an official stock exchange. The level of apathy was disturbingly high. When questioned, most people seemed reluctant to seek help or even shop around. A quarter of savers had not even checked the rate paid on their deposit account over the past three years, few savers consider the product of more than one provider for a personal pension, although several dozen similar products are available, and few savers read the **key features document** that by law has to accompany every endowment and pension policy that is sold.

If you drift into retirement, it may not be the enriching experience you had anticipated

Seven Stages to Financial Freedom

If you have given scant thought to retirement planning as yet, and might therefore enter this, arguably the most crucial period in your life, in a poor financial state, do not despair. Although you may not achieve an ideal result, you will certainly make a noticeable improvement to your finances by following the seven stages outlined in *Financial Freedom*.

When you begin by preparing your unique blueprint and add plenty of enthusiasm, major improvements quickly emerge. Then you gain the confidence of being fully in control of your financial affairs.

If you are tackling retirement planning from scratch, or feel uncertain how to proceed, I suggest you begin by reading through the first six Stages of *Financial Freedom*, for a broad overview of how your plans should progress. Stages 1 to 6 discuss the main issues and principles you need to consider, set out in a logical order. Within each Stage, there is a clearly described series of steps. Depending on your personal circumstances, some of these Stages will be more important than others. After your preliminary reading, take time to work through the areas that most apply to you. When you are more familiar with the key issues set out in Stages 1 to 6, you will be ready to move on to Stage 7. The natural progression that takes you through the seven Stages is shown in the diagram on page viii – it is your planning path to financial freedom.

The Path to Financial Freedom

We begin with Stage 1 – Step into Retirement. Adopting a positive attitude to plan your financial future is the essential first ingredient for success. Whatever you do, avoid just drifting. Stage 2 examines putting both your financial and your real house in order so you are better prepared for your life in retirement. Stage 3 looks at the vital need to build your future sources of secure income, especially your pension. Stage 4 covers creating a lump sum of capital investments to supplement your pension. This Stage provides an indispensable flexibility to your finances. Stage 5 covers the often neglected area of preparing for life, whether the problems are due to dying too soon or living to a ripe old age. Stage 6 considers ways of passing on the nest egg you have built up. Finally, in Stage 7, we tackle the detail, with a practical guide to covering all the key issues previously explored in Stages 1 to 6. Topics covered in Stage 7 are cross referenced back to earlier Stages, to help you select any individual item you want to examine in more detail.

Financial freedom is a truly liberating attainment at any time of life, but it is doubly important for retirement. Achieving financial security right throughout your retirement can provide you with a tremendously exciting hobby which brings its own rewards. Not only will it allow you to develop new skills, but in addition, you will have extra funds to spend and a capital cushion to rely on, no matter how long your retirement lasts.

So let us get started right away by setting out on Stage 1, preparing yourself to step positively into a financially successful retirement.

'Society has produced a medical revolution which extends human life but has failed to create an accompanying financial revolution which sustains it in dignity.'

President John F. Kennedy

Step into Retirement

*'Joseph Fouché's exile lasted more than three years, and the
lonely, inhospitable island to which he was sent is known
as Poverty.'*

Joseph Fouché, Stefan Zweig
(Fouché was Minister of Police for Napoleon)

Retirement can be a daunting prospect. After a long, busy working life are you nervous about the arrival of endless free time? What will you do each day when you finally throw off the work disciplines which are almost second nature? Perhaps you are frustrated by rigid schedules, but as they disappear, do you sense only a great emptiness ahead?

Step 1
Adopt a positive
attitude

DANIEL DRIFTS INTO RETIREMENT

This thought recently struck me when I met Daniel. His whole working life was spent in regional journalism. With two years to retirement, he was relying on his **final salary** (or **defined benefits**) **company pension**. He had not given his future finances much thought. His interests lay in music and rugby, but he had few hobbies. He thought he might fill his days playing golf or spending time with his grandchildren. I wondered how well he would settle to such idleness after years of demanding, twelve-hour working days.

Whether you make plans for it, or ignore it, retirement is bound to bring a massive transformation to your lifestyle. Yet how much more alarming to discover that retirement brings a financial strait-jacket, in addition to a sudden lifestyle readjustment. When your working life is phased out are you worrying that the funds for an enjoyable retirement are missing? Unlike Daniel, perhaps you do not have the guarantees of a final salary company pension after forty years in the same job? In one respect, most people are like Daniel; they either totally

STAGE 1 STEP INTO RETIREMENT

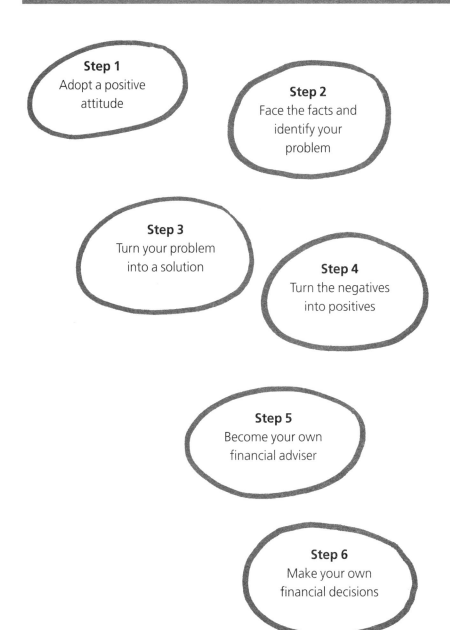

Step 1
Adopt a positive
attitude

Step 2
Face the facts and
identify your
problem

Step 3
Turn your problem
into a solution

Step 4
Turn the negatives
into positives

Step 5
Become your own
financial adviser

Step 6
Make your own
financial decisions

MOVE TO STAGE 2

ignore the financial issues or simply do not know how to judge whether their finances will cope successfully with a prolonged period of leisure time.

Adopt a Positive Attitude

So we start with the first planning Stage: adopt a positive attitude to your forthcoming retirement and resolve not to drift into it in a state of ill-preparedness. If you can face realistically all the relevant facts about your finances, it will free up the paralysis that may have prevented you from dealing with them properly in the past. Managing your money effectively will never be more crucial to your well-being than now, as you contemplate the loss of your regular income. It sounds easy, but in practice, it can be difficult to move from simply worrying about financial problems to actually tackling them. I know, because I faced this cruel test myself during 1989.

'The biggest change in my life in the past four years has been having four children, not having all this money.'

Daniel Dell, 33-year old CEO of Dell Computers, net worth $5.5 billion in 1998

Step 2
Face the facts and identify your problem

MY EXPERIENCE

In the late 1980s, I plunged into debt in a self-publishing venture which meant a great deal to me at the time and still matters a lot, despite the huge losses incurred. There was credit card debt, a rising bank overdraft and a large remortgage on our house. The debts were mounting, but I could not tackle them. I paid the minimum monthly amount on the credit card and stopped opening the monthly bank statements. I couldn't face the gut-wrenching sight of staring at the bank debt figures. As I could not repay the money outstanding, I reasoned that there was no point in knowing how big the debt was, nor how it was growing. I was too overwhelmed by its very existence, to think positively about eliminating it. I could not trouble my husband, as he was extremely busy at work and I felt I should resolve the impasse myself – but when? And how? My days were haunted by useless worry over debt, while the problem continued to grow. Although I owed tens of thousands of pounds, I did not know the exact figure simply because I was too paralysed to examine the detail.

When I tell people this story, they always ask how much money I owed, and I reply that I honestly don't know as I never counted up the full total. Why? Because the debt was a giant negative and I finally realised I didn't *need to know* how *big* it was, I only needed to know *how to get out of debt and into credit again*. What I needed was a plan of action to do just that.

The Turning Point

You may find this an odd excuse, but when you face a major problem, your strength comes from deciding on an overall solution before getting immersed in details. For money problems the solution has two prongs. First, decide on a plan of campaign, and second, put it into action and monitor your progress until you achieve the results you initially set yourself. In my case, the turning point came when I recognised the positive – I could escape the debt, without knowing the negative – its true size, but I do not recall the trigger event which finally set me free. Whatever it was, I did eventually start thinking positively about escaping from debt, and that galvanised me into planning an action campaign.

'It is always vital in the midst of apparent disaster to try to spot the point where action matches problems to be solved.'
Fund Manager's Diary, *Investors Chronicle*

Faced with financial worries, you may wonder if you are about to embark on retirement in a sadly unprepared state. But as my story shows, you can lay out a sensible path to follow so you can overcome a poor starting position. The essence of financial planning at retirement is fivefold:

1. Face the facts.
2. Identify the problems.
3. Plan your solution and then,
4. Act upon it.
5. Lastly, monitor your progress, so you can turn your cherished plans into reality by dealing with the inevitable setbacks decisively, as soon as they crop up.

So how did my problems get resolved?

It took a year of action to turn my plan from a train of thought into reality. Of course, there were hiccups along the route, but it is only now, in retrospect, that I can see what a happy turning point my action plan was. Central to this rescue was the move to a smaller house and a strict adherence to the chore of monthly budgeting. Over the next seven years, the freed-up money enabled me to improve our fortunes so we could enjoy a good retirement. I decided to invest in the stock market to rebuild our funds and this transformed our finances. We repaid most of our debts. It took me over six years to build a growing portfolio of investments - my investment family. With this portfolio, I finally achieved the financial security so dear to my heart and the secret for this transformation was my decision to act. I turned the negatives into positives.

One of my father's favourite sayings was:
'You make your own luck.'

Turn a Problem into a Solution

Once you embark on a positive plan of action, your future can be exciting. There may be setbacks, but thinking positively helps you to overcome them. It is the key to turning your problem into a solution. Look how it worked for me when we moved to a smaller house. I was driven to act by my all-consuming debt, but as we shall soon see, moving to a more appropriate house is one of the first essentials in sensible retirement planning, although such planning was a secondary issue for me in 1989. Facing up to the problems of any debt is a top priority, but the full state of your finances during your fifties must be a central part of your planning. In my case, plunging into massive debt had a fortunate ending, serving as the crucial starting point for my own retirement planning programme. I was doubly fortunate because I tackled all the right financial Stages as part of my escape from debt, without fully appreciating I was thereby acting out the most sensible retirement plan. In retrospect, I now realise that without my serious brush with debt we would have simply ambled into retirement in a most unfocused way, just as Daniel was doing.

Step 3
Turn your problem into a solution

Of course I would caution against simply drifting into any financial situation, but my story shows that if you can turn the negatives into positives, even a shocking starting point can be happily rectified. A practical master plan is the bedrock of financial planning when you approach retirement. Few people will enjoy a perfect financial position. For most, compromises may be necessary, depending on your personal preferences or priorities. To avoid the pitfalls of drifting, you must first consider all the relevant facts about your finances as they apply both prior and at retirement. This allows you to identify the problems, plan a solution and then act upon it. To ensure you tackle the process in the right order, it is helpful to think about it as seven Stages to achieving financial security - precisely the theme of this book.

Turn the negatives into positives and appropriate actions will emerge

A Future Unlike Your Past?

Retirement can be a thirty-year holiday if sufficient funds exist, but will you personally have those funds? You may need more than just luck to enjoy twenty or more years of free leisure time. As everyone has a unique starting point and individual needs, it is essential that you know how to figure out how much money will be enough for you, for there is certainly no fixed amount to satisfy some general rule.

Step 4
Turn the negatives into positives

So what is financial security? How much capital will make *you* feel financially secure? How can you build it? And how long will it take? These are the questions you must tackle as part of the process of stepping successfully into your retirement. We will consider them in detail in Stage 2 and you can then begin to make suitable plans.

Whatever your attitude to financial planning was in the past, even if you managed somehow to avoid it entirely, the reality of a comfortable retirement rarely happens by accident; you must follow a set plan to make the best possible use of what might be limited resources. If you do not plan you might become prey to an unscrupulous financial salesman or adviser, eager to part you from your savings.

Cast your mind back to your childhood. Were you lucky enough to obtain a good grounding in money skills from parents or teachers? If not, are you now worried by the need to handle large sums of cash? Do you see yourself as a financial drop-out with little or no idea about financial planning? Are you one of thousands who think, 'I should do something – about my savings, my pension, my investments,' but, sadly, thinking about it is as far as you get? Do you have a mental block when you should be dealing with your money?

If you recognise yourself in this description, you may end up as one of many millions who drift into retirement without giving it due thought, only to find you are slowly descending into poverty.

It is impossible to avoid contact with money. More family and marriage disputes centre on money than any other cause, more even, surprisingly, than on problems over sex. Of course, money is not, nor should it be, the focus of your life, but oddly enough, it becomes more important the less of it you have. With adequate funds, whenever you want money to spend, within reason, for unplanned luxuries, money worries won't cross your mind. But suppose you don't have enough cash to pay the heating bill, or buy tomorrow's lunch? How will you feel if you have to go and ask a stony-faced social security official for income support? Many pensioners have told me they feel like scroungers when facing this ordeal. Over three million pensioners received income support in 1998, living on a modest sum of around £72 for a single person or £110 per week for a couple.

Managing money is a skill. It involves more than just choosing a few growth shares

We all need money, but in retirement this need becomes acute as your regular income source disappears. This indisputable fact means embarking upon retirement demands a change in your lifestyle, whether you want it or not. This then, is a crucial time to plan, and may pose many questions. Are you vague, even terrified about facing it now? Perhaps you think you do not have enough savings to rely on and worry that it is too late to catch up. Are you one of millions who dislike working with numbers or hate the very idea of dealing with money? Do you have no idea where to start or what your goals should be? Faced with such questions, you may be worrying that you are ill-equipped to enter retirement.

Fortunately, even if you think this might apply to you, it need not be a total disaster. However, it may take more time and effort to achieve a good result, as you pull yourself away from your unfavourable starting position. The essence of financial planning at retirement is to proceed along your seven Stage plan to financial freedom. So how will you set about doing this?

Seven Stages to Planning

However unsatisfactory your starting point, the first step is to have a master plan. Few people will become millionaires in their lifetime, even if they regularly play the lottery. So for most retirees, a top priority to achieving security is to develop a personal blueprint. Using the seven Stages to plan your route to a successful retirement provides exactly that. Following these seven Stages is a wonderful tool to carve out financial security for you and your partner. It is your passport to future planning, lifting you away from the gloom uncertainty brings.

Preparing your plan is a big confidence-booster, even if your finances are in a mess, because you know you can progress methodically through the seven Stages in order to improve your financial situation. This is not a 'get-rich-quick' book. On the contrary, if you are in your fifties as I was when I took control, you will feel far more optimistic about the outcome if you take plenty of time to consider your plans. Adopting a 'get-rich-slowly' attitude worked well for me and can work very well for you too.

The seven Stages to financial freedom is your catch-all plan because it starts with your current financial situation. This, inevitably is the centre-piece for all your future planning. Do you want to move to a smaller home to reduce your living costs? If so, your finances play a key role in that equation. Do you plan to buy a second home, perhaps to ease into, in later years when the time finally comes to sell your large family home? Again, all the finances involved must be considered. Have you belatedly realised that you do not have enough hobbies to fill your time happily? Once more, finance matters as you plan for part-time work or learning new skills.

You cannot escape reality. Without a fat cushion of funds to rely on in retirement, the future may be just as tough as it was working every day for forty years. When your reliable monthly salary is replaced by a far smaller

'Discontent is the want of self-reliance: it is infirmity of will.'
Ralph Waldo Emerson

pension income, having other cash sources is central to your planning agenda. From my interviews with pensioners, I believe it is not too melodramatic to suggest that this planning can literally spell the difference between happiness and misery during a long retirement.

There are many negatives about managing money. You must turn these negatives into positives. This is easier than you think. Embarking on retirement is a perfect opportunity to transform your relationship with your money. If you can face your fears about handling it successfully, you can discover how to take genuine control over your own financial destiny. These lessons will carry you through retirement and you will easily achieve the security you crave.

You need to tackle your fears, apathy or ignorance, and wake up to a stunning truth. Few experts will manage your money or make it work for you better than you can yourself. You may be sceptical about accepting that idea, so we will shortly look at it more closely, to see how it measures up in practice. Indeed, by the time you reach retirement with the additional free time it offers, relying on yourself is a far more effective and I believe, quicker, route to financial security than relying on others, whoever they are.

Relying on Others

For the over-fifties, a long tradition of relying on the welfare state is deeply rooted. Growing up with it has left many reluctant, perhaps unable, to take direct control of their finances. America lacks an all-embracing welfare state, forcing people to be more self-reliant. They have always known that they must plan for their own retirement and pay for their children's school and college education. With the cash crisis in the welfare state, our future may follow the American pattern, but if you were not taught money skills at school or university, you may have no idea how or where to start. Feeling inadequate to the task ahead, perhaps you hope you will be lucky in your choice of experts to rely on, even though you have heard of many financial disasters that turned millions into victims, because they relied on 'experts'. For decades, the British have been a nation of savers, immensely shocked by this seemingly unending series of financial scandals.

'The world is full of schemes aimed at parting the gullible from their money.'

Clay Harris, *Financial Times*

Many consider the stock market a risky home for savings. The City of London has the reputation of a cosy insiders' club using obscure, jargon-ridden language. Whereas savings accounts in the bank or building society are easily accessible, easy to understand and widely known as 'safe' havens for cash. In 1998, over £500 billion was sitting idle in deposit accounts because the British are natural savers, and are not investors by nature. So they ignore the obvious **risk** that inflation is eating away the value of their money all the time it sits in a deposit account.

Are you among the millions who are too scared to manage their money alone? Have you been lulled into a false sense of well-being, expecting someone else to sort out your finances? This financial wizard you expect to help has many guises – the government, your partner, husband, accountant or offspring. Relying on someone else to solve your money affairs can be doubly traumatic if there is a death in the family, as Mary sadly discovered.

MARY'S FINANCIAL MUDDLE

Mary Clarke was in her late sixties when her husband, Gordon, was rushed into hospital in a diabetic coma. Their only daughter lived abroad and Mary was shocked and of course devastated when Gordon died two hours after being admitted. He had always managed the family finances and Mary had no idea about his money.

The day before the funeral she began to suspect her husband's finances were in a muddle. She found some papers in an old shoe box, and others crammed into a broken box file. They did not have a shared bank account and she could not find his will. Fearing she could not afford expensive accountant or solicitor's fees, she decided to sort the mess out alone, without having any idea of her true financial position, little realising that it would be six months before she had sorted out her finances.

She was worse off than she had expected, but her saddest reflection was, 'Now I know the facts, what I most regret is never having taken any interest in our finances while Gordon was alive. At least I might have persuaded him to keep things in order, so it would have been sorted out much faster.'

When you lose your regular income and depend on pensions, investments and savings to meet all your future needs, the greatest risk you face is any loss to your capital. Avoiding the task of managing your own finances could be the most risky act you take if it leads you into the open arms of a scheming adviser. Senior citizens who are naive about their personal finances have repeatedly proved easy prey to greedy salesmen.

> *'A few days before my 55th birthday, three teenage bank managers sit round the dining table explaining what they plan to do with my money. My wife and I agree that they should do it, but ask them to tell us as little about what they are doing as possible, except how much money they are making for us. They seem rather shocked, but I think it is called "empowerment" and they should be thrilled.'*
>
> Tom Rayfield, *Financial Times* (1 April, 1998)

Relying on Experts?

Reading Tom Rayfield's first experiences of early retirement, from which the above quotation is taken, momentarily stunned me. Was he seriously ready to face retirement with such a trusting faith in his bank and its teenage managers? At fifty-five, he probably will enjoy another twenty to thirty years of active life. Yet with no regular salary coming in, preparing his financial future was something he seemed quite happy to leave in the hands of three young bank managers.

Sadly, a string of British financial scandals has made me very wary, since millions of unfortunate investors have been mis-sold pensions, **additional voluntary (pension) contributions, investment bonds, home income plans, UK gilt-edged investment funds** (investing in bonds issued as loans by the government to cover its borrowing) and even boring, safe, endowment and ten-year savings plans.

By 1998, the mis-selling of personal pension plans to around two and a half million people during the 1980s was headline news. This raised awareness among the general public, to alert them to the dangers of relying solely on expert advice. But, perversely, the main effect was in the reduced numbers of personal pensions bought, and this at a time when state pensions were dwindling in value.

Become Your Own Adviser

You should heed the experiences of previous victims. Sadly, most victims genuinely believed they were safely putting their affairs in expert hands being unwilling or unable to manage alone. Yet once confronted by an enormous financial mess, many were forced, like Mary, to tackle their own problems. Compiling fat dossiers of letters and documents, they waded through masses of complicated facts and figures, to understand the basis of their claims for compensation.

Step 5
Become your own financial adviser

Ironically, familiarity with all these mind-blowing details turned many frustrated victims into reluctant 'experts'.

There have been many British financial scandals, but two which directly affected the retired were the 1988 Barlow Clowes fraud and the mis-selling of home income plans in the 1980s.

The Barlow Clowes Company collapse was an unexpected shock to eleven thousand retired people whose **independent financial advisers** had placed their savings in the company's off-shore funds, misguidedly thinking they were earning high returns on 'safe' **UK government gilt-edged stock**. This investment fund was licenced by the British regulatory authorities, yet the

'The IFA (independent financial adviser) Hall of Fame is littered with an A to Z of flamboyant crooks ... who can forget Peter Clowes, founder of the gilt-edged Lear Jet Fund, or Roger Levitt, the bow-tied, eternally suntanned salesman who has reinvented himself as a New York boxing promoter?'

Paul Ham, *The Sunday Times*

swindle duped all those involved – the authorities, financial advisers and the long-suffering investors.

When this disaster hit the headlines, the mis-selling of home income plans was already one of the biggest scandals in British financial history. Home income plans were very popular in the 1980s. By unlocking some of the equity in their homes, the elderly obtained additional income without the bother of moving house. This scandal brought incalculable misery. Many died before receiving compensation and thousands more were burdened by debt and still seeking redress in 1998.

The ugly truth is that once you have parted – even innocently – with your hard earned savings, fate can deal you a cruel blow if you relied completely on an expert. Many are undoubtedly trustworthy and reliable, but history shows the path to financially secure retirements is littered with horror stories of elderly people persuaded to part with their savings. Millions of pensioners have fat savings accounts or large untapped equity values locked into their mortgage-free homes. This is a tempting lure for irresponsible financial advisers. They see the opportunity for rich pickings from clients who are trusting by nature and easily confused by the complications of most financial products. Home income plans of the 1980s variety are no longer sold, being superseded by more reliable versions, but many victims continue to suffer from their traumatic ordeal.

'Millions of pounds have been lost in recent years by investors who staked their hopes on currency speculation, obscure US shares, "strategic metals", exotic fowl such as ostriches, and new manifestations of familiar pyramid and Ponzi schemes.'

Clay Harris, *Financial Times*

Seek Advice but Make Your Own Decisions

Financial advice is available from either **tied agents** or independent financial advisers (IFAs). Tied agents work for one company, are trained to sell only that

Step 6
Make your own
financial decisions

company's products and are legally forbidden to give advice about other competing products on the market. While the products they sell may be good, they are the only ones the agent knows about. He will not be able to tell you how his company's products compare with perhaps hundreds of similar products sold by competitor companies. You must obtain that information yourself. A salesman selling only one company's products is not impartial.

There are around twenty thousand IFAs in Britain, qualified to give independent advice across the whole range of products. They are legally obliged to give 'best advice' when making recommendations. Given the vast numbers of products from which to make choices, many IFAs operate best-advice product panels. These whittle down the range by selecting around ten products or funds only from each available sector. Critics claim this system tempts the adviser to favour high commission paying products and so undermines their complete impartiality. But the enormous field does require some sifting so there may be a place for panels, as long as you know they are being used.

About 95 per cent of IFAs have only the basic required qualification - the financial planning certificate - but they can go on to upgrades through further study, assessment and exams. They are regulated by the PIA (Personal Investment Authority) which requires every adviser to undertake continuous professional progress to keep up with the never-ending changes in the financial markets.

Confusion on Charges

Charges are another area of confusion for investors. Usually advisers give 'free' advice to you, the client, and receive commission from the insurance or fund management company if you buy a product. Recent new regulations on commission disclosure has exposed the high cost of many products, increasing public disquiet. As every type of product carries a different commission structure, no blanket rule will say when you are better off negotiating a fee for advice and receiving back the commissions due. In general, long-term savings contracts, (a pension or endowment policy set up to run for twenty-five years) and lump sum investments for over £15,000 command high commissions. For these products, a negotiated fee could be cheaper.

'Fees are there because a lot of people quite rightly do not trust financial advisers. Fees give a client peace of mind that commission is not the driving force behind the advice given.'
Roddy Koln, a member of the Personal Investment Authority board

Although commission rates and fees vary widely, an illustration might help. Arranging a pension policy through a fee-paying adviser for a thirty-five year-old spending £200 per month to retire at sixty involves costs ranging from £500 to £600, and takes about six hours of an adviser's time. A similar policy set up through a commission-based salesman could cost £1,500 to £1,600 plus continuation commissions, usually of 2.5 per cent a month.

Continuation commissions are only paid after the policy has remained in force for a certain period, often two years, but they then continue throughout the lifetime of the policy.

Once you realise how large some commissions are it makes sense to discuss the charges openly with your adviser. Negotiating often produces a better deal. Sadly, many people get lured into buying policies from a friend newly starting up in financial services. His company will teach him that asking friends to buy policies is a good way to get started. Be very careful if you buy policies or investment products from friends or family working in the insurance industry. You may face awkward problems later. You will not want to complain or create trouble for a friend, no matter how unsatisfactory your policy turns out to be.

Even using a fee-charging adviser carries pitfalls. Buying from a life insur-ance salesman avoids paying VAT on commission, but when you pay fees, they are normally paid in advance, can start from £50 an hour depending on the IFA company you use, and a 17.5 per cent VAT charge is then added. As with all professionals, the quality of advice varies. You should use a firm you either know, or one which has been recommended by a friend or relative. You might try a solicitor, as lawyers increasingly deal with financial prod-ucts. They charge fees, returning all commis-sions to the client. How to choose a financial adviser is covered in Stage 7 on pages 166–7.

'Fees tend to occupy the high moral ground but there are pros and cons … Fees do not automatically mean discounted or cheap advice.'

Chris Wicks, a fee-based adviser at Kidson Impey Scott Lang

Future Mis-selling Scandals?

While problems still face millions of investment victims from past mis-selling scandals, a new danger now lurks.

As almost 30 per cent of the population is over fifty, they present a lucrative target. More financial resources are focusing on this potentially rewarding mar-ket, which includes many of the most comfortably off sections of society. Salespeople learn how to market a whole range of products to the wealthy over-fifties through seminars and conferences focusing on their financial needs. Courses charge from £350 to £500 for a one-day seminar. Such high fees mean companies expect employees to recoup the cost and make big profits selling products to this target market.

Pay Commissions?

Financial product	Typical commission structure	Example – approximate figures for 35 year-old Total commissions
Life Cover	Year 1 – all annual premium + 2.5% per month after 4 years if the policy is in force	£100,000 cover for 20 years. Costs vary (£16 to £20 per month: £215 to £450 + 39p per month after 49 months)
Pension	Year 1 – 50% of annual premium + 2.5% per month after 2 years if the policy is in force	£200 per month for 35 year-old, to run to age 60: £1,500 + £5 per month after 26–28 months in force
Endowment	Year 1 – 75% annual premium + 2.5% of premiums after 3 years	£225 per month to save £100,000 after 20 years (mortgage repayment): £2,000 + £5.60 after around 32 months
Peps (Isas may be sold by i) a cheap route through banks and supermarkets or ii) as for Peps, through financial advisers	3% of initial investment + 0.5% annual commission	£6,000 lump sum in a unit-trust-based Pep: £180 + annual 0.5%. Some companies pay around £90 up front commission

Pay Fees?

Initial consultation fee	Hourly rate	Cost of yearly review
Free, or about £100	£50 to £150 + VAT	£100 to £1,000

Delegates at such seminars are bombarded with information on how to reassure the frightened fifties, beset by financial worries about managing their money through retirement. Make no mistake, you are in their sights. They intend to overcome your fears and sell you the products they want you to buy. As the regulatory processes in Britain are imperfect, it is a case of BUYER BEWARE. What they are offering may not be right for you. It is an unfair contest: they are fully trained and you are not, so you need to know in great detail what you may gain or, more importantly, lose, from whatever they try to sell you.

Seek Out Sound Advice

Knowing how expensive it is to train successful financial salespeople, you begin to realise how important it is for you personally, to take more interest in future financial decisions. However attractive the scheme, pause, consider and, if in doubt, desist. If you are offered a financial scheme that sounds highly advantageous, be even more cautious. Schemes offering high returns are the most risky; generally it is impossible to make high returns on fairly safe investments. Making high returns usually carries extra risk. Many of the most tempting schemes offer unsustainably high returns, perhaps concealing an element of fraud. This certainly applied to the Barlow Clowes Company. When tempted by high returns on a scheme, always look for pitfalls.

> *'People no longer feel secure in their jobs, nor are they confident that the government will look after them in retirement. So this puts pressure on people to save more - hence the demand for financial services.'*
>
> Roger Nightingale, economist

If in doubt, discuss the proposition with someone whose advice you trust; a family member, colleague, solicitor or accountant. It is *your* money, so you should be absolutely certain that you have made the right choice before you sign up. Your doubts may mean missing out, but rest assured, there are endless opportunities to put your money safely to work.

Sadly, the tendency to be suspicious of any investment that requires a financial adviser or putting money into the stock market, has made British people fearful of managing their own money, and equally fearful of relying on experts. So most people just stay with the 'safe' saving options, even though, as we shall see in Stage 4, by not keeping pace with inflation, these are far from safe. If you do this, it could be the worst of all possible outcomes during retirement, especially if your cash resources are limited.

INTRODUCING GEORGE AND FREDA BLAKE

To set you thinking along the right lines, we shall follow the fortunes of George and Freda Blake, who have another nine and eleven years respectively before retirement.

George is fifty-one and his wife, Freda is forty-nine. They have two unmarried children, Alice, aged twenty-seven and Henry, twenty-five, both living away from home. The Blakes live in a large three-bedroomed house in York.

George, a local authority librarian, earns £24,500 a year. He hopes to retire at sixty, in November 2007. Freda worked full-time early in their marriage but took a long period off to bring up the children and care for her invalid father at home. She began working again in 1993 as a part-time secretary, earning £6,500 a year.

Through the following Stages, we will watch them tackle their financial planning, as they attempt to become their own financial advisers and make their own financial decisions.

In Summary

For everyone planning future finances, including the Blakes, retirement is an unavoidable turning point, a time to rethink and reorder your whole lifestyle as well as your finances. To make the transition both smooth and rewarding, you need a master plan. The seven Stages to financial freedom will make a big contribution to these plans. They form a logical progression, taking you through all the steps required to improve your financial position in retirement. Now you have adopted a positive attitude, let us turn to Stage 2, putting your house in order.

Key Points to Remember

STAGE 1: STEP INTO RETIREMENT

1. Adopt a positive attitude: don't drift into retirement.
2. Face the facts and identify your problem.
3. Turn your financial problems into a solution.
4. Turn the negatives into positives.
5. Making money is a skill which you can learn.
6. Follow a blueprint investment plan to map out your route.
7. Use seven Stages to retirement as a 'get-rich-slowly' action plan.

'The more I practise, the luckier I get.'

Stephen Riley, Chief Executive, Denby Pottery

Put Your House in Order

Your only long-term plan should be the intention to become financially secure

Do you ever think how many thousands of pounds your pay packets put into your bank account during your lifetime? A forty-year career with several pay rises can produce over a million pounds, plus perhaps, bonuses or cash gifts worth thousands more. Of course, that's only theory. In practice, you have to live on your earned salary.

Every month, there are endless outgoings, for food, rent or mortgage, household and transport expenses, the costs of raising your children, buying holidays, clothes, presents and sundries. Working for your living is precisely that – working for the cash to live on day by day. This regime creates a totally different lifestyle to one with a stable source of **unearned income** to rely on.

Today, almost everyone of working age expects to work for their living. But this idea was unfamiliar to Jane Austen's contemporaries as portrayed in her novels. Equally, before 1914, the young Agatha Christie lived comfortably on interest from UK government bonds (gilts) inherited from her father and she did not need to work.

Live like a Lord on unearned income

Retirement – A Time of Reckoning

However, whether earned or unearned, people allocate their income in various ways. Do you spend every penny? Perhaps you spend more than you earn, running up overdrafts or credit card debts. Are you frugal, saving some money each month?

To plan a successful retirement, treat it as a financial day of reckoning. Now is the time to work out how much of that million-plus that you earned while working will be there for your future when pay cheques disappear. The acid test on how you manage your money cannot be delayed when you retire, as Mrs Urquhart's story shows.

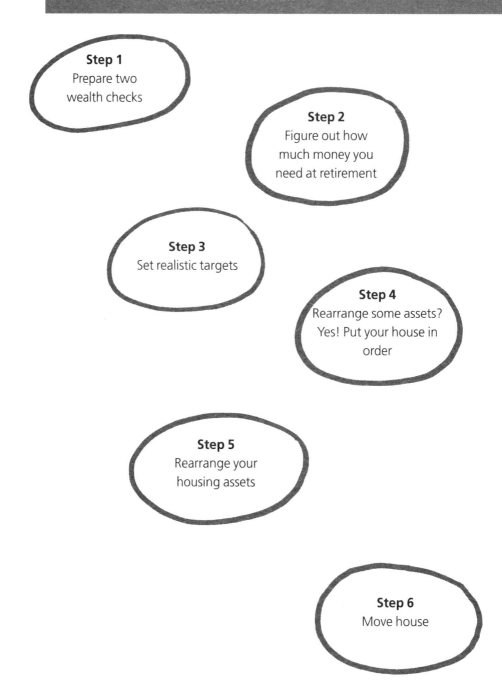

STAGE 2 PUT YOUR HOUSE IN ORDER

Step 1
Prepare two
wealth checks

Step 2
Figure out how
much money you
need at retirement

Step 3
Set realistic targets

Step 4
Rearrange some assets?
Yes! Put your house in
order

Step 5
Rearrange your
housing assets

Step 6
Move house

MOVE TO STAGE 3

MRS URQUHART'S DEBT DILEMMA

I met Mrs Urquhart when I was an insurance broker in the early 1980s. A widow in her sixties, she lived in a comfortably furnished flat, relying on the with-profit **investment bonds** her husband left her. But she was slowly cashing them in to meet her spending debts, regularly run up to pay for clothes and entertainments although tough interviews about her overdraft with the bank manager upset her. Periodically, she bowed to his pressure, surrendering another bond to pay her debts.

> '*Start saving and investing early. It's a great habit to have.*'
>
> Warren Buffett, America's wealthiest private investor. He grew $100 in 1956 to over $36 billion by 1998

She accepted she was hopeless at managing money. But at her age, she was not eligible for a home income plan and refused to move. I often wondered whether she continued her carefree spending and still retained her capital until she could qualify for a home income plan.

Build a Financial Pyramid

The root of Mrs Urquhart's dilemma was her inability to master her finances. A head-in-the-sand approach can be lethal for preserving your capital. The seven Stages to financial success is the route to take to avoid this unsatisfactory outcome. It applies to everyone, as does the idea of building a financial pyramid. I used this pyramid image in *The Money Maze*, a personal finance primer for learning money skills to better manage your money.

Although everyone should build a pyramid, whether they are twenty or seventy, the emphasis changes for different phases in life. On approaching retirement, pyramid building acquires a sharper focus, first to improve your pension which will be your replacement income, and second because saving becomes less important than having sound investments to rely on. How you build your own financial pyramid is covered in Stage 4.

Sadly, in Britain, millions of people have far too little capital in retirement. Ideally, you can rectify this by planning well ahead, allowing at least five to ten years, but twenty would be better. With plenty of time, you may alter course early, if necessary, so you reach a secure outcome when you do retire, even for a retirement spanning thirty years.

If you are still working in your sixties, or are recently retired, you may face different problems to people with several years of planning time ahead. Everyone should begin by examining their current position, but your planning will be affected by whether you are retired now, or an aspiring retiree with many years for planning.

Exploring this begins in earnest here in Stage 2. But we start by assuming you have several years of useful planning time ahead. That knowledge is valuable; it becomes part of the planning process itself.

The Starting Point

Your plan of action always starts from your current financial position. It considers your overall situation: including whether you are married or single, the state of your health and if your housing arrangements are appropriate to your future possible needs. These factors form part of the final equation underpinning your master plan. But at the outset give yourself some achievable targets, tailored to meet what you see as your own special needs.

How you do this will become clearer as we progress through Stage 2. It covers the twin elements needed to put your house in order: your financial house as well as your real house, since rearranging your housing is only one part of this exercise. Statistics show that a house in Britain is the largest financial asset most people own. If this applies to you, now is the time to decide whether all the money tied up in your home is working for you or lying idle and out of reach. However, to decide if a change of housing will help, you must review all your finances to judge how they might look at retirement. Hence, putting your financial house in order means looking at your real housing situation as part of the total picture.

You cannot judge how your finances will cope in retirement if you do not know today's full picture. This sounds obvious, but people rarely approach their retirement plans from this starting point. You must know where you are now, in order to chart a successful route to financial happiness into your sixties and beyond.

The Full Financial Picture

Stage 2, therefore, will help you put your financial house in order by exposing your overall finances. It takes you through the logical sequence outlined in the planning path on page 26. *Step 1* compares your current situation with your estimated finances at retirement to judge how they will change between these two dates. *Step 2* follows on to figure out how much money you will need at retirement. From this step you will rapidly see if you might face a shortfall at retirement. If so, *Step 3* helps you set realistic targets to improve your forecast situation, while *Step 4* explores ways to rearrange some assets as another route to improving your retirement prospects. Following on from this assessment, if you want to rearrange your housing assets, *Step 5* works through options which don't involve moving, while *Step 6* explores housing options that do.

'You have to count the pennies to make every penny count.'

Suze Orman, financial planning expert

It is better to review your house as part of your financial position in your forties to sixties rather than wait until you reach eighty-plus. Moving house then could be unmanageable. An early housing assessment might resolve an income shortfall, as Mrs Urquhart hoped. Sadly, many people are like Roger and Elsie and leave this important decision until it is far too late to act.

A LOST OPPORTUNITY TO MOVE

In their late forties, Roger and Elsie bought a two-bedroom house, repaying their mortgage over the next twenty years. They made several improvements; building a garage, a large sun room and a garden patio. Their biggest alteration, a loft extension, allowed their daughter Susan, her husband John and their two grandchildren to stay for weekend breaks. The additions cost a few thousand pounds, but after rampant inflation during the 1970s and 1980s, their house, bought for £2,750 in 1957, was worth £70,000 in 1985 when the retired couple were in their late seventies.

Susan then tried to persuade them to move to a flat to reduce their overheads and eliminate the problem of stairs to reach the bathroom and bedroom. Although they both still enjoyed reasonably good health, they disliked the idea of living in a flat. In 1990, John was posted abroad taking his family with him. Now Roger and Elsie are in their nineties with no close family nearby. Roger has had a mild stroke and Elsie suffers from angina and arthritis. Neither is fit enough to climb the stairs so the bed is downstairs in the lounge. The gardening they enjoyed is now too much work. The large sun room and the whole upstairs part of the house are never used but the opportunity to move to a more suitable home has long gone.

Assess Your Financial State

To establish your full financial situation, you can do some calculations. These paper exercises will give you a complete financial overview for two set dates; today, and the expected date of your retirement. Even if this date is ten or more years ahead, you still need a rough estimate of how your finances will change by then. It doesn't matter greatly if your estimates are vague. As you progress towards your expected retirement date, you can update early forecasts. Regularly reviewing your financial state should be part of your monitoring routine so you remain totally in control of events as your retirement date draws nearer.

Step 1
Prepare two
wealth checks

Follow the five-point guide to see how your finances will shape up on current plans. Then, examine some alternative options, to see if you can improve your prospects. A detailed layout of the five-point guide is shown on pages 168–71 of Stage 7.

Five-Point Guide to Forecast Your Financial Needs

Begin by preparing a complete financial overview for two dates; today, and your expected retirement date.

1. Compile today's budget.
2. Prepare today's **net worth** list.
3. Compile your estimated budget at your planned retirement date.
4. Prepare your estimated net worth list for your planned retirement date.
5. Compile a gains and losses list.

Having completed your five-point guide, it is far easier to identify any possible retirement income or capital shortfall. From there, the realistic targets you need to set follow almost automatically since closing the shortfalls in effect, sets these targets for you.

Compile today's budget
i) Collect together all your pay slips, bills and bank statements over the last year.
ii) List all your income (money coming in) and expenses (money going out).
iii) Calculate the current income/expenses totals for today. Is there a positive or negative cash balance? This is called the **cash flow**.
iv) If you have a negative balance, plan a budgeting campaign, (covered extensively in Chapter 3 of *The Money Maze*).
v) If you have a positive balance, can you redirect part of it to increase your current savings?

Prepare today's net worth list
Today's net worth gives a picture, at a glance, of the total value of the **assets** you own after taking account of all your debts (**liabilities**):
i) List all your existing assets, including your house, car, cash in the bank, policies, jewellery and any other saleable valuables you own.
ii) Put a rough value on each asset, exact values are not necessary.
iii) Add up the total value of them all.
iv) List all your outstanding debts including your mortgage, bank loans, store and credit card debts, overdraft.
v) Deduct the total of your debts from the total value of your assets to obtain a balancing figure. This balance is a rough estimate of your current net worth.

Compile your estimated budget at your planned retirement date
i) Calculate the total income you are likely to have on retirement, such as a monthly pension, consultancy fees, one-off jobs or part-time work, spouse's income.
ii) Calculate all the expenses due to end on retirement: a) mortgage repayments; b) pension contributions; c) insurance policy premiums linked to work, e.g. permanent health insurance; d) savings.
iii) Calculate the estimated income and expenses totals situation for your retirement date.
iv) Establish whether there is a shortfall on the income.

v) Calculate a target income level you will need, based on your estimated list of retirement expenses.

Prepare your estimated net worth list for your planned retirement date
i) List all your estimated assets at your forecast retirement date. If they are existing assets, add a conservative percentage increase to allow for growth over the intervening period for your house, cash in the bank, savings or policies and other valuables. Put a rough value on each asset at retirement.
ii) If you are building a pension fund through a personal pension, do not include its total value in your net worth list *at retirement* as this fund will be used to buy your guaranteed **annuity** then. However, you can include 25 per cent of the forecast fund at retirement, as this is the amount of your fund you can **commute** into a tax-free lump sum. These points are covered in Stage 3.
iii) Add together all these assets to find the total value.
iv) List all the debts you expect will still be outstanding at retirement, including your mortgage, overdraft, bank loan and credit card debts, if applicable.
v) Deduct the total of your anticipated debts from the total value of your estimated assets to arrive at a forecast balancing figure.

Achieving a comfortable retirement needs a special plan that deserves to be treated as such

Compile a gains and losses list
For the two dates, now and at retirement, list the evident gains plus the obvious losses in your financial situation.

This five-point guide will help you figure out your money needs at retirement. It also exposes shortfalls in income or capital which might occur then, based on current plans.

Step 2
Figure out how much money you need at retirement

If your present budget reveals you are spending more than you earn and you have built up debts, think about how you will cope in retirement. Running debts in retirement is expensive, unless there is a known future lump sum to pay them off, perhaps an inheritance or some tax-free cash you will get when you take your pension. If your present net worth is a small positive figure, but you have about ten years until you retire, by focusing on ways to increase it, as I did, you can build a bigger nest egg for the future.

AROUND THE WORLD . . . IN DEBT
Big debts are a burden at any time of life, but in retirement they may become insurmountable. Sam and Gladys discovered this in their mid-sixties. They were enticed into applying for a credit card, even though they lived on pensions and had never previously had a card. After two years, Sam was offered

a higher credit limit and the couple decided to take a round-the-world trip. This was a splendid once-in-a-lifetime adventure, but so, sadly, was the problem of repaying a £6,500 credit card debt. After weeks of anxiety the card company withdrew their card and credit facility. But the five years of monthly payments to repay the debt was a miserable blight on their lives.

The exercise of preparing two net worth estimates, for now and at retirement gives a quick picture of all the valuable assets, or possessions, you own after deducting all your debts. You need not know precisely what your house, jewellery or car is worth, or the exact figure owed on your mortgage or other debts. This paper exercise provides an overview. Deducting your total debts from your total assets produces a rough estimate of your current and future net worth.

Suppose your house is worth £60,000, your mortgage is £55,000 and other debts are £7,500. Your net worth would be negative at –£2,500, as shown below.

Net Worth Calculation

Value of asset £	Value of liabilities £	Net worth £
House 60,000	Mortgage –55,000	
	Other debts –7,500	
Total assets 60,000	**Total debts –62,500**	**Net worth –2,500**

Few people know what it feels like to lose $100 million (£60 million) but then few know what it is like to have made $150 million in the first place

Mark Andreeson, founder of Netscape, has done both

Figures for the future are guesses, but compiling your retirement wealth check is still worthwhile. At a glance, you see roughly what your budget of income and expenses, and your net worth will look like at your retirement date. Comparing the two schedules, for now and ten years hence, gives an instant 'snap shot' of your estimated retirement situation. You can judge how much money you will need, whether your forecast pension will cover your estimated expenses after deducting those that will disappear, and whether there is likely to be a shortfall.

If the retirement estimates look attainable, they immediately give you a target income figure that you will need to reach by your retirement date. If the figures look unsatisfactory, unless your estimated expenses can be reduced or your forecast income can rise, you know you will have to make positive changes to achieve a realistic balanced budget by then. If you have twenty years to retirement, you could tackle this five-point guide in two phases; one for ten years ahead and a second when you get to within ten years of retirement. On-going monitoring of your progress is essential to ensure you reach your set targets.

To help you assess any major changes you need to improve your retirement estimates, compiling a list to show the financial gains and losses involved, will complete the full assessment of your situation at your two chosen dates. This assumes you continue with your current plans right through to retirement. The whole five-point guide, however, is designed to help you decide how to introduce changes at an early stage, so you can improve your retirement position. In Stage 7, on pages 168–71, we will examine the detailed route for preparing your budget and net worth lists.

'I am afraid I have always taken it (money) for granted, even before my inheritance.'

The Marquis of Bath inherited £23 million, at the age of 18

WEALTH CHECKS FOR THE BLAKES

We introduced George and Freda in Stage 1. They have nine years to plan for George's retirement. Their two grown-up children no longer live at home.

To clarify the five-point guide, we will now compile two wealth checks for the Blakes, to see them operating in practice. Stage 7 provides a step-by-step guide for you to do your own wealth checks.

The 1999 Financial Situation

The House
The Blakes bought a large three-bedroomed house in 1982 for £55,000, paying a deposit of £5,000. They have a twenty-five year **repayment mortgage** on which they pay interest and also pay off the capital throughout the whole term which ends in December 2007. In 1999, the house was worth around £160,000.

The Pension
George earns £24,500 a year gross and plans to retire at sixty, in November 2007. He is building his own fund through a **personal pension** and pays £150 each month into it. A recent valuation shows his fund is worth £33,700 with a forecast value of £85,000 at sixty. If he takes a full pension and no cash lump sum, his pension is forecast to be £7,225, but the actual amount depends on **annuity rate** levels in 2007. George's pension options are fully covered in Stage 3.

Freda's Income

Freda began working again in 1993 as a part-time secretary for a small company, earning £6,500 a year. She has no pension and has only paid national insurance contributions for six years so her state pension will be very small.

Savings

The Blakes have saved £4,500 in a joint bank deposit account. They add £60 each month: George saves £35 and Freda saves £25. Freda has 100 Abbey National shares which came as a windfall in 1989 when the building society converted to a bank. She gets a **dividend** twice a year from these shares. The yearly dividend has risen steadily since the company floated on the London **Stock Exchange**.

The Car

In May 1997 the Blakes bought a second-hand car for £9,800, with a five-year bank loan for £9,500 ending in May 2002. The monthly loan repayments are £180, (£2,160 a year). Most banks offer three-year car loans, but George arranged a five-year deal. With a three-year loan the monthly repayments would be around £330, (£3,960 a year).

Protection

1. George has a **Permanent Health Insurance policy** (PHI) which would pay a small benefit if he is off sick for more than three months while he is in work. This costs £45 a month.
2. Twelve years ago George bought £5,000 of life assurance, paying a premium of £21 per month. This is a **term assurance** policy, ending on his seventieth birthday, in November 2017.
3. Their mortgage will be completely repaid in 2007, but they did not buy a **joint mortgage protection policy** when it began in 1982. This would pay a sum of £50,000 if either one of them dies before the mortgage term ends. This was a risky omission as Freda would have had to continue paying the mortgage while supporting two young children if George had died with the mortgage still outstanding. Freda, has some protection from George's growing pension fund, worth £33,700. If George dies before sixty, Fred will receive its full value.

> *'It is better to be certain of a good result than hopeful of a great one'.*
> Warren Buffett

Freda's 1999 Situation

In 1999, the mortgage owed was about £20,000, so Freda's financial state if

Freda's Situation if George Dies in 1999

Item providing cash	Amount in 1999 (£)
George's pension fund	33,700
George's Life policy	5,000
TOTAL CASH	38,700
Outstanding Mortgage	−20,000
Final Cash Situation	**18,700**

George dies looks tough, since her income is only £6,500 a year. She would have £33,700 to pay off £20,000 of outstanding mortgage, plus £5,000 from the life assurance policy.

However, over the next nine years, Freda's protection will improve as George's pension builds up and the mortgage debt falls.

George's 1999 Situation

When thinking about protection too few people factor in both partners, even when both work. If Freda dies in the next few years, George would lose her £6,500 income but as she has no life assurance, he must live on his income and eventually, on his pension. While George is working, if he earns £24,500, that, plus bank interest and dividends (he will inherit Freda's Abbey National shares) would be around £24,809. His expenses on food and various items might fall by a third, but he would have some high expenses: repaying the mortgage, his car loan, pension premiums and tax.

Five-Point Guide for the Blakes

With all these facts assembled, we can apply *Step 1* and compile two wealth checks for the Blakes, hoping to reveal at least one early solution to any financial short-fall they may face at George's retirement date, which is not obvious without preparing wealth checks. Then they can move to *Steps 2* and *3*; first, to figure out how much money they need by 2007 and second, to set themselves realistic targets for that date. To compile their wealth checks, we follow the five-point guide shown in the diagram below.

The Blakes
Step 1
Prepare two wealth checks

Five-Point Guide to Forecast the Blakes' Financial Needs

1. Compile today's budget.
2. Prepare today's net worth list.
3. Repeat with their estimated budget for November 2007.

4. Compile their estimated net worth list for November 2007.

5. Compile a gains and losses list.

George and Freda's Two Budgets – For 1999 and 2007

Items	1999 (A)			2007 (B)		
	Monthly (£)		Annual (£)	Monthly (£)		Annual (£)
	George	Freda	Combined	George	Freda	Combined
INCOME	2,041.67	541.67	31,000	602.08	541.67	13,725
Interest			261			729
Dividends			33			53
Totals	**24,500**	**6,500**	**31,294**	**7,225**	**6,500**	**14,507**
EXPENSES						
Mortgage	360		4,320			
Food	170		2,040	187		2,244
Household	220		2,640	242		2,904
Car/transport	140		1,680	154		1,848
Car loan	180		2,160			
Holidays	127		1,524			1,676
Entertainment	100		1,200	110		1,320
Cigarettes/beer	120		1,440	132		1,584
Clothes	75		900	82.50		990
Insurance	66		792	21		252
House Insurance			408			448
Extras	184		2,208	200		2,400
Savings	35	25	720			
Tax NI	540	80	7,440	60	60	1,440
Pension	150		1,800			
Totals			**31,272**			**17,106**
Surplus/Shortfall			**+ 22**			**- 2,599**

Notes for estimating the 2007 budget: We must make a few assumptions to give us a guide for the 2007 situation. i) All expenses in 2007 grow by around 10 per cent from 1999. ii) Abbey National dividends grow by 5 per cent a year, from £32.50 in 1998 to £53 by 2007. iii) Mortgage payments, savings, pension and PHI premiums end in 2007 and they pay less tax. iv) Their bank deposit savings grow at 5 per cent a year, rising from £4,500 in 1999 to £15,320 in 2007 because they continue to put £720 each year into the account.

Comparing the Two Budgets

The two estimated budgets reveal a drastic change in the Blakes' financial position when George retires in 2007. Their combined income will decrease by more than half, from £31,294 to £14,507. If Freda stops work at sixty, in 2009, their finances look worse, with income falling to £10,907 and George will not receive his state pension until November 2012 when he reaches sixty-five.

The Blakes' Annual Income in 2009

Income items	Annual value (£)
George's pension	7,225
Freda's estimated state pension – £55 per week	2,860
Interest on bank savings (£766 interest + £56 dividends).	822
Total income	**10,907**

Retirement reductions in expenses

Some of the Blakes' annual expenses will end in 2007; the car loan payments of £2,160 end in 2002 and they will pay less tax, making a total reduction of £15,540 in their expenses.

Thrift is a great source of revenue

As the total reduction in expenses when George retires is more than half their 1999 combined income, you might think their future looks fine. Without inflation, it could be. However, there has been some inflation every year over the past sixty years, so it cannot be ignored. With a low rate of inflation each year, most of their expenses will rise by that amount or more. Column B in the 2007 budget shows a shortfall of £2,599. With continuing inflation, the shortfall will increase each year but George's pension is permanently fixed at £7,225 with no increases to allow for rising inflation. We will look at George's pension options in Stage 3 on pages 67–9. Finally, their car will be over ten years old and perhaps, more expensive to run, but there is insufficient income for a new car loan of £2,000 each year.

Annual Expenses Ending as George Retires £

Item	Value (£)
Mortgage payments	4,320
Pension premiums	1,800
PHI premiums	540
Savings	720
Car loan repayments	2,160 (end in May 2002)
Tax	6,000
Total reduction in expenses	**15,540**

If George dies after his seventieth birthday

If George dies after his seventieth birthday in November 2017, Freda's financial situation will be difficult. She will only have her state pension as the term policy will have expired worthless, and George's pension ends on his death. This looks worrisome, but on the plus side, she will own the whole house, mortgage-free. By 2018, it could be a valuable asset, although house prices may not continue to rise in the future as they have in the past.

'A world might be created with budgets.'

Napoleon Bonaparte

The Blakes' two budgets show their expenses exceed their income in 2007. They might need to budget, a topic discussed in detail in *The Money Maze*. Keep records of all your income and expenditure and set spending limits for a few months to reduce your overspend. This is incredibly tedious. You or the Blakes might find budgeting a tiresome chore, so another idea is to reduce outlays on a pet extravagance: clothes, alcohol or theatre visits, perhaps. The Blakes might tackle spending on entertainment, cigarettes or beer. A voluntary regime now, may avoid compulsory belt-tightening in 2007. Alternatively, they could try to raise extra cash by:

1. Rearranging some existing assets.
2. Taking an extra part-time job (Freda).
3. Moving to a smaller house.
4. Taking in a lodger (notify the mortgage company).

Having compiled the two budgets, we now examine the Blakes' net worth lists, for 1999 and 2007. That might reveal ways to reduce their 2007 income shortfall. The net worth lists are shown on page 39.

**The Blakes
Step 2**
Figure out how much money you need at retirement

In column (B), at first glance, a forecast rise of only £10,850 over nine years looks modest, while if there is no gain in the value of the Blakes' house, column (A), their total net worth will fall –£5,150 between 1999 and 2007. The puzzle of why the figures are not better after nine years of further savings is due to the fact that while George is working, his accumulating pension fund is a source of capital: it acts as life assurance for Freda. For her it is money in the bank until George buys his annuity at sixty. If he dies before he retires, she receives the full fund. However, in November 2007, George will use the whole

'The most important thing money gives you is freedom. If I were to lose it, my worry would be that I would lose the ability to set my own agenda and have to start working for a living.'

The Marquis of Bath

George and Freda's Net Worth for 1999 and 2007

(A) No gain in house   (B) 10% gain in house value

Assets	1999 value £	2007 value £ (A) no gain in house	2007 value £ (B) 10% gain in house	Comments
House	160,000	160,000	176,000	
Car	5,000	1,500	1,500	Loses value
Pension fund	33,700	Nil	Nil	Capital converted to income via annuity on retirement
Life Assurance	5,000	Nil	Nil	Term policy ends 2017
100 Abbey National shares	1,000	1,200	1,200	Assumes around 20% growth in 9 years
Bank Deposits	4,500	15,300	15,300	Assumes 5% interest and £720 added to the fund each year
Totals	**209,200**	**178,000**	**194,000**	
Debts				
Mortgage	20,000	Nil	Nil	Mortgage repaid in 2007
Car loan	5,400	Nil	Nil	Car loan repaid in May 2002
Credit Card debt	1,250	600	600	
Total Debts	**26,650**	**600**	**600**	
Net Worth	**182,550**	**177,400**	**193,400**	
Estimated Gain/Loss		**–5,150 Loss**	**10,850 Gain**	

fund to purchase an annuity. This becomes his fixed income through retirement. But say he died in 2008, without taking any extra options to protect that income when he buys the annuity, this income would cease on his death.

The Capital/Income Link

George's accumulating pension fund acts as deferred pay. However, when George buys his annuity he will convert his *capital* (around £85,000 by 2007) into *income*. This accumulated capital item on his net worth statement will literally disappear. Unless he buys a five-year guarantee to ensure his pension is paid out for five years, even if he dies before 2012, his whole capital fund is lost to

'Business is all about putting out money today to get a whole lot more back later.'

Warren Buffett

39

both him and Freda. George's pension options are examined in Stage 3 on pages 67–9.

By 2007, the outstanding mortgage and car loan debts should be eliminated. If they continue to save £720 every year, their bank deposit account should grow from £4,500 to about £15,300. But even if the house rises 10 per cent in value, the loss of the pension fund as capital dominates the net worth picture at retirement. This illustrates the importance of having balanced savings by your planned retirement date, a point covered in Stage 4.

However, there is some flexibility in the Blakes' savings plans, because by 2002 their car loan will be fully paid off and £2,160 a year can be reallocated to improve their prospects for 2007. Comparing the two budgets and net worth statements for 1999 and 2007 highlights some interesting points as

Estimated Retirement Gains and Losses for the Blakes

Gains	Losses
1. The mortgage will be fully paid off: they can live rent-free.	1. Too much of their wealth is locked up in their house.
2. Their house is a **real asset.** It gains in value if there is inflation.	2. They face an income shortfall of about £2,600 in 2007.
3. They will own their car, debt-free.	3. The car will be over ten years old, but there is inadequate income for a new car loan.
4. They can buy an annuity with George's pension fund as a replacement income.	4. a) After 2007, Freda loses the protection of George's accumulated pension fund. b) After 2017 she loses £5,000 of life assurance protection.
	5. Freda has no personal pension and will lose the benefit of George's pension when he dies.
	6. There is only a small savings account of £15,300, too little for emergencies or luxuries.
	7. If either partner dies, the other may have to work, or move to a smaller house to replace the lost income.

shown on the gains and losses list below, which is item 5 in the five-points guide to forecast their financial needs.

Setting Realistic Targets

The gains versus losses exercise quickly reveals the Blakes will have more losses than gains in 2007. They can see that without making any changes to their current plans, they probably face an income shortfall of around £2,600 in 2007, rising in each following year. They will not have saved enough free money. About £15,300 on deposit is too little to provide planning flexibility.

The Budget Shortfall

The budget exercise showed that their expected annual expenses will be around £17,106 by 2007, so they immediately know they must budget for an income of at least £17,100 to £17,500 by that time.

The Blakes
Step 3
Set realistic targets

The Capital Funds Shortfall

By 2007, they should have saved about £15,300. They need at least an extra £2,600 annually, to cover the income shortfall. An additional sum of around £50,000 in their bank deposit account would produce £2,500 in interest at 5% a year, giving them approximately the extra income they need, but it would not solve the rising income shortfall from 2008 onwards.

Filling the Blakes' Income and Capital Shortfalls

Shortfalls	Solutions
1. Income – **£2,600**	1. Save an additional £50,000 by 2007 (interest at 5% produces £2,500 a year)
2. Capital – **£50,000**	2. Examine the Options: (a) Save car loan cash: £2,000 from 2002 to 2007 – only raises about £14,280 (b) Move to a smaller house

---

Identifying the income and capital shortfalls immediately takes the Blakes to *Step 3*, setting realistic targets. For, if they want to maintain their current lifestyle after 2007, they will have an income shortfall of at least £2,600 and they need an additional £50,000 in capital to create that extra income from interest on a bank deposit account. *Steps 2* and *3* of putting your financial house in order, follow one another logically. So now we can compile a table for *Step 3*, to show how the Blakes work out their 2007 targets. To achieve more security, they need to plan for a yearly income of at least £17,500. When George retires, they should have about £16,500 in shares and deposits, but they need an extra £50,000 of capital. This would increase the capital in their 2007 net worth statement to £66,500 by 2007.

'I love being busy. I hope they carry me out of an office, not a rocking chair. I intend to go on for ever. I am not even thinking of retiring.'

Morton Mandel, chief executive, Premier Farnell

Retirement Targets for the Blakes

Asset	2007 Value on current plans £	Shortfall £	2007 Targets £
Annual Income	14,507	2,599	17,500
Capital fund	16,500 (bank account plus 100 Abbey National shares)	50,000	66,500
Net worth	**193,400**	**50,000**	**243,400**

If you spend time compiling your two wealth checks, any shortfall on either income and capital will emerge, from which it is a natural step to set these shortfall figures as realistic targets to be corrected by your expected retirement date. In Stages 3 and 4, we will follow the Blakes rectifying these shortfalls.

Endowment or Repayment Mortgage?

During the early 1980s, many people used endowment mortgages to buy their houses. Over 80 per cent of mortgages were linked to endowments, compared to over 30 per cent in the 1990s. As an exercise to illustrate the difference this might make for George and Freda, we will look at how their wealth checks would have changed if they had taken out an **endowment mortgage** instead of their repayment mortgage. Borrowers on a repayment mortgage gradually repay the outstanding capital on the debt, so that during the last fifteen or so years, the amount of interest they pay gradually reduces. When the mortgage term ends, their debt is completely paid off. With an endowment mortgage, a long-term savings policy is taken out at the start to run alongside it throughout the whole term. Every month the borrower pays interest on the full loan (without paying off any capital) plus a separate premium on the endowment policy. None of the capital is repaid until the term ends. The hope is that after twenty-five years, the endowment policy will be large enough to repay the entire debt. During the early 1980s, advisers were of the opinion that these plans would pay out a surplus after repaying the loans.

SUPPOSE THE BLAKES HAD AN ENDOWMENT MORTGAGE

Suppose the Blakes took out their endowment policy in 1982, and paid a premium of £60 each month to build up a fund of £50,000 to pay off their mortgage in 2007. They would pay interest on the whole loan, but to keep things simple, we will assume it is the same amount they are currently paying, (£4,320 a year). In practice, however, their monthly payments should be lower, as they are not repaying some of the capital each year. A joint endowment policy includes joint life cover on the first death for both parties, so the loan is repaid on either death before maturity. George could therefore have dispensed with the £5,000 term assurance policy.

To re-examine the expenses and net worth picture for the Blakes assuming they had an endowment mortgage, we will adjust their 1999 expenses in the simplest way. This will show how their positive net worth position for 2007 might differ. Again, these are rough estimates just to see how the financial picture would change for different financial products.

We can do a straight swap with the £60 each month which will now pay the endowment policy premium instead of being saved in the bank. But the Blakes can still save £21 a month in the bank because they do not need to pay the premium of £21 on the £5,000 of life cover for Freda. By 1999 we will assume they still have £4,500 saved in the bank, but it will only grow by £252 (£21 × 12) each year. With added interest, by 2007, their bank account will have grown to £9,899 instead of £15,300. However, by 1999, the endowment policy will have added seventeen years of guaranteed **annual bonuses**. It could be worth about £17,500. If the policy runs to maturity in 2007, a large, but not guaranteed **terminal bonus** will be added.

> '*I remember saving up for things when I was a boy and getting a wonderful thrill when I eventually had enough to buy what I wanted.*'
>
> John Madejski, founder of *Autotrader* magazine and owner of Reading Football Club

If the Blakes surrender their policy earlier, the **surrender value** will be less than the estimated value because costs spread over twenty-five years will be condensed into the smaller number of years up to their surrender date. During the 1990s, a second-hand market arose, as endowment policies were surrendered, because they play a valuable role in financial planning for many people. If you must sell an endowment policy before it matures, get a quote from the specialist policy companies, rather than surrender it to your insurance company. You may receive 25–30 per cent more cash. Details of companies in this market are given in Stage 7 on pages 189–90.

> '*Money will never buy the affection of other people. All said, I would still rather have money than not, but nobody should ever think it will be the answer to all their dreams.*'
>
> John Madejski

Annual bonuses added each year smooth out valuation fluctuations as, being guaranteed, once they are added, they cannot be taken away. The big terminal bonus is usually around 30 or even 40 per cent of the fund value by maturity. For the Blakes in 2007, it could be around £16,500 if the fund grows to reach the targeted £50,000 they had hoped for in 1982. However, the terminal bonus is not guaranteed and many endowment policies underperformed other equity-based investments during the 1990s. The poor record was due to annual bonus reductions made by insurance companies in the 1990s. The companies blamed this on a decline in long-term investment returns.

The outcome of poor returns in the 1990s means millions of borrowers with long-running endowment policies face sizeable shortfalls in the lump sum due to pay off their loans when the mortgage ends.

As possible shortfalls could be a problem you might face, we will look at how the Blakes cope on an endowment mortgage. If they had an average endowment policy their expected cash value by 2007 could be as low as £35,500 assuming standard rates of investment growth, instead of the forecast £50,000. To cover this shortfall, they must increase their policy premiums, or make additional savings elsewhere. Insurance companies who have identified a shortfall usually alert policyholders when they send out annual bonus notices each year.

It is possible that forecast estimates could be too pessimistic on the eventual outcomes, as average maturity values for twenty-five-year endowment policies were good in 1998. A £30 a month twenty-five-year average policy maturing on April 1 1998 produced a payout of £62,065, 3 per cent up from 1997. A pro-rata figure for a £60 a month policy suggests a payout exceeding £120,000. However, these policies began in April 1973, just a few months before the start of a severe global recession. The recovery began in 1975, and the next twenty-three years were excellent for equity-based investments. The **FTSE All-Share index**, with dividends reinvested, rose almost 140-fold to December 1997, while the growth without reinvesting the dividends was 44-fold. A notional £1,000 invested in 1975 in the FTSE All-Share index with dividends reinvested would have returned almost £120,000 by December 1997.

With such excellent market conditions, several insurance companies will exceed the average performance for twenty-five-year endowment plans. However, while there was over twenty years of strong growth for equity-based investments, it is rash when planning retirement to expect this to continue into the future. Better to be cautious. If returns for the next few years are lower, more saving will be needed, not less.

'I think anybody who is miserable now will still be miserable after winning the lottery. Money alone will not make you happier, you will just find something else to worry about.'

Elaine Thompson, winner of £2.7 million in the National Lottery, December 1995

The Blakes

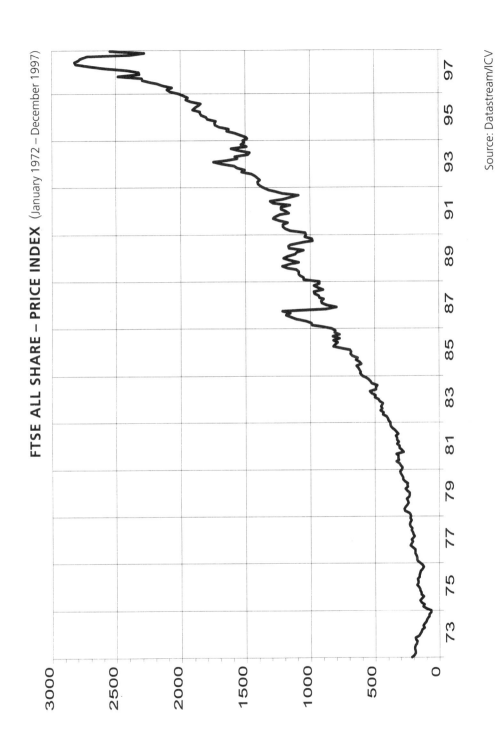

FTSE ALL SHARE – PRICE INDEX (January 1972 – December 1997)

Source: Datastream/ICV

To assess the differences, we rework the Blakes' net worth figures for 1999 and 2007, using the endowment rather than repayment mortgage calculations. Because they still owe £50,000 on their mortgage, their net worth in 1999 is £17,500 less than with their repayment mortgage where only £20,000 is still outstanding. (£182,550 – £165,050 = £17,500). In scenario (A), a possible shortfall of £14,500 will completely wipe out their bank savings of £9,899 and still leave them with another £4,601 to find. This would be a poor start to George's retirement. The loss of £7,551 in their net worth in (A) is due to the loss of the accumulated pension fund, plus the endowment policy deficit, but they would be £25,051 worse off than with their endowment mortgage (£182,550–£157,499 = –£25,051).

In scenario (B), there is still a large drop in their 2007 net worth compared

George and Freda's Net Worth for 1999 and 2007 With an Endowment Mortgage

Assets	1999 Value £	2007 Value £ (A) no growth	2007 Value £ (B) 10% growth	Comments
House	160,000	160,000	176,000	
Car	5,000	1,500	1,500	Loses value
Pension fund	33,700	Nil	Nil	Capital converted to income via annuity on retirement
Endowment policy	17,500	35,500	39,050	Life cover until 2007
100 Abbey National shares	1,000	1,200	1,200	Assumes around 20% growth in 9 years
Bank Deposit	4,500	9,899	9,899	Assumes 5% interest and £252 added to the fund each year
Totals	**221,700**	**208,099**	**227,649**	
DEBTS				
Mortgage	50,000	50,000	50,000	Mortgage repaid in 2007
Car loan	5,400	Nil	Nil	Car loan repaid in May 2002
Credit card debt	1,250	600	600	
Total debts	56,650	50,600	50,600	Full mortgage still to pay (£50,000)
Net worth	**165,050**	**157,499**	**177,049**	
Estimated Gain/Loss		**–7,551** **Loss**	**–5,501** **Loss** **(on £182,550)**	

to the repayment mortgage route due mainly to the shortfall of £10,950 in the endowment payout. The figure again exceeds their estimated bank savings. To remedy this, the Blakes must begin investing the freed-up car loan cash to pay off their mortgage debt: £2,160 a year will become available from May 2002, when the car loan is fully repaid.

While these are only rough guesses, this exercise shows how crucial it is to make early estimates of your assets and debts at retirement. They show how easy it is to drift blindly into unexpected financial shocks. In Stages 3 and 4, we will examine pension and capital building ideas for the Blakes but we will use the original net worth schedules, assuming they had a repayment mortgage.

Consider Rearranging Your Assets

As you go through the five-point guide to forecast your financial needs at retirement, you move through *Steps 2* and *3* of putting your house in order. You can figure out the shortfalls and set the obvious targets. If your esti-mated gains and losses table looks as lopsided as the Blakes don't despair. The purpose of these exercises is to give you a full picture, so you can make improvements to your prospects.

Step 4
Rearrange some assets?
Yes! Put your house in
order

If the Blakes begin in 1999, they have another nine years to get their finances in better shape for retirement. In their case, a shortfall of £50,000 looks depressing so they should now consider rearranging some of their assets.

Studying their two wealth checks, their problem looks obvious: they have too much cash locked up in their home and far too little as a capital sum to give flexibility in retirement. In Stage 4, we will explore ways the Blakes, and you, can rearrange existing assets to improve the forecast situation.

However, it is clear the Blakes could find extra cash by releasing funds from their house. So we will now examine the available options. They can either reorganise their finances while staying put. Or they can move house in order to release further funds.

'In the developed world, thanks to all-rapid change, today's average citizen enjoys a higher standard of living than a king did 200 years ago. Only, more often than not, he is not enjoying it as much as he might, as he is too worried that it might all disappear at the click of a mouse.'

The Economist

47

Pay Your Mortgage off Early?

Although repaying their mortgage is not a problem for George and Freda, they could pay it off in 1999 by buying a smaller house outright, in order to release money for investing prior to retirement. The debate about paying the whole balance off early often concerns many people when they retire. Saving on the interest due and the capital repayments each month sounds sensible when you are organising your retirement budget. You might eliminate your whole debt and save thousands of pounds by paying off your mortgage early.

Step 5
Rearrange your housing assets

However, there are other issues and, like many aspects of retirement planning, there are advantages and disadvantages. Any decision depends on your special circumstances. It obviously helps to do full wealth checks, as set out earlier. How you assess your situation is shown in Stage 7 on pages 171–8.

Revised Home Income Plans

More than a decade after the scandal of home income plans, improved variations began appearing, as rising property values during the 1990s meant an estimated £900 billion or more was available to fund them. By unlocking cash tied up in their homes, these plans are invaluable to cash-strapped retired people not wanting to move, although many people are deterred by knowing they will pass less of their assets to their families on death. These plans are most suitable for older people living in expensive houses, because one drawback is that if your circumstances change and you would like to move house in the future, your options may be more limited, as a large part of the value of your existing home is tied up in the home income plan. There are three main types of scheme, all involving some complexity, so seek expert advice. Details on home income plans are covered in Stage 7 on pages 174–6.

> *'All insurance is a form of betting, an insurance company is only a glorified bookmaker, you have to weigh up the odds.'*
>
> John Cusson, on his Stalwart Assurance reversionary plan, *The Times*, May 1998

Step 6
Move house

Your financial assets must start working constructively for you once you are no longer working for them

Choose Between Two Homes

Many people approaching retirement consider buying a small house as a holiday home, in Britain or abroad. This might serve as a transition period for deciding whether the smaller property is an acceptable home before the larger property is sold. You have an adjustment period, to get used to living in a small property, while continuing to occupy your larger family home, before the big move is made. We will look at buying a property abroad as a second home in Stage 7 on pages 172–4 including options to finance it. However, taking decisive action on moving in retirement can cause problems if it is not well planned, as the sad story of Bruce and Margery White illustrates.

BRUCE HAS A MOVING SHOCK

Bruce and Margery were civil servants who had met at work and married in their late thirties. They both had superannuated pensions to enjoy when they retired in 1980. They lived very comfortably in a modern, expensive bungalow in the Lake District but Margery came from Devon and in 1978 she inherited a small cottage there from her father. During the 1980 recession the Whites decided they could not afford the upkeep on both properties. But which one should they sell? Bruce preferred to sell the cottage as he had no friends in Devon. Margery had relatives and friends in Devon and wanted to keep the cottage.

After a year, as the expenses mounted and were a drain on their pensions, they began to worry. Then, a buyer emerged for their bungalow, and the decision seemed to have been made for them. They would keep the cottage and sell the bungalow.

Two months after the move to Devon, Margery had a massive heart attack and died within twenty-four hours. Bruce was devastated. He had no children and had hardly settled into the cottage and had made no friends. Whenever I spoke to him, he was distraught over his losses; his world had fallen apart. Within two years, Bruce moved back to his roots in the Lake District, but it took several years to rebuild his life.

While it is impossible to anticipate such disasters, Bruce's story shows how central it is to your planning to be sure about moving house and to avoid being swayed by lesser issues unless there are no alternatives.

Cash in on Your Home

Moving house is a monumental upheaval. This and divorce are the two most stressful events in domestic life. Nevertheless, reassessing your housing needs as part of your overall investment plans is worthwhile for retirement planning. Although it is sometimes useful to have extra bedrooms, you might find a smaller house, flat or bungalow will suit you better. When you compile your forecast retirement budget, you may

A big advantage of home ownership is the income boost you get by repaying the mortgage during your working life, so you can live rent-free during retirement

find, as I did, that your finances would receive a useful boost if you unlock some of the capital tied up in your large family home.

MR SHROFF STAYED PUT

I suggested exactly this to Mr Shroff in 1981. He lived in a luxurious house in an expensive Manchester suburb. He was two years from retiring but he had not saved for a pension. His accountant asked me to explain how selling his huge house to invest some of the freed-up capital in long-dated gilt-edged stock would give him a fairly safe fixed income. In 1981, interest rates of 12 per cent were available, and his accountant wanted to prepare a gilts portfolio to substitute for his missing pension.

While you are still fully mobile and perhaps living with an active partner, it makes sense to review all the possible options in your housing situation

Neither his wife, accountant nor I could budge him from his view that a prestigious home was a good investment. However true that may be, living in a large house with expensive overheads is a luxury that doesn't make sense for a family without a pension. But Mr Shroff wouldn't budge. His financial pyramid looked very unstable with a huge commitment to his house, no pension and little cash to live on in retirement. He was in his late sixties in 1981, and I often wonder how he finally resolved his dilemma. Another home income plan, perhaps.

Consider a Safe Shelter

Moving into **sheltered accommodation** is another alternative. This is a group of warden-controlled properties, each comprising a basic set of rooms: a living room, one or two bedrooms, a small kitchen and a bathroom. They could be new purpose-built homes, or part of newly converted, older houses. This accommodation is ideal for young retirees living alone. Twenty-four-hour warden services provide reassurance. There is someone to call quickly in an emergency, to organise minor repairs or to carry out the chores the elderly find difficult to tackle alone.

The market for sheltered housing in Britain has become a large, complex sector. However, do not move into sheltered housing too early; one of my friends did just that and felt uncomfortably young compared to other residents. She moved out again within three years.

Many schemes are available, with possibly more choice in the future, to satisfy increasing demand. Sheltered housing details are covered in Stage 7 on pages 176–8.

HOUSING CHOICES FOR THE BLAKES

Three, possibly four of these housing options might suit George and Freda Blake. Any of them would create more cash either now or at retirement, so they merit further investigation:

1. They could move to a smaller house right away (in 1999).
2. They could move in 2007, when the mortgage is repaid.
3. They could consider a home income plan. This option only applies to the over-seventies.
4. They might buy or rent a warden-controlled property.

The Blakes may decide to wait to see how their plans develop, but by investigating their options at the outset and storing the findings, quicker actions will be possible when the time looks right.

Whatever route they take, their choice depends on individual preferences, since three of their options mean waiting until they are closer to, or are actually in retirement. To illustrate how to judge their options, we will look at what they might gain by moving in 1999.

Benefits of Moving Early for the Blakes

Suppose they sold their house for £160,000 in 1999 and bought a smaller property for £120,000 including all costs. They could repay their mortgage of £20,000 and have a cash sum of about £20,000 free to invest. The Blakes will then live rent-free, giving them an additional £4,320 every year to invest, from January 2000 to December 2007; an extra £34,560 over eight years.

Cash released by moving in 1999
Free cash from selling house: £20,000
8 years of mortgage repayments saved: £34,560 (£4,320 × 8)
Total cash released: £54,560

If between January 2000 and December 2007, their total savings of £54,560 grew by a modest 5 per cent each year, they could build a capital sum of £72,865. A growth rate of 7 per cent would lift their savings to £81,789 by the end of 2007.

Prospects for the Blakes by Moving House in 1999

Item	Value in 1999 £
House	160,000
Less mortgage	−20,000
Money for smaller house	140,000
Cost of smaller house	120,000
FREE CASH	**20,000**
Money saved on mortgage	34,560 (4,320 × 8 = 34,560)
Total money invested	54,560
Capital Fund by 2007	
(5%)	**72,865**
(7%)	**81,789**

We will look at ways to make these savings of £54,560 grow in Stage 4, but it is clear that rearranging their assets by moving to a smaller house might transform the Blakes' prospects. When we set realistic targets for them we wanted to build a capital fund of £50,000 by 2007. By creating £20,000 in 1999, plus the opportunity to redirect mortgage repayments over eight years into savings, they have an extra eight years to invest to make a substantial improvement to their financial situation before they retire.

In Summary

Building secure foundations by adjusting your housing arrangements at retirement, covers a large range of different factors and options. However, even when your housing needs are suitably addressed, there is still the all-important matter of a secure and adequate income once your regular salary ceases. Acquiring this is the second building block for your retirement financial pyramid. We will discuss it in Stage 3, to which we now turn.

Key Points to Remember

STAGE 2: PUT YOUR HOUSE IN ORDER

1. Your long term plan is to become financially secure.

2. Build a financial pyramid to acquire a balanced group of assets for retirement.

3. Use the five-point guide to forecast your financial needs: identify any shortfalls.

4. Set yourself realistic targets for income and capital at retirement.

5. Consider different options for raising more money if necessary.

6. Rearrange some assets to raise more cash.

7. Consider various options for your housing needs.

'The retirement planner's biggest challenge is to ensure an adequate pension.'

Touche Ross, financial advisers

Build an Income to Rely on

'Saving for your retirement is not a simple affair. Many people get bogged down in the intricacies of regulation and legislation and keep putting the decision off. But this decision cannot be put off indefinitely.'

Peter Davis, Group chief executive, Prudential Corporation

In Britain, sadly, the pensions industry is a mess. During the 1990s, pension legislation, regulation and advice fell far short of acceptable standards, although pension planning is arguably the most important investment issue future retirees face. A reliable pension plan is the one financial product almost everyone of working age needs. Yet recent publicity over the ten-year-old mis-selling scandal – with an estimated 2.4 million victims in 1998 – has destroyed public confidence in the industry's ability to provide good products.

For this reason alone, if you become your own financial adviser you can reap huge benefits by retirement. Here, we follow a logical series of steps to help you master this complicated topic. We begin with a description of available pension types, the main background information. Then, in *Step 1* you calculate what size pension you need, in the context of *Step 2*, in which you assess whether to commute the allowable lump sum. Knowing what size pension you need, you move on to *Step 3* – is there an income shortfall? *Step 4* helps you find a good personal pension plan. Accumulating your pension fund is only half the task if you must then buy an annuity with it. *Step 5* covers this important issue and *Step 6* tackles finding the best annuity. A new option, income drawdown, needs careful assessment, described in *Step 7*.

Insufficient Pension Planning

The state pension is **unfunded**, or pay-as-you-go. Today's workers pay the pensions of today's pensioners through their taxes. It worked when more people died young or lived a few years into retirement, but it is unsatisfactory now. Pensions saved by individuals, by whatever scheme, are **funded** or investment

STAGE 3 BUILD AN INCOME TO RELY ON

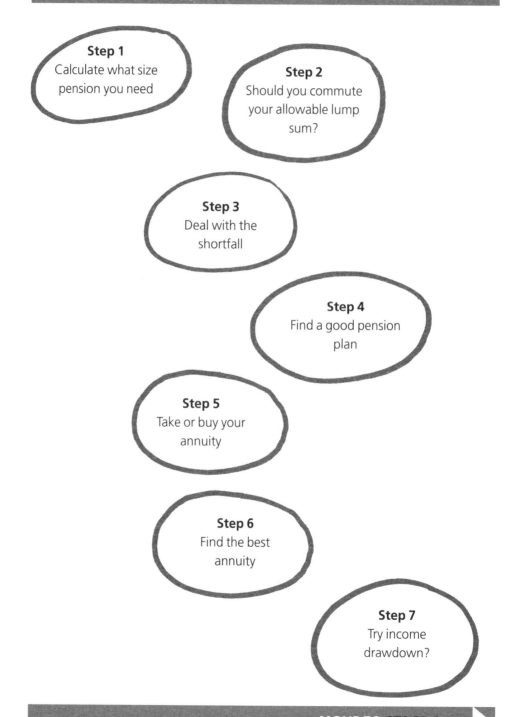

Step 1
Calculate what size pension you need

Step 2
Should you commute your allowable lump sum?

Step 3
Deal with the shortfall

Step 4
Find a good pension plan

Step 5
Take or buy your annuity

Step 6
Find the best annuity

Step 7
Try income drawdown?

MOVE TO STAGE 4 ▶

linked, relying on accumulating a fund which will ultimately be used to buy the pension.

According to the NatWest Pensions Index in 1998, about 13 million people will retire with a pension worth £106 or less a week, a figure on which millions of pensioners now struggle to survive. Almost 21 per cent of workers will retire on a pension of around £179 a week, well below half the average earnings of £420 per week in 1998.

> *'The Index is really aimed at making people take notice of the problem.'*
>
> Joanne Hindle, pensions development director at NatWest Life

A government study in 1998, reported that pensioner inequality will rise sharply up to 2025, even if state-provided income support rises in line with earnings, rather than inflation. However, despite these dismal findings, the group found that although the value of the state pension is falling, it will remain an important part of pensioners' income by 2025. For all but the top 20 per cent of pensioners, the modest state pension accounts for at least a quarter of their income.

The problem of inadequate pension preparation by millions of working people is partly due to the inflexibility of most policies. The enormous available choice added to complex regulations, make people wary of acquiring a long-term commitment for fear they later discover it was a poor choice. This is what happened to Stella, when she decided to transfer her personal pension to another pension provider.

STELLA'S PENSION SHOCK

After saving £80 a month for just under four years in a personal pension plan, Stella discovered, when talking to colleagues at work, that her plan was one of the worst for high charges and poor returns. She decided to transfer to the pension provider her friend was with. When she rang the company running her plan to request a transfer value she found to her horror that she would get back £2,850 less than she had paid in. Now she faced a no-win situation – she could either continue to pay into this below par plan or transfer what remained of her four years of premiums at a large loss.

Information Stella Needs
When she told me this sorry tale, I made some suggestions:
1. Ask the salesman who sold her the plan to calculate what size fund she must build to buy an annuity, equal to two-thirds her estimated final year's salary at retirement. This annuity is her guaranteed income for life.
2. Ask what size premiums she must make to reach this size fund.

She was even more shocked to learn she should be paying £250 per month in premiums to meet these estimates. She was unsure whether or not to transfer the pension. However, there was a third solution, which she ultimately took:

A Third Option for Stella

1. Reduce her premiums down to the lowest allowable amount at the annual review. This was £20 per month and her annual review was two months ahead.

2. Find a reliable independent financial adviser to choose a company with lower charges and a consistently good performance record. This is better than blindly starting another pension with the company her friend uses.

3. Begin her new plan with the £60 per month balance of her existing premiums. She then has two policies, giving her more flexibility and spreading her investment risk.

4. She must think seriously about increasing her premiums to £250 a month to build the fund size she needs for a secure retirement.

'A house and pension are the two biggest assets that most people acquire during their working lives but unfortunately they do not usually see their pension in this way. Otherwise they would not be content to put just £30 or £50 a month into it.'

Steve Bell, pensions expert at Scottish Life

Pensions Benefits

There are probably thousands of people facing similar pension dilemmas to Stella. Yet despite all the drawbacks, accumulating a pension fund offers four important benefits, although only two apply to everyone.

1. A pension is undoubtedly the best way to create a replacement retirement income. As a secure income, it is more reliable even than your regular salary, as you may lose your job. A pension, once set up, is guaranteed to be paid until you die, even if you live abroad. The certainty of pension income is its greatest saving virtue. It is clearly valuable, but we shall see in Stage 4 that there are other ways to build a replacement income, if your pension plans are inadequate.

2. A pension has several major tax advantages, enabling your fund to grow faster than other forms of saving.

   a) Your contributions are deducted from your income before tax, so you can invest an extra 20, 23 or 40 per cent more cash (depending on your top tax rate).

   b) You pay no **capital gains tax**. This is payable on gains made outside tax-free schemes when selling assets above a legal allowance (£6,800 for the financial year 6 April 1998 to 5 April 1999).

c) At retirement, you can take 25 per cent (30 per cent for **retirement annuity plans**) as a tax-free lump sum. This valuable concession is termed commutation.

These tax advantages are so beneficial that limits are applied to the amounts of income you can pay into a pension fund. These limits, listed in Stage 7, rise with age for personal pensions. However, when you take your pension on retirement you pay tax at source.

3. There are substantial guaranteed benefits for employees of final salary company schemes. Government funded **superannuation** schemes for civil servants and government employees are even better.

4. Personal pensions are flexible as they can be drawn any time after the age of fifty.

Build a Pensions Staircase

To exploit this age rule, arrange a series of different policies with different companies, using different retirement dates, to create a pensions staircase. Every few years another plan is used to buy an annuity, providing increasing income as your retirement progresses. Using several companies avoids the risk of relying on one policy with a poor investment performance.

A pensions staircase with several policies, avoids the legal requirement to take each fund in its entirety. If Stella increases her premiums to £250 per month, a pensions staircase would give greater flexibility and diversify the risks.

> *'We are in the rather unhappy position where people have lost a great deal of confidence in the financial services industry as a competent adviser in times of need, or as trustworthy guardians of savings and investment.'*
>
> Frank Field, minister for welfare reform, 1997 to 1998

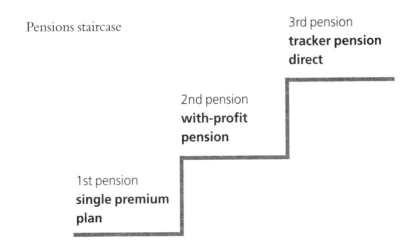

Pensions staircase

1st pension
single premium plan

2nd pension
with-profit pension

3rd pension
tracker pension direct

Inadequate State Pensions

Newspapers have highlighted the low, and falling level of state pensions. Younger people are urged to save for retirement. Starting early can make an enormous difference to the amounts you need to save, because money growing over twenty or thirty years increases by **compound growth**: dividends reinvested or interest paid on the money saved adds to the money already saved, so you don't have to save as much as is necessary over a shorter period of only ten to fifteen years. This is good news for younger people but unhelpful for those with ten years or less to make up pension shortfalls. However, compound growth works for all savings plans, if you begin at around age forty or fifty to build tax-free cash for retirement, a point covered in Stage 4.

The maximum basic state pension in 1998 for a single person was about £3,663 a year, £70.45 per week. The increase to £75 per week applied only to about a million pensioners with no other income sources. There was no firm figure for maximum **Serps** payouts, (state earnings-related pension scheme, discussed below) best guesses suggest around £4,000 a year.

In 1998, *The Times* asked Charles Levett-Scrivener, of financial services group, Towry Law, to analyse the state pension as a percentage of average incomes. He calculated the state pension in 1998 was 15.4 per cent of the average male weekly wage of £420. It would fall to under 8 per cent of an average weekly wage of £3,868 by 2050.

Average earnings of £3,868 a week may sound ridiculous to people currently earning £400 to £600 a week. The figures may assume inflation continues as in the past, a dangerous assumption. However, since 1948, British people have become almost three times better off. In 1948, my father, a company managing director, earned £48 a week or £2,500 a year. If his wage had kept pace with inflation it would have risen approximately twenty times by 1998, to around £960 a week or £50,000 a year. However, most company managing directors earn well in excess of £50,000, as skilled peoples' incomes have grown faster than inflation since 1948.

If you retire at sixty in 2007 and live to eighty-five, who can say what living conditions and average earnings will be in 2032? The only certainty is to recognise the looming cash crisis future retirees might face if they do not have a growing pot of money, or a large and growing second pension in retirement.

'People should know that on current policies their state pensions will represent very modest proportions of their likely earnings if they are going to retire in thirty or forty years' time.'

Tom Ross, City pensions consultant

The Serps Conundrum

Few people understand Serps: what is it? Should you be in it or not? Serps is a state-run pension scheme to top up the state pension. It is paid for from a proportion of your national insurance contributions for employees earning over £64 a week. The self-employed or unemployed are excluded; only company employees are eligible. The ceiling is earnings of £485 a week above which no contributions are allowed. The size of the ultimate benefit you obtain relates to your earnings between these two limits. Calculations on your Serps pension are complicated as a complex formula is applied.

Everyone can opt out of Serps via an occupational pension or a personal plan. If you opt out, national insurance contributions continue to be deducted from your pay but part of them go into your pension fund as rebates. The decision to contract out or not is complicated. It depends on your age, sex and salary, your views on how good your pension provider's investment returns will be, and the size of your national insurance rebates. Experts think that men over 50 and women over 45 should be in Serps, even if they contracted out earlier. Around 6 million people have used personal pensions to contract out of Serps on the assumption that personal pension providers invest your national insurance rebates to give better growth than occurs within Serps. However, the government abolished the right of pension funds to reclaim **advance corporation tax** on dividends they receive within those funds, from April 1997. This measure made it harder for providers to outdo Serps, by reducing the investment returns they achieve. Issues concerning Serps are covered in Stage 7 on pages 182–3.

'Millions face sharp falls in income on retirement as the basic state pension, which is linked to the rise in prices, and Serps, the second-tier state earnings-related pension scheme, fall farther behind the rise in average earnings.'

We all need pensions – the prospects for pension provision, Government Report, 1998

Types of Pension Schemes

With small state pensions, we must look at the private plans available, as most people rely on these. Although the government plans to introduce stakeholder pensions, perhaps by 2001, at the time of writing this book there were two main types:

1. Occupational schemes, run by employers for the benefit of their employees, which include: a) Final salary (defined benefits) schemes. b) Money purchase (defined contributions) which are usually group personal pension schemes run collectively by the employer.

2. Personal pensions which an individual saver buys from an insurance or pension company.

Final Salary Company Schemes

About 11 million people, less than half the working population, are fortunate enough to belong to company final salary schemes, also called defined benefit schemes because all the many benefits to be provided are defined by the scheme's rules when the employee joins. His ultimate pension depends on just two factors:

1. How many years he works for that company.
2. His final salary.

The pension is a predetermined percentage, usually 1/60th (it varies in different schemes) of final salary for each year the employee is in the scheme.

These company schemes provide many guaranteed benefits: a widow's pension, a death-in-service lump sum payment for the widow, perhaps two or three times salary on death, **indexation** of the pension by a set amount, say 3 per cent, or in line with the **Retail Prices Index** (which measures the amount of inflation in the economy). The employer makes monthly contributions throughout the period of service, usually around 12 per cent, while the employees pay, on average 5 per cent.

To illustrate how excellent these benefits are, suppose George Blake earned £24,500 a year in a final salary scheme. If he died in 1999, Freda would receive a death-in-service lump sum benefit of perhaps three times his annual salary. This would give her £73,500 (£24,500 × 3 = £73,500) instead of £33,700 in his personal pension fund. Even if the death-in-service benefit is only twice his salary, Freda would get £49,000. She would also be entitled to a widow's pension from George's company, which she would not get from his personal pension fund.

Another advantage is that the ultimate pension value is linked to your final salary. Worries over stock market crashes or annuity rate levels, two major concerns for people with personal pensions, are avoided as the employer bears all the risk.

However, among the drawbacks, job mobility ranks highly. To enjoy the maximum two-thirds pension you must stay forty years with one company. Few people achieve this. Men average twenty two years in one job, and women sixteen. If you lose your job or move voluntarily, your pension will not continue to grow at the rate it did when you and your employer paid in contributions. You can transfer it to your new scheme but penalties are imposed which reduce the amount transferred.

A state pension linked to prices, not average earnings, means pensioners totally fail to enjoy the rising prosperity of the nation

About half existing schemes, called **integrated company schemes** allow for the state pension in their calculations, so your final pension will be lower than your total salary. A ceiling of 15 per

Final Salary Company Schemes

Advantages	Disadvantages
1. Benefits are guaranteed.	1. Few people stay forty years in one job.
2. Many defined benefits are included.	2. Pensions that are left in a scheme when an employee leaves grow very little.
3. The employer bears the investment risk.	3. High transfer fees reduce the fund on moving jobs.
4. The employer makes generous contributions (12 per cent).	4. Cannot build a two-thirds of final salary pension with integrated company schemes.
5. Pension is linked to final salary, not stock market performance.	5. Limits of 15 per cent on employee contributions may prevent job-movers building a large enough fund.
6. Pension can be two-thirds of final salary.	6. Cannot take pensions early and continue working for the same company.
7. Company-run AVCs are cheaper than **free-standing AVCs** (FAVCs) run by outside companies.	7. Less flexible than personal pensions.

cent of income limits employee contributions into company schemes. If you have several job changes, you may not be able to increase your contributions enough to overcome the loss in the growth of your funds. Regular job-movers or people in integrated schemes, should address the shortfall by topping up funds with AVCs (additional voluntary contributions). Despite the advantages, few employees use AVCs.

Money Purchase Company Schemes

This is the other main occupational pension scheme. However, 'money purchase' just describes the way the fund is built. Both your contributions and those made by your employer in a group scheme, buy a range of investments – mainly equities – to increase the fund size. Your investment fund is used on retirement to buy a guaranteed annuity: the larger the fund, the larger the annuity it will buy.

Your employer may run a money purchase scheme along lines similar to, but less attractive than, a final salary scheme. It may be a group personal pension scheme, which is becoming popular because although the employer makes regular contributions to your fund, that is his only risk.

A survey by the Association of Consulting Actuaries in 1998 found that almost one third of companies run a group personal pension scheme, paying in less than money purchase or final salary schemes. Final salary pensions were declining, to 30 per cent of companies, from 38 per cent in 1996.

A few money purchase company schemes offer life assurance, (in addition to the value of your fund if you die) and disability cover. These benefits are optional and depend on your employer. The average combined employer-employee contribution is only 9.3 per cent, which is lower than most final salary employer contribution levels. This will produce a pension of just under half final salary at retirement. Again, AVCs can improve the prospects or make up contribution gaps.

The majority of the employer's and employees' contributions are invested into equities, which show the best long-term returns. Employees shoulder all the risks of a big stock market fall in the year they retire. Another worry is that falling annuity rates reduce the value of the annuity bought at retirement.

These schemes are called **defined contributions** because the only definite feature is the level of contributions made. You cannot know the final size of your pension at retirement because the several unknowns include the investment performance of the company running your policy, and the investment conditions at the time you retire.

While group schemes are meant to be portable, in practice, this is impractical. Job-movers can take their money purchase scheme with them, but it is most unlikely another employer will take it on, as too many employees move jobs so the administration effort is unmanageable.

High charges punch big holes in the funds of paid-up personal pensions, those to which the policyholder has ceased to make contributions

Personal Pensions

If you take out a pension on your own, you buy a personal pension, yet another form of money purchase pension. It is similar to a group scheme, although it does not receive contributions from your employer. Your contract exists between you and the company running your plan. Although all the risks and responsibility now lie with you, there are compensations. You can choose the company you want to manage your fund, rather than having to accept the company your employer chooses and most personal policies are flexible.

You can buy your annuity while continuing to work until age seventy-five or vary the premiums you pay from year to year. You can also pay in irregular one-off lump sums. Some plans allow unlimited premium holidays without penalties. You can take your fund at any age after fifty, while still working, and use more than one company, to spread your investment risk.

Adventurous self-employed investors, or certain employees, can choose

a **Sipp** plan (**Self-invested personal pension**). It can be funded by

Money Purchase Company Schemes

Advantages	Disadvantages
1. The employer pays a 9.3 per cent contribution.	1. Benefits are not guaranteed.
2. The pension is portable but this is impractical.	2. No defined benefits are included.
	3. The employees bear all the investment risk.
	4. The employer's contribution is lower than in final salary schemes.
	5. The pension is not linked to final salary.
	6. The pension may be adversely affected by stock market fluctuations.
	7. Most employees only build a pension equal to half their salary.
	8. Job-movers may find their new company uses a different pension provider and cannot continue with their previous plan.
	9. Penalties are incurred by moving funds to a new company pension.
	10. Employees cannot choose the pension provider. This choice is made by the employer.
	11. Running costs may be higher and performance lower than if you choose your own pension provider.

transferring existing policies, making new contributions or a combination of both. Sipps allow planholders even more flexibility than traditional policies, including a wider investment choice: you can put commercial property into your Sipp.

There are two major uncertainties:

1. Personal pensions rely on stock market investments to boost their performance, so your pot may be subject to a sudden downturn in the market in the final months before you take your pension. Ways to avoid this are discussed on page 183.

2. Falling annuity rates reduce the size of the annuity you can buy. We look more closely at this problem on pages 85–7.

Personal Pensions

Advantages	Disadvantages
1. You always keep control.	1. No employer contribution to increase the growth rate of your fund.
2. You can vary your contribution levels.	2. You bear all the investment risks.
3. There is more flexibility in the terms.	3. No guaranteed benefits.
4. You can add extra options: waiver of premium, life assurance protection.	4. You need very large premiums to build a fund equal to two-thirds of final salary.
5. Your policy may allow premium holidays.	5. Your funds may be exposed to stock market collapses.
6. You can take your pension at fifty and continue working.	6. Your annuity depends on prevailing annuity rates.
7. You can use several pension providers to spread investment risks.	
8. Your pension is unaffected if you move jobs.	

Different Pension Types Compared

Neither money purchase or personal pension schemes are as good as final salary schemes because the only defined area is in the amount of contribution you or your employer makes. All the reassuring guarantees of final salary schemes are absent with money purchase schemes. As personal pensions have many disadvantages, choosing a good plan is a vital issue covered on pages 78–84.

What Size Pension Do You Need?

As state benefits are small, building your pension fund is the second main block in your retirement financial pyramid. We saw in Stage 2, how owning your home gives you a valuable asset. While most people willingly take on a large mortgage, perhaps paying £200 to £500 a month to buy their home over twenty to thirty years, the average pension contribution a month is around £30 to £50. Too few people begin serious pension planning until well into their thirties, or later. As the state pension falls in value this could be a monumental disaster within two decades, since a second pension to supplement the basic state pension will be essential for maintaining a decent retirement living standard.

Step 1
Calculate what size pension you need

Aim to build a pension at least two-thirds your final salary. We have seen how difficult it is to achieve this for people with group or personal money purchase schemes. For all these savers, plus late starters and people with large domestic commitments, this level of pension may be unattainable. However, after deducting the expenses that end on retirement, a pension equal to two-thirds your final salary should provide a reasonable excess of income over your remaining expenses. Even at this level, a pension alone may not cover expensive items, like holidays or new cars.

As you work through the seven Stages to a successful retirement, you should set yourself a target to try to achieve two-thirds of your final salary, if possible. If this is impractical, focus on building up a lump sum of capital to supplement your less-than-adequate pension. How you do this will become clearer in Stage 4.

> *'I constantly think I am going to retire this year, but it never happens.'*
>
> Nicola Horlick, joint managing director of Société Générale Asset Management UK

Commute For Cash Now

Most people expect the whole of their growing pension fund will buy their annuity. Under present legislation, everyone is allowed to commute 25 per cent of the accumulated fund as tax-free cash and this concession offers valuable planning flexibility. However, 30 per cent can be commuted for earlier retirement annuity plans begun before 1988. Many of these retirement annuities incorporate guaranteed annuity rates. These are so much higher than current annuity rates, if you have one of these pre-1988 plans, it may be worth ignoring the commutation option and using your whole fund to buy your annuity.

Step 2
Should you commute your allowable lump sum?

Your annuity usually ends when you die. If you take your full allowable tax-free lump sum, at least 25 per cent of your fund can be used in a variety of ways outside the pension constraints. You can:

1. Pay off big debts.
2. Buy expensive items, say, a garden swimming pool or world travel.
3. Build up a capital fund by saving it in a tax-free **Isa** (Individual savings account) beginning April 1999.
4. Bequeath it to your family or a charity on your death.

If you commute your tax-free cash, only 75 per cent of your accumulated fund will be available to buy your annuity with serious consequences for your income in retirement: if you spend your lump sum or repay debts, your long-term pension income will be much smaller than if you use your whole fund to buy your annuity. However, if you save the whole 25 per cent cash when you commute your pension, you can build up flexible capital outside your pension.

Creating such a fund is Stage 4 of the planning path to financial freedom. Saving the tax-free lump sum preserves your planning flexibility.

The Shortfall Now

An estimated 7 million people, over a quarter of the workforce, have neither occupational nor personal pensions. In 1998, an independent panel, the Pensions Review Group, forecast that 5 million people face an income drop of over 50 per cent at retirement due to inadequate pension savings.

Step 3
Deal with the shortfall

Within a final salary company scheme employees may achieve a retirement income of up to two-thirds of their final salary. Yet since 1988, when pension scheme membership ceased to be compulsory, about 20 per cent of new employees have chosen not to join. This means a loss of the employer's contribution, so employees took a pay cut by opting out, although few would have realised this consequence.

Poor information for employees underlies this faulty decision; as does the low take-up of AVCs, which reduces the size of a final pension fund as AVCs allow employees to top up their company pension. In 1998, the annual survey by the National Association of Pension Funds (NAPF) showed that on average only 15 per cent of company scheme members make AVCs. Yet only 8 per cent of men and 4 per cent of women, (about 1.32 million people) achieve the maximum allowable pension.

AVCs became the issue for a possible mis-selling scandal during 1998, when surveys showed pension and insurance salesmen had discovered this lucrative, virtually untapped market. Initial estimates suggested 50,000 to 60,000 cases could require compensation totalling up to £100 million. By selling free-standing AVCs (FAVCs and FSAVCs, run by the salesman's company not the employee's company) they made high commission. However, the employees lose, because costs of FAVCs are much higher than AVCs run internally by company schemes. High costs result in a poorer performance for the invested funds. The problem arises because companies do not inform their employees about the cheap AVCs run within the company scheme. Employees must make the effort themselves to discover these options. AVCs are covered in Stage 7, on pages 181–2.

For people with personal pension plans, hoping to achieve two-thirds of final salary, advisers suggest they pay 15 per cent of their income into their plan from age twenty-five. This is clearly impossible for most youngsters who will be saving for shorter-term needs of car purchase, or a house deposit.

Unfortunately, the longer the delay, the higher the contributions need to be, due to the loss of compound growth. Money left to grow for thirty years produces a much larger pot than money growing over a shorter period, as interest earned (or dividends reinvested) in the early stages earns its own interest later on. By waiting until age forty-five, you would have to save 40 per cent of your income, probably an unrealistic target.

> *'People know they should be doing something about their pension but they are afraid of being ripped off by the high charges imposed by pension providers.'*
> Harriet Harman, Social Security Secretary, 1997 to 1998

GEORGE BLAKE'S PENSION SHORTFALL

On their current plans, the Blakes are among those millions who will see a 50 per cent drop in their income when George retires. We compiled a retirement budget for George and Freda in Stage 2 on pages 35–42, showing that the fall in their incomes in 2007 puts them squarely into that category.

The pension shortfall
In 2007 the Blakes' combined income falls from £31,294 to £14,507 (a 53.6 per cent fall). If George's income stays unchanged at £24,500 until he retires, we can calculate an annuity equal to two-thirds of his salary.
Annuity of two-thirds income is *£16,333*.
(£24,500 × two-thirds = £16,333)
Based on a 7 per cent a year growth rate, the annuity forecast by his provider is *£7,225*.
For 2007, George's annuity shortfall is £9,108.
(£16,333 – £7,225 = £9,108)
If George's income rose to £25,750, his pension shortfall would be £9,925, as the table shows.

Pension Shortfall For George Blake

(Assumes pension at retirement of £7,225)

Salary in 2007 £	Two-thirds final salary £	Pension shortfall £
24,500	16,333	9,108
25,750	17,150	9,925

On these figures, although he may not want to increase his pension premiums, George should explore options to reduce his shortfall. To close it, he must work out what premiums he needs to produce a pension of £16,333 by 2007, which is equal to two-thirds his income.

For simplicity, we will assume £10 of pension fund buys £1 of pension. Although this was a valid assumption in 1997, rapidly falling annuity rates during autumn 1998 mean this gives too optimistic a forecast for future annuity values, especially for young retirees at sixty and women who generally live longer than men. However, it gives a guide on how to proceed.

The final fund shortfall

The forecast for George's final fund value in 2007 is £85,000.
To obtain an annuity of *£16,333* he needs a fund of *£163,333*.
(£100,000/£10,000 × £16,333 = £163,333).

A fund of £163,333 is almost twice his forecast accumulated fund of £85,000. As this is such a huge increase, we can look at the premium increase George would face if he built his fund to £100,000 for a pension of around £10,000.

Pension Fund Shortfall For George Blake

(Assumes accumulated pension fund in 2007 of £85,000)

Fund size in 2007 £	Annuity in 2007 £	Fund shortfall £
85,000	7,225	
163,333	16,333	78,333
100,000	10,000	15,000

Closing George's Shortfall

On a forecast growth rate of 7 per cent, George planned to build his fund from £33,700 to £85,000 between 1999 and 2007. To build his fund to £100,000 he must increase his total premiums over the next nine years.

The premium increase

He pays annual premiums of *£1,800*.
From 1999 to 2007, he will add total premiums of *£16,200*.
(£1,800 × 9 = £16,200).
To build a £100,000 fund, he needs total premiums for the next nine years of *£19,059*.
(£16,200/85,000 × 100,000 = *£19,059*).
This will increase his annual contributions to *£2,118*.
(£19,059/9 = £2,118). George saves £420 a year in the bank. He could pay this £420 into his pension.
His future premiums would then be *£2,220*.
(£1,800 + £420 = £2,220).
Depending on the level of annuity rates prevailing in 2007, if George

increased his contributions to £2,220 annually, he might achieve a pension of around £10,000. This calculation assumes he does not commute his pension to take the 25 per cent tax-free sum to which all pension savers are entitled when they buy their annuity. If George does commute his 25 per cent tax-free sum, his pension fund will be only £75,000 and his annuity will fall to about £6,375. We will look at the effects of commuting his tax-free lump sum on page 72.

Building George's Pension Fund
(Assumes he adds extra cash to his annual premium of £1,800 for nine years)

Fund size in 2007 £	Total premiums to add £	Increase in annual premiums £	Extra annual cash to find £
100,000	16,941	2,220	420
163,333	27,670	3,459	1,659

To build a final fund of £163,333 for an annuity of £16,333, the Blakes would have to make big budget sacrifices to find an extra £1,659 in premiums every year. However, in May 2002, the car loan will be repaid, releasing another £2,160 a year. George could then increase his pension contributions. The Blakes should explore other options for improving their finances before making a final decision. We will do this in Stage 4, when we examine ways for them to build their capital resources.

> *'Two-thirds of policyholders stop contributing to their [personal] pension before it matures.'*
>
> Paul Ham, *The Sunday Times*

Compare the New Retirement Forecasts
We can calculate the effect of diverting £420 a year from bank savings to increasing George's pension premiums, to see how it alters the 2007 wealth check figures.

The wealth check changes in 2007
The expected £15,300 in the bank account would only reach *£10,454*.
George's pension would rise from £7,225 a year to *£10,000*.
Their combined annual income would rise from £13,725 to *£16,500*.
(George's £10,000 + Freda's £6,500)
Their annual interest would be *£523*.
The Abbey National dividend would be *£53*.
Their total annual income for 2007 therefore, is *£17,076*.
This is an improvement of £2,569 over the estimated £14,507, but if their retirement expenses stay as forecast at £17,106, they would still have a small debit of £30 in 2007.

We saw in Stage 2, that George set a target of £17,500 for his retirement income. If he aims for a pension of £10,000, he will not have completely met this target. These figures are estimates: but they give a guide on possible outcomes by taking different savings routes. Doing these exercises helps to clarify your thinking about which route will be best for your personal circumstances. The global economic crisis of autumn 1998 made a further detrimental impact on annuity rates, indicating how important it is to update your forecasts regularly.

George and Freda's Revised Budget for 2007

Items	1999 Annual £	2007 Annual £
Income	31,000	16,500
Interest (at 5%)	261	523
Dividends	33	53
Totals	31,294	17,076
Total Expenses	**31,272**	**17,106**
Surplus	**22**	**–30**

Where You Save Makes a Difference

These calculations show that over nine years, an extra £420 a year, totalling £3,780, saved in George's pension pot could lift his fund by about £15,000 (from £85,000 to £100,000). This £3,780 saved in the bank would increase the deposit account by £4,846 (from £10,454 to £15,300). This difference is over £10,000: it shows how crucial it is when you have only limited resources, to put your savings to work in tax-efficient schemes. The figures highlight the attractive tax advantages pensions enjoy, giving a faster growth rate for additional money saved. These calculations assume 7 per cent a year growth for the pension, a cautiously low rate, and 5 per cent a year for the deposit account, which could be too optimistic.

Similar advantages of faster growth should work in any tax-free investment, such as the new Isa plans (Individual savings account), if equity markets continue to rise over the long term. Some financial advisers suggest saving the maximum allowed in an Isa is an attractive alternative to saving within a pension as Isas are more flexible, surviving after death (although the tax-free status ends on the death of the fund's owner).

Weigh up the Options

Thinking through the possible alternatives gives the Blakes two choices for improving their finances in 2007.

1. Move to a smaller house in 1999 and invest some of the capital released.

We saw, in Stage 2, that moving in 1999 could give them capital of about *£72,865* by 2007, from which they could draw an income of around *£3,640,* assuming 5 per cent in interest, as a supplement to George's pension. In Stage 4 we will compare that result with the possible benefits of waiting until 2007 before they move.

2. Remain in their present house but pay part of their monthly savings (£35) into George's pension fund, instead of into the bank. This would boost George's pension in 2007 from an estimated £7,225 to about £10,000, an increase of over 38 per cent in his expected retirement income although if annuity rates continue falling his pension could be lower than £10,000. (£10,000 − £7,225 = £2,775/£7,225 × 100 = 38.4%)

George has only nine years before he buys his annuity. If his personal pension plan invests in equity-based options, he must protect his funds as retirement nears.

Protect Your Fund Ahead of Retirement

As you approach retirement, monitor your accumulating fund if it is invested in equities. Begin switching out of equities into a deposit fund within five years prior to retirement to avoid exposure to stock market fluctuations. In the last two or three years before retirement, move all your funds into a cash or fixed interest fund. This might adversely affect the final size of your fund as the rate of growth falls to about 5 per cent (bank interest is paid gross in pension funds), but you will have more certainty about your final fund size and need not fear a market collapse when you buy your annuity.

SHOULD GEORGE BLAKE COMMUTE FOR CASH NOW?

How would commuting 25 per cent of George's total fund affect the size of the annuity he buys at retirement? Again, only rough estimates are possible. Actual figures depend on annuity rates in November 2007 when he reaches sixty. The rough forecast is a guide to help the planning process.

Commute 25 per cent of George's £85,000 fund in 2007
His tax-free cash sum would be *£21,250.*

His remaining fund left to buy his annuity would be only *£63,750.*

If he chose a fixed annuity, paying the same annuity each year until death, his reduced fund would buy an even smaller annuity, perhaps about £5,420, instead of £7,225 which he would get with his full fund of £85,000.

However, a fixed annuity of £5,420 a year gives no guarantees. If he wants the annuity to be paid for five years, even if he dies earlier, it will be smaller, as it will be if he opts for indexation to allow for future inflation. Nor has he provided a pension for Freda after his death. All these extra options reduce his initial annuity.

The picture does not improve greatly if his total accumulated fund is £100,000 and he commutes 25 per cent as cash, receiving *£25,000*.

Now, his reduced fund of £75,000 would buy a fixed annuity of around *£6,375*.

Again this would be fixed, and excludes valuable extras, such as a five-year guarantee, indexed payments to offset inflation, or a pension after his death for Freda.

'Having a second pension is not a guarantee that you will be well off in retirement, but it does seem to be a necessary condition.'

Tom Ross, City pensions consultant

Commuting 25 per cent of George's Fund as Cash in 2007

Fund in 2007 £	Tax-free sum £	Fund left £	Fixed annuity £
85,000	21,250	63,750	5,420
85,000	Nil	85,000	7,225
100,000	25,000	75,000	6,375
100,000	Nil	100,000	10,000

The loss to George's accumulated fund

Buying an annuity is another risky aspect of pension planning. Figures show how dying early would affect the Blakes' capital situation. We will assume George's annuity is guaranteed for five years, and for simplicity, assume this reduces his pension by £1,000.

If he is paid £6,225 a year for five years, by 2012 he will have received *£31,125*.

(£6,225 × 5 = £31,125)

1. If George dies at sixty-five, his fund would have lost *£53,875*

(£85,000 – £31,125 = £53,875)

2. If he dies at seventy, he will receive *£62,250*

The loss to his fund falls to *£22,750*

Even at age seventy, he will not have recouped the total £85,000 investment in his accumulated fund. These figures can be considerably improved if George commutes 25 per cent of his accumulated fund at the outset and saves this cash each year in an account growing at 5 per cent.

Commuting cash to save

From his fund of £85,000, George takes a cash sum (to put either into an equity-based fund or a deposit account). His initial fund is *£21,250* (£85,000 × 25% = £21,250).

The residual fund is *£63,750* which would pay a fixed annuity of £5,420.

George pays £1,000 for a five-year guarantee which reduces his annual income to £4,420.

1. *If George dies at sixty-five,* he would have received *£22,100* (£4,420 × 5 = £22,100).

The commuted sum of £21,250 would grow to *£25,830*

His total return would therefore be *£47,930*

(£22,100 + £25,830 = £47,930)

If he dies at sixty-five, his fund would have lost *£37,070.*

Although this is better than taking his whole fund as an annuity, he is still losing money.

However, on his death, Freda would inherit the account worth £25,830. This is a far better result than losing £53,875 outright if George died after drawing only five years of pension.

2. *If George dies at seventy,* his reduced pension would have paid out *£44,200.*

The commuted sum of £21,250 would have grown to *£34,615.*

His total return would therefore be *£78,815.*

At age seventy, on this savings regime, George would still not break even on his accumulated fund but his cash lump sum of £21,250 growing for ten years at 5 per cent, would be worth £34,615, which again, would be passed on to Freda on his death.

To see the power of long-term saving, we can look at the total fund position when George reaches seventy-five in 2022, taking the same exercise one stage further.

3. *If George dies at seventy-five*, his reduced pension would have paid out *£66,300.*

The commuted cash sum of £21,250 would have grown to *£44,179.*

His total return would therefore be *£110,479.*

He would be making an overall profit of £25,479 after fifteen years. And if

'What are the major misconceptions people have about the stock market?'

Jack Schwager (author of *Market Wizards* and *New Market Wizards*)

'They tend to confuse short-term volatility with long-term risk. The longer the term, the lower the risk of holding equities.'

Richard Driehaus (Manager of the Driehaus Small Cap Fund)

Money Saved and Total Annuity Received by George

Fixed annuity from 2007 to death, £6,225 for 5, 10 or 15 years (£)	(yrs)	Funds saved from 2007 to 2012, 2017 or 2022 5% interest (£)	Total amount received (£)	Shortfall/excess over £85,000 pension fund in 2007 (£)
31,125	(5)	Nil	31,125	-53,875
62,225	(10)	Nil	62,225	-22,750
21,100	(5)	25,830	47,930	-37,070
44,200	(10)	34,615	78,815	+6,185
93,375 (6,225 × 15)	(15)	Nil	93,375	+8,375
66,300 (4,420 × 15)	(15)	44,179	110,479	25,479

George dies at age seventy-five, although Freda will lose his pension, she will have the free capital of £44,179 to rely on, plus her mortgage-free house.

These calculations are only a guide to possible outcomes to illustrate the benefits that are derived from commuting the largest allowable tax-free lump sum. George may spend some of his cash, or put part of it into low-risk areas where his interest will be below 5 per cent and he must pay tax on his annuity income. However, if George does take a smaller pension, building up his capital ahead of retirement will be even more important, to boost his annual income.

The exercise may look tedious, but whenever you are exploring different financial options, the safest course is to examine the possible results of each one in turn. We have seen the benefits of commuting the 25 per cent tax-free cash on retirement even if these are only rough estimates.

'Once retirement dawns, you still cannot get your hands on the capital, beyond that doomed lump sum, let alone bequeath it to your descendants. You are forced to convert these savings into an annuity income, which dies with you or your spouse.'

Graham Searjeant, *The Times*

Pension Problems Aplenty

Although it is important to build a large pension fund, a whole raft of problems apply; there are at least seven major snags, but possibly more. I discussed pension defects in *The Money Maze*, but a brief summary is included here because the problems impact on retirement planning.

The major defects you should be wary about are as follows:

1. Pensions are inflexible. Minimise this problem by building a pensions staircase.

2. There is no real growth in your pension after you have taken it. With no other source of income your standard of living will fall as the years pass.

3. The pension is not transferable: it dies with you. You can compensate by buying a joint annuity to protect a surviving spouse, but this reduces the size of your initial annuity.

4. Despite the advertising hype, it may be a bad investment bargain. You must live more than ten years to recoup the full fund you accumulated while working.

5. Tax is deducted at source, which hampers cash flow.

6. Very high charges applied on personal pensions damage performance, which means poor returns.

7. Constantly changing conditions are a pension planner's nightmare. The government introduces endless changes and changes in interest rates directly affect annuity rates.

Unfortunately, the inflexibility of most plans is a major problem. They cannot be surrendered early as would be possible with endowment policies, and if you stop your contributions, policies are frozen (that is, '**paid up**') until retirement. When a personal pension, intended to run for twenty or more years, is made paid up after three years, huge penalties will be taken from your fund, as you have changed the originally agreed contract terms.

Surveys repeatedly show most people rarely read their policy documents. However, your pension is a legally binding contract, hedged around with a host of restrictions and penalty clauses. Many people only appreciate these limitations after they have been paying premiums for two or three years. If they then stop their contributions, they discover the huge costs involved. Figures show around a fifth, or 20 per cent of pensions are made paid up within the first three years while this rises to 60 per cent within the first five years. This is a terrible waste of savings and a sad reflection on the carefree way many people are beguiled into entering blindly into rigid, expensive, long-term plans.

'You are starting from a very imperfect position in terms of people's knowledge of the welfare state, as well as financial services.'

Mark Boleat, director-general of the Association of British Insurers

75

From the start, your cash is locked up in a fund out of reach until you buy your annuity. However, on death before retirement, most final salary schemes pay generous death-in-service benefits and money purchase schemes usually pay out the whole accumulated fund. This may not apply to some **with-profits** pension policies begun in the 1970s and 1980s, as I learned when I did a financial wealth check for the Johnsons.

HOWARD'S PENSION LET-DOWN

Howard and Brenda Johnson ran a small corner shop, selling newspapers, confectionery and stationery. Howard, in his early fifties, planned to take his pension at sixty in 1990, but would continue running his shop as he had two sons to educate. On my visit in 1983 to review his pension I noted his with-profits policy with a major insurance company was forecast to provide an annual pension of around £4,000 in 1990. Like most endowment policies, a with-profits pension pays annual bonuses to smooth out the troughs and peaks in the market with a substantial terminal bonus on maturity.

However, under the terms of Howard's policy, it would only pay out a return of his premiums plus interest if he died before sixty. There was no return of the total fund he had built up over the years. The Johnsons were shocked to learn this as they had made contributions for over ten years. They had not read the policy document and the salesman who sold them the pension had not explained how this contract worked. The longer the pension fund builds up the bigger the potential loss to the policyholder, as returns of the premiums plus interest deny him all the fund's growth. This defect obviously left Brenda vulnerable, as most of their money was tied up in their business.

Howard wanted to make additional provision for Brenda.

Additional protection for Brenda
He would need capital of *£80,000* to create an income of *£4,000* a year. (£80,000 on deposit earning 5 per cent a year, would provide £4,000 a year in interest).

The compromise
At fifty-three, Howard could not afford high premiums for £80,000 of life cover. He compromised with term assurance for seven years of *£30,000*.
This would end when Howard reached sixty, when his expected £4,000 annual pension would begin.
A sum of £30,000 on deposit at 5 per cent, would only give an extra income of *£1,500*.
But it was better than nothing.
And so, sadly, this is exactly what it proved to be.
I lost contact with the Johnsons after the term life cover policy was set up,

but I later learned that Howard had died within three years of my visit, so his widow received the £30,000 of life insurance money in addition to the return of the premiums plus interest, on Howard's with-profits pension.

Howard's early death reveals another major flaw with pensions. As we saw with calculations for George Blake's pension, these contracts are a bad bet for people who do not live out an average life expectancy. And since your fund is not transferable and dies with the pensioner, it cannot be passed on to your surviving spouse or heirs.

Avoid Pension Limitations

I think the loss of the fund on death is one of the major disadvantages of pensions, especially since people in Britain are not good at saving. The inability to pass money down the generations prevents people acquiring funds that have already been built up within a family. You avoid this by building capital outside a pension.

> *'What seems like an adequate pension now will be a pittance in thirty years. Between 1967 and 1997, the Retail Prices Index increased by 897 per cent. If you had taken out a level-rate annuity in 1967, paying you £2,000 per annum – a good income then – you would still be trying to live on £2,000 a year today; in real terms a tenth the value of your original pension.'*
>
> Ross Clark, *The Sunday Times*

Other ways to beat the non-transferability of pensions must be established at the outset, when you buy your annuity.

1. Always commute 25 per cent of your fund, even though the balance will be much smaller unless your plan includes a guaranteed annuity rate.
2. Take a joint life annuity.
3. Take a smaller pension for you, plus one for your surviving spouse. All choices must be made at the outset; they cannot be changed at any future date and every choice reduces the amount of annuity your fund buys.

Then, although your pension funds grow rapidly in a tax-free environment, on retirement, tax is taken every year at your top rate on your annuity, denying you the use of the tax funds on a short-term basis. Unless your pension is indexed for inflation, it remains fixed throughout your retirement, even if inflation continues and your expenses rise in line with it. A long retirement on a fixed pension can be a recipe for miserable poverty in later years.

High Charges Mean Poor Performance

The structure of your policy is obscure, so you may not realise the high level of charges you pay, even if you read the key features document that providers are obliged by law to send you before your policy comes into force. This important document summarises all the core information on costs and investment risk in the policy you are buying, but evidence shows that most people rely on the salesman or adviser who sells them the plan. In one survey 65 per cent of people could not recall receiving a copy of the key features document. Unfortunately, as his high commission makes up a large part of the costs, the adviser will be torn between his loyalty to you as a client and his need to boost his salary by selling you this policy. Many honest advisers work in the financial services industry, but it seems quite obvious that some might be unlikely to point out the high charges, unless you know about them and ask the adviser directly. If you broach this issue, your adviser may be willing to share his commission with you, perhaps giving you a 50 per cent return of the commission. To benefit from this when buying a traditional pension, you should invest all the rebated commission in your new plan, rather than pocketing it. This solution is applied more often now people understand the impact of high charges. However, you may not get impartial advice unless you deal with a fee-charging adviser, rather than one who earns commission.

The high level of charges taken by most companies on money purchase and personal pension plans is considerable. In the first two or three years of a personal pension, perhaps as much as 80 per cent of your premiums may be taken as charges, so finding a low charging plan is important.

Find A Good Personal Pension

Figures comparing the effect of charges appear frequently in the financial sections of the weekend press. There are striking differences between the projected maturity values of personal pensions when charges are taken into account. However, wading through the detail of over one hundred different policies to find low charging plans is time-consuming and complicated. Try to use a company with a consistently strong performance record, over at least five years, plus a reasonable charging

Step 4
Find a good pension plan

'The public do not know which are the low-charging companies and which are the high. About 1 million plans are sold each year, mostly to people who cannot judge what they are buying.'

John Chapman, co-author of *Kitemarking or Benchmarking?* New Policy Institute

structure. Many companies fall into this category: Mark Batersley, deputy editor of *Money Management* magazine suggested some that qualified in 1998, but entrants on such lists vary each year. He recommended Eagle Star Direct (not its traditional pension operation), Colonial Direct (not its traditional pension), Equitable Life, Gartmore, Professional Life, Rothschild Asset management, Scottish Widows Direct, Wesleyan and Winterthur Life. Virgin was not included, as it did not have a five-year track record in 1998.

In summer 1998, a survey by *Money Marketing* revealed the huge differences in charges between the lowest cost pensions companies and the highest. The survey asked pension providers to project a fund for a thirty-year-old investing £100 a month until retirement at sixty-five. The following table shows the wide range involved, assuming a growth rate of 9 per cent each year:

High and Low Charging Plans Compared

Charges	Fund Size Achieved
No charges	£283,867
Lowest charges	£250,000
Highest charges	Below £200,000

Many of the cheapest charging pensions were with **mutual** companies, owned by their members, not by shareholders, so profits are not paid out as dividends. The two cheapest pensions were with mutual companies, Friends Provident and Equitable Life. Other mutuals among the top ten were NFU Mutual and National Mutual. However, more recently, **direct** pension providers have entered the market. Confusingly, some of them are subsidiaries of traditional pension providers who continue to charge as before on their traditional pension policies. Competition from direct providers could improve the outlook on all pension charges. Direct companies offer pensions by telephone, substantially reducing administrative costs.

Cheap Personal Pensions Options

With so much choice and almost an equal amount of confusion, how can you decide which pension to buy? Can you sift through the hundreds of pensions on offer? If your company runs a company scheme and you are not on board, ask for information so you can decide whether to join. Once you belong to a company scheme, it is illegal to own a personal pension, unless you earn other income outside your company income, perhaps from consultancy work. If you suspect you will not be able to stay in one job or might change jobs five or six times before you retire, think about buying a personal pension. You will lose the employer's contribution and all the guaranteed benefits, but these would be reduced, perhaps by 30 per cent if you make several job changes. For personal pensions, if you are in your forties or fifties, choose a plan which gives you the best possible chance of building your fund as fast and successfully as you can. It is far easier now to buy a cheap personal pension but you should be willing to do some preliminary investigations. Plenty of information appears in the financial pages of the broadsheet newspapers where many companies advertise.

Choices For a Good Personal Pension
1. Serial single premium plans – 5 per cent charges at most to start each plan.
2. Direct **tracker** pensions – performance has beaten most **actively managed funds**.
3. Investment trust pensions – much lower charges.
4. Direct pensions – with telephone providers.

'There are recurring single-premium plans, paid on a monthly basis, but every premium is treated as a single premium with no advance commission and which are therefore a better deal.'
John Sheffield, independent financial adviser with AIS Pensions

Direct providers take you through your whole pension situation over the telephone. Most of them only offer cash or tracker funds (which track a particular stock market **index**). But for novice investors, or those without the luxury of a long period in which to save, they offer a simple solution to pension planning. Many mutual companies have a good reputation for low costs. This applies also to the lesser known investment trust companies. Some traditional companies sell **annual recurring single premium pensions** which avoid the high cost structures of twenty- to thirty-year plans. Financial advisers may not volunteer information on these as they will only earn commission of around 5 per cent of the premium instead of the 50 to 80 per cent of your first two-years' premium earned by selling traditional policies. Angela's story explains how they work.

ANGELA'S PENSION SHORTFALL
Angela was a contract nurse, who had worked outside the National Health Service since she was twenty-seven, so she did not contribute to the government's superannuated pension scheme for nurses. As a divorcée living alone, on reaching fifty she suddenly realised she might not be able to retire at sixty as she had hoped. One of her patients was an independent financial adviser who offered her advice on buying a pension.

He thought Angela should build a fund of £100,000 over ten years. She bought a series of annual recurring single-premium policies into which she could make monthly contributions. They are treated as one-off plans and do not carry the hefty charges that ten- or twenty-year policies impose. Her annual charges were 5 per cent of her premiums.

Angela builds a Pension Staircase:
In 1990, Angela began saving with a single premium of *£2,000*.
By 1995 she increased her annual premium to *£5,000*.
She split this sum between two companies, to guard against one not producing as good a return as the other.
Paying £5,000 a year from her salary was a big commitment.
By December 1996 her pension fund had grown to about *£40,000*.
By 2000, she could possibly exceed her goal of *£100,000*.

Her total contributions of around £35,000 over ten years could build a fund of around £100,000. As a 23 per cent tax-payer, she could have saved around £10,000 in tax over that period (for part of the ten-year saving period her tax rate was higher than 23 per cent, as the basic rate tax was 25 or 24 per cent). The true cost of building her pension was therefore around £31,000 (£35,000 – £8,000 = £27,000). If her fund reached £100,000 she would have made a return of over 370 per cent on her contributions.

If Angela retires at sixty and lives to eighty-five, her pension investment of £27,000 will produce a return of £200,000 in regular annuity payments of £8,000 over twenty-five years. However, if her pension is fixed at £8,000 annually, what might it be worth in 2020, when she will be eighty with probably another five years to live? To ensure she is not locked into a frozen annuity that lags inflation, she must either take an indexed pension or try to build up capital as an additional supplement.

If you are within ten years of retirement and planning to start your first personal pension or are looking to diversify your funds by starting a second plan, contributing with single lump sums rather than by regular premiums carries lower costs and should therefore achieve a better performance. However, if like George Blake, your plan has been running for several years, the cheapest option may still be to increase the premiums in that policy rather than set up a new one, because most of the heavy initial charges have already been taken from the plan. If George's plan does not have a good performance record, he might still benefit by starting a second plan. Before you act, investigate which of these two options would be best.

The Tracker Route

Many direct, mutuals, investment trust companies and traditional insurance companies now offer low cost tracker pension funds. A tracker fund just tracks a recognised index, usually a benchmark index for the UK stock market, like the FTSE All-Share index, used by Virgin Direct and Legal & General, among others. The FTSE All-Share index is one of several indices used as a yardstick by professionals so they can judge their investment performance against that of their competitors. There are several indices for each stock market but each tracker fund will only track one.

Trackers became popular in the 1990s because surveys show very few professional fund managers, perhaps only 10 per cent, beat the benchmark index. Managers who run actively managed funds make their own share selection, hoping to outperform the market while tracker funds are passive; their share selection is automatic, including only those shares listed in the index being tracked.

The tracker fund manager designs his portfolio to mirror the return achievable if he owned all the company shares in the index he tracks. An exact match is impossible, as he pays commission when buying or selling shares. However, he receives dividends on shares in the fund, but these are not included in index calculations.

The FTSE All-Share tracker tracks over 830 shares, so is less risky than the FTSE 100 which tracks the top 100: a big drop in one of over 830 companies will have a smaller impact on your savings

Trackers are popular because:

1. Despite high charges too few active fund managers even match the performance of the key benchmark indices, let alone manage to beat the relevant index. Trackers avoid this problem.

2. Automatic selection removes the need for expensive professional analysts, reducing costs to investors. Trackers are cheaper to run and charges to investors are smaller. Reduced charges can improve investment performance because more money is invested rather than paid out as costs.

Keep Tracking

History shows that over long periods the stock market rises more than it falls. By keeping your money in the market long term, in a fund that closely tracks it, your money will enjoy each rise every time the market starts moving higher. However smart you are, catching every rise is almost impossible. So leaving your money in the fund ensures it is there when the next great upsurge begins. This effect removes much of the uncertainty of actively managed funds and explains why trackers are popular.

You know in advance that your fund will closely follow the index performance, both up and down. Certainty in investing is rare. Using a tracker is an effective way to reduce risk, for both amateurs and professionals. However, the growing popularity of trackers carries a threat. During the 1990s strongly rising markets beguiled many people into believing that markets always rise. These investors will be sorely disappointed if the market has a serious fall. You must understand the main risk the tracker reduces is investment uncertainty. So how does it work in practice?

In October 1987, prices suddenly plunged. The tracker funds fell to reflect that. While this looks scary, it has two positive aspects:

1. If you realise in advance that this will happen, you won't panic when it does. You will know that a 20 per cent plunge is a rare market occurrence. It could be a buying rather than a selling opportunity, as was indeed the case in 1987.

2. If the market dropped by around 20 per cent, the trackers fall roughly in step, but risky actively managed funds might fall more than 20 per cent, as the manager will be holding shares he hopes will outperform the market.

This happened during the panic sell-off in October 1987. Huge drops of 40 or 50 per cent occurred in some specialist fund unit trusts, following one country, such as Australia, or investing in one sector or type of business, say, smaller companies or commodities. The FTSE 100 index suffered a two-day drop of 500 points, nearly 22 per cent.

'Everybody remembers the dark side of the 1987 crash, but they tend to forget what a great buying opportunity it was.'

Graham Hooper, investment director at Chase de Vere

With tracker funds, you know that a fall in line with the index will be roughly the full extent of the drop your fund will experience. And if you stay invested, you can profit from the next rise, whenever it begins. However, if prices enter a prolonged decline, the saver near to or in retirement might lose a serious amount of his investment. You must be aware of this possibility over the next decade or two as the global economy has become weaker than in the recent past. Some tracker pension plans allow you to move your funds into a cash fund during the last few years you are building your fund, to avoid exposure to volatile market movements.

The Sting in the Tracker Tail

The increasing popularity of trackers coincided with the big rises in the stock market. Trackers successfully beat the performance of most actively managed funds, thereby enhancing their popularity. The last big downturn in global markets was over twenty-five years ago, from 1972 to 1974, and undoubtedly, many people have become too complacent that markets just keep rising. There is no guarantee that the

Trackers are eminently suited to all types of investor. Why drive yourself crazy learning to be clever at picking shares when the tracker does it for you?

excellent results seen during the 1990s will continue, but this should not deter serious long-term investors, as history is on their side. Over the past eighty, fifty or even twenty years, equities have outperformed every other financial investment. For this excellent reason, trackers can be used for building up a capital sum, as we will see in Stage 4.

Poor Performance Means Poor Returns

The problem of high charges is more important than simply a matter of getting a good deal. High charges make a huge difference to the growth of your fund, especially if those charges continue running, at a lower rate, over a period of twenty or more years.

If your fund performs badly, it produces a smaller pot from which you have to take your pension. The differences can be enormous, according to CAPS, an independent research company that monitors the performance of pension fund managers. Good managers produce returns that are 50 per cent better than the poor managers. In 1998, CAPS statistics showed that PDFM, one of the biggest pension fund managers, returned only 19.7 per cent over the previous year, while the top performers achieved over 30 per cent during the same period.

Performance figures show that, in general, the pensions industry is failing its clients. Most of the premiums paid into personal pensions are invested in the stock market in one of two ways; through a with-profits fund (which pays annual bonuses to smooth out the troughs and peaks in the market) or a **managed fund**, similar to a unit trust and riskier than a with-profits fund because it does not smooth out stock market ups and downs. The performance figures for both types of fund were disappointing: both had fallen short of the FTSE All-Share index. A personal pension set up in 1983 in the average managed fund, with contributions of £200 a month, would have built a fund worth £82,000 after fifteen years; a with-profits fund would have been worth £108,000. However, a FTSE All-Share index tracker fund would have generated £140,000. These differences are so vast, people must take note when saving for retirement, so everyone can aim to improve the ultimate size of their pension, by recognising how vital it is to put your funds into a plan that will perform well, not poorly.

One third of the money paid into some personal pensions is being pocketed in charges and expenses, with costs at the highest-charging companies at twice the level of the cheapest

To spread the risks, opt for two or three different policies; for example, a tracker, a with-profits fund and an annual recurring single premium plan, to form three levels for your pension staircase.

Poor returns have a direct adverse effect on the size of the annuity you can buy if you are in

a money purchase or group personal pension scheme: the bigger your pension pot, the larger your pension. This is especially important when annuity rates are low. If the fund performance is poor, your pension will be dealt a double blow: you have a smaller pension pot available to buy your annuity, but as rates are low, your small fund buys an even smaller annuity.

Annuities Under Pressure

And finally, there is the thorny issue of annuity rates to which we have referred earlier, so now we will look at how this affects your pension. Annuities are the end product for everyone using a money purchase company scheme, a group personal pension or for self-employed people buy-ing personal pensions. If you have built up a fund with any of these pensions, your scheme will provide a pension based on what the money available in the pension fund at retirement will buy. Employees with company final salary schemes need not worry about buying compulsory annuities on retirement although they might consider buying a **purchase life annuity**, to increase their income, covered in Stage 7.

Step 5
Take or buy your annuity

Since 1990, annuity rates have fallen by over 35 per cent, jeopardising the annual pension income of all prospective pensioners, faced with the dilemma of buying their annuity as rates decline.

We need not dwell on the reasons for the recent decline, but as it is a factor in pension planning you should have some idea of the forces driving annuity rates down, so you can adjust for your future retirement date. Annuity rates are linked to the **yield** on UK government gilts (which is the interest paid on the bond). Demand for gilts is rising. Major demographic changes and falling interest rates lie at the heart of the decline:

1. As the government tries to reduce its debts, gilts become more scarce.
2. People live longer, creating more demand for annuities.
3. There are more pensioners, which increases the demand for annuities.
4. Falling interest rates reduce annuity rates (1987–1998).
5. Long-term interest rates are falling across Europe with the introduction of the single European currency.

These underlying reasons may not seem important to prospective retirees, deciding on whether to defer taking a pension until they are sixty-five or sev-enty. However, this complicated mix of reasons is bad news for people buying annuities. If these trends operate over two or more decades, rising annuity rates may be delayed.

During August of 1998, the problem of falling stock markets and falling annuity rates gave a sharp reminder to people approaching retirement of the risks involved. One estimate suggested that a man with a pension fund worth £100,000 on 20 July, when the FTSE 100 peaked, would have seen his fund value fall to £87,384 by 14 August. An annuity purchased with that depleted fund would provide an income of approximately £1,000 a year less because of the three week drop in share prices which was accompanied by rising bond prices. This further depressed annuity rates, because the bond price and its yield move in opposite directions.

One way to improve your annual retirement income would be to consider a **with-profits annuity**. These are linked to stock market performance and annuity rates there have not fallen as far as annuity rates on conventional annuities. However, the resultant income is not guaranteed because it fluctuates with the markets, so pensioners might want to split their fund between a with-profits and a fixed annuity. If you create a pensions staircase, it automatically offers the option of an annuity staircase, making further increases in annual income possible throughout a lengthy retirement.

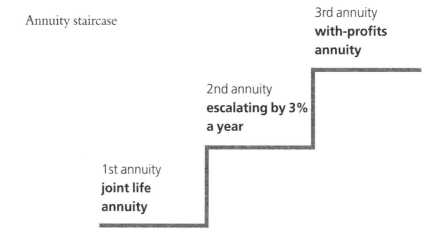

Annuity staircase

1st annuity
joint life annuity

2nd annuity
escalating by 3% a year

3rd annuity
with-profits annuity

Step 6
Find the best annuity

Too few people with personal pension plans realise that they do not have to buy their annuity from the company they built their fund with. Everyone can shop around to find the best annuity on offer for their requirements. This may mean transferring your fund to another company to buy the annuity. As with every other aspect of pension planning, there is a huge range between the worst and best annuity rate for people, even with the same requirements. Searching for the best annuity is extremely important now because annuity rates are falling.

To ensure you get the best possible deal, use a specialist company. There are now several such groups who give detailed advice on what will be best for you. They will not advise you on the right time to buy your annuity, but once you make this decision, they can then find you the best annuity deal taking your special details into account: your age, sex and whether you want your annuity to cover indexation, a five-year guarantee, a joint pension or a pension for a surviving spouse. Special annuities are available to cope with particular circumstances: **immediate care annuities** can be arranged to pay an income for life in return for a lump sum, to help fund long-term care. Several companies specialise in offering **impaired life annuities**, which pay a higher than normal income for life for people with illnesses that reduce life expectancy. Ways of tackling annuity purchase are covered in Stage 7 on pages 183–5.

'The average investor may well think that the investment risk [of income drawdown] is greater than the potential reward.'

Nick Bamford, director of Informed Choice

Falling annuity rates are very serious for people with personal pensions. Many have postponed retirement hoping to build a bigger fund. But they may never get back what they have already lost through falling annuity rates. Calculations showed that deferring annuity purchase by just one year, from 1996 to 1997, knocked 10 per cent off a pensioner's annual income.

Try Income Drawdown?

Falling annuity rates are important when deciding whether to keep your pension fund invested long past your due retirement date. Rising share prices throughout the 1990s tempted people to delay taking their pensions, hoping their funds will grow much larger so producing a bigger pension when they finally take it. Legally, you do not need to buy your annuity until age seventy-five. Even in the average unit trust, share prices have grown over 200 per cent since the crash of October 1987. The temptation is to defer buying an annuity, hoping for continuing double digit growth in your accumulating fund, which will be largely invested in equities.

Step 7
Try income drawdown?

Income drawdown schemes were introduced as a half-way house for taking a pension. The contract allows you to invest the cash in your fund as you please, and take an income, within certain fixed limits. Commissions on these schemes are highly attractive to salesmen, being around 5 to 6 per cent of the value of the original fund, but this puts additional strains on the ability of the fund to grow. Think carefully before taking income drawdown as it ties you into a legally binding contract which cannot be altered once begun. The problem of investment risk still applies, if your funds remain in the stock market.

It is more useful for relatively young retirees with alternative sources of income and works best for large pension funds, which stand a better chance of continuing to grow, even after some income is taken.

Income drawdown schemes were introduced in 1995 and around 300,000 had been sold by summer 1998, when the earliest contracts came up for review. The government **actuary** resets the maximum income that can be drawn from the fund every three years, based on gilt yields. As these fell between 1995 and 1998, the early drawdown investors were facing losses by mid-1998. In 1995 a sixty-year-old man with a pension fund worth £100,000 could have drawn a maximum income of 10.3 per cent or £10,300. By August 1998, the maximum limit had fallen to 9 per cent or £9,000. To maintain the higher level of income, the underlying pension fund would have needed to be worth £114,444 by August 1998, after £30,900 had been withdrawn for the three years of income. If annuity rates continue falling, this option spells ultimate disaster when a pension must be taken by age seventy-five, regardless of its size.

'Loose money may stimulate more rapid economic growth, but that has little, if any, appeal to pensioners.'

Barry Riley, *Financial Times*

Even with a big accumulated pension fund and other sources of income, this option could still be risky as the outlook for annuity rates is unclear. I believe the greatest benefit from your pension is its certainty. As future levels of annuity rates are not foreseeable, by taking income drawdown you have sacrificed this enormously important feature of your future pension: its value can no longer be assured. At retirement, if your pension turns out to be lower than you had hoped, at least you will know where you stand. You can then focus on making supplementary plans to improve your financial situation. It is precisely because there is usually no one complete answer to achieving financial security that you need to build a well balanced financial pyramid to overcome the limitations of any one investment. You need a family of investments to cover your future needs.

Having seen some of the problems and difficulties that accompany the search for building a safe, reliable pension, I hope you can appreciate why pensions alone are not a perfect panacea. This in fact, is exactly why you should also aim to build a sizeable capital sum to supplement your pension. Examining how to do this takes us on to Stage 4.

Key Points to Remember

STAGE 3: BUILD AN INCOME TO RELY ON

1. The level of the UK state pension is below the official poverty line.
2. Opt back into Serps at age fifty-two (for men) or forty-five (for women).
3. Calculate the forecast shortfall in your pension income. If it is less than two-thirds your estimated final salary, then:
4. Revise your pension contribution level to correct the pension shortfall.
5. Learn about the details of your pension policy.
6. Annuities are under pressure as rates are falling.
7. British pension policies are no panacea. Aim to build a capital sum to resolve some of the worst deficiencies.

Create a Lump Sum For Capital

'Immediately after the New Year, the postman brings the biggest cheque I have ever received – tax-free lump sum part of pension. I decide to splurge out on a new computer.'

Tom Rayfield, *Financial Times*
(1 April 1998)

If you were George or Freda Blake, you might now feel a little anxious, even depressed. You live in a comfortable house and had previously had no thought of moving, yet to free up some money to make life easier in retirement you know you should be thinking about moving into a smaller property, although you would much prefer to stay where you are. However, a move during retirement might become inevitable. The big question is: should that move be now or later?

Moreover, while George is saving for his pension, the Blakes have discovered that to build a pension to replace his regular income, more saving is urgently required – twice as much as now, in fact, to achieve a pension worth about two-thirds his forecast final salary. On their present budget, spending cuts are needed to fund the extra premiums, without which, they face a pension short-fall. However, as we saw, pensions have numerous drawbacks.

Fortunately, there is no need to be depressed, for you are now at Stage 4 of retirement planning. It offers great opportunities to improve your financial prospects while keeping other options open, and follows logically from the Stages already covered.

Planning Flexibility With Stage 4

Stage 4 is the 'trouble shooter' element for retirement planning, following a series of steps to build a family of assets. Your home may be an **illiquid asset** (difficult to sell quickly) and your pension too small, but building capital has few constraints. Stage 4 flexibility can bring financial freedom as you move from one step to the next, outlined on the planning path on page 90. In *Step 1,*

STAGE 4 CREATE A LUMP SUM FOR CAPITAL

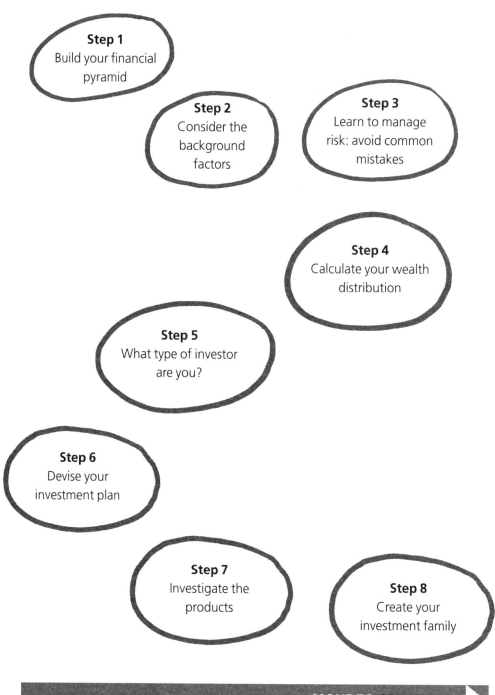

Step 1
Build your financial pyramid

Step 2
Consider the background factors

Step 3
Learn to manage risk: avoid common mistakes

Step 4
Calculate your wealth distribution

Step 5
What type of investor are you?

Step 6
Devise your investment plan

Step 7
Investigate the products

Step 8
Create your investment family

MOVE TO STAGE 5

we discuss building your financial pyramid, as mentioned in earlier Stages. It is central to plans for balancing your assets. *Step 2* covers the background factors with a direct influence on your saving or investment decisions. *Step 3* shows you how to manage risk and avoid the common mistakes most novice investors make. In *Step 4* you calculate your current wealth distribution. If this is lopsided, you move to *Step 5* – deciding what kind of investor you are. Knowing this, takes you on to *Step 6* to devise your investment plan based on your investment family. To create that, *Step 7* investigates the products to consider and *Step 8* shows you how to put these products together to create your investment family.

> *'My secret of success is never to get excited when things go right, or depressed when they go badly.'*
>
> Tim Martin, Managing director of J D Wetherspoon

Build a Balanced Financial Pyramid

Building a successful financial pyramid creates a balanced group of assets: the heart of your planning. I used the image of a pyramid for building a secure future in *The Money Maze*, which deals with the key issues of learning money skills for better management of your money. For every age group, the three basic essentials of your financial pyramid are buying your own home, building up a large pension fund to become your replacement income in retirement, and accumulating capital to supplement your pension and pay for special events.

> **Step 1**
> Build your financial pyramid

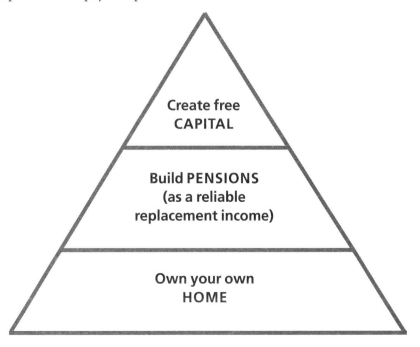

Everyone, whether they are twenty or seventy, needs to build their own financial pyramid, but as you approach retirement, your pyramid needs a sharper focus because you are about to rely on your pension and capital: increasing your income and saving more capital will be difficult. Few people can build a perfectly balanced pyramid with each block pulling its full weight because few know how to create a sensible family of investments. However, even if an ideal result is elusive, by focusing on these three basic essentials you will be more in control of your future and better equipped to cope with unforeseen outcomes.

Create some free capital
1. Emergency cash.
2. Life assurance.
   i. term
   ii. whole-of-life
3. Unit and investment trusts.
4. Company shares.

Benefit From a Lump Sum

If you are happily settled in your house or have an excellent pension, you may think Stage 4 is unnecessary. However, the future is always uncertain, so extra options are worthwhile. Building more capital brings many benefits:

1. It provides added flexibility for future planning.

2. This cash will not die with you, which is the fate for most pensions or annuities.

3. You can pass it on to a surviving spouse, other members of your family, or gift it to charity.

4. If your pension is small, capital is a useful supplement for large outlays, and special items.

5. If your pension is fixed in value, a fund of real financial assets can compensate. Equities provide a rising income stream and may also grow in value, increasing your wealth. I call this happy outcome, 'having your cake and eating it'. Freda's Abbey National shares illustrate this idea. Floated as a bank in 1989, Abbey National's dividends grew steadily in value. Rising dividends provided extra income, but the shares themselves increased from 130p at flotation in 1989 to 1139p on 17 July 1998.

6. Investing in real financial assets helps to outpace inflation. Suppose, like George, you retire on a fixed pension. Over a twenty year retirement, inflation might average about 3.5 per cent a year. That seems manageable, but over twenty years, the purchasing power of your pension – the amount of goods and services it will buy – will roughly halve. Your money is fixed, but the price of goods rises, so it buys less. Britain has a poor inflation record. If inflation was

Warren Buffett's company, Berkshire Hathaway, has produced annual compound returns in excess of 25 per cent for almost thirty years. It has multiplied its original investors' stakes more than 1,000 times

7 per cent a year, far from an outrageous level on past evidence, your pension would halve in only ten years. In such conditions, capital that can grow faster than inflation at 3.5 or 7 per cent each year would help you maintain your standard of living through retirement.

7. A capital fund is ideal for dealing with unplanned future needs. As capital offers so many advantages, you can now see why commuting the full allowable amount of your pension as a tax-free sum is important. It gives extra flexibility that you might need in future.

LUMP SUM BONANZAS

Donald and Mildred Othmer were ordinary folk. Donald was born in Omaha, Nebraska. As a child, he earned pocket-money picking dandelions from neighbours' lawns. He became a professor of chemical engineering at Polytechnic University in New York and Mildred, his wife, was a teacher.

When they died in their nineties, they had amassed an estate worth $750 million (£470 million) and bequeathed millions to charities and institutions, including the Polytechnic University in New York.

They grew their fortune by investing their savings with an old family friend from Nebraska: Warren Buffett, the world's most successful private investor. Investing in Berkshire Hathaway, Warren Buffett's company, defies the rules of investment diversification. All the investors who put their savings in his funds became multimillionaires over more than thirty years.

Stable Prices, Inflation and Deflation

When you create an investment family, you become your own fund manager. No one will safeguard your capital as carefully as you will once you gain the skills. Acquiring them is easier than you think if you follow the logical steps outlined here, beginning with some background information on factors affecting how you save and invest.

Step 2
Consider the background factors

Back in the nineteenth century, long spells of stable or falling prices enabled middle class families to live comfortably on income from their **Consols** or **War Loan stock**, both of which are examples of **non–redeemable** UK government gilts (that is, loan certificates issued by the government with no fixed maturity date and so they can still be bought today). Before 1914,

Agatha Christie, the fiction crime writer, lived on the income from gilts she inherited from her father. She did not need to earn her living until the First World War ended in 1918, when high inflation accompanied financing the war effort. Sadly, she was not alone in finding the value of her investment income declining rapidly.

Right through this century, high inflation has played havoc with the savings of people relying on **fixed interest** investments such as bank deposit accounts and government bonds, both favourite investments for pensioners. In their annual study, Barclays Capital showed a gilt bond, like Consols and War Loan, which cost £100 in 1918, had lost 97 per cent of its value by December 1997 in real terms (that is, after taking account of inflation). Even if the holder had reinvested all the income received, rather than simply spent it as income, and had paid no tax, the £100 would only have grown to £115 after inflation over almost eighty years. The story for cash in deposit accounts is equally dismal.

Since 1945, there have been certain periods of very high interest rates when gilts and cash on deposit did provide good short-term returns. We cannot know whether another such period will return.

The poor result produced by the 1998 Barclays Capital survey is due to the high levels of inflation we have suffered through most of this century. It averaged 2.25 per cent during the first fifty years and a shocking 6.5 per cent every year since 1950. Compare this dreadful outcome with the performance of inflation during the lifetime of Agatha Christie's father. *The average rate of inflation was just 0.07 per cent for fifty years, from 1851 to 1900.* Agatha Christie would have been able to enjoy the same standard of living when she inherited her father's bonds early in this century, as he enjoyed throughout his lifetime. The reason was that the income from a gilt purchased in 1851 would still buy virtually the same value of goods in 1900 as prices stayed so stable.

Compare that outcome with my childrens' experience. As a student in the 1950s I lived through a short period with minimal levels of inflation. This contrasts dramatically with the inflation explosion my children grew up with. While I could just about get by on a very frugal budget of £1 per week as a student for five years, from 1955 to 1960, the equivalent, £20 a week in 1998 money, is nowhere near the figure of around £80 to £100 a week most students now spend on living expenses. However, many economic factors move in cycles so could we one day see the return of that idyllic 1850 to 1900 scenario or even my experiences of the 1950s? It would certainly be good news for pensioners.

Inflation is a boon to debtors and a curse to savers

Inflation is the great enemy of pensioners in retirement. It results in a corrosive destruction of the buying power of money. The amount of money stays the same, but what it will buy when you spend it may be less. While inflation reduces your spending power, it also reduces the value of a debt. Inflation is a boon to debtors and a curse to savers. This is the main reason why mortgage borrowers saw such splendid returns on their housing investments when inflation was high in the 1970s and 80s. Mortgage debt shrank in real terms as this real asset, their house, was rising in value, roughly in line with inflation. Although inflation was fairly low in the latter part of the 1990s, it could return at higher levels. Any form of fixed interest product, whether it is a government or **corporate bond** (which is a loan issued by a company) or a deposit account in the bank or building society, compares unfavourably with real financial assets during a period of rising inflation.

However, during a period of falling prices, called **deflation**, fixed interest investments are not only 'safe', they become more valuable because the amount of your money expressed in numbers, stays unchanged while prices continue to fall. This means each pound you own buys more goods and services than it did a year before. With deflation, fixed interest investments become more valuable, because they are 'capital secure'. Your capital stays unchanged in value as prices fall against it. It is safeguarded from the volatility that affects equity-based investments.

Variable Impacts of Inflation

With inflation, rises in the values of consumer goods vary. Some goods rise higher or faster in price than others, as we saw with the huge change in student costs comparing the 1950s with the 1990s.

If inflation is 3.5 per cent a year for ten years and you save £50,000 in the bank for those ten years, earning 3.5 per cent each year after tax deductions, interest earned on that money should just cover the rise in inflation, but only if you do not withdraw any cash to spend. You may not be exactly back where you started, because different consumer goods change in price at different rates. How you fare depends on what you buy.

If you help a child through university, you would find rent, food, books, clothes, transport and entertainments had all risen, adding greatly to students' costs. But if you bought a computer, you could probably buy a far more advanced model for far less than would have been possible ten years earlier, as goods improving in quality or technology fall in price, even if inflation is rising.

Many real assets, like antique furniture or carpets hold their value, as do real financial assets, like houses, or shares in companies where profits grow every year, perhaps faster than inflation. Houses, publicly quoted shares or private, fast-growing companies are examples of real financial assets. They usually outpace inflation.

Suppose you wanted to buy a house with your £50,000 after a ten year period with 3.5 per cent inflation a year. Houses in desirable areas you might want to move to may have risen by more than 3.5 per cent a year, so £50,000 would not be enough to buy the same house outright that was possible ten years before. There could be a shortfall of several thousand pounds.

*'Consider the numbers: 2% growth over 30 years gives an 80%
increase in the value of a capital sum; 10% growth over 30 years
gives a 1645% increase. We are talking about a difference of 20
times. It is scarce wonder that people might have been confused about
real values during the inflationary process.'*

Roger Bootle, *The Times*

Equities For Long-Term Growth

Among the real financial assets that most people acquire, a home or successful
business are typical examples. However, millions of people own shares or equities in public companies quoted on the London Stock Exchange, even though
few realise this, since they do not own them directly. Shares in companies, like
Marks & Spencer, BP, Glaxo Wellcome or Barclays Bank are core investments
bought by insurance companies and pension fund managers. Their funds must
grow, as vast sums are required to pay out on policies at maturity, on surrender,
on death or as pensions to millions of policyholders. Company shares are real
financial assets forming the main bulk of institutional portfolios because
evidence shows they have the best chance of outpacing inflation.

Buying good **blue chip** shares and holding them for years pays great dividends for patient investors and people investing for retirement if they have a
long saving period before retirement. Figures for the FTSE 100 index support
this idea. The FTSE 100 was introduced in 1984 at 1000; by July 1998, it had
reached 6179. This means if you had invested £1,000 in a FTSE 100 tracker
fund in 1984, it would have grown to £6,179 in fourteen years, a rise of 518
per cent. This growth includes recovering from the October 1987 crash,
although the index took two years to return to and then pass its July 1987 peak.

The chart of the FTSE 100 index on page 97 shows this fourteen year
performance. However, we must avoid the error of reading the past with the
benefit of hindsight. The future may be very different and retired people must
be alert to that possible danger.

If there was a serious global recession, share prices could fall, perhaps for
many years. This would be disastrous news for retired people dependent on
their funds and with limited time to rebuild them. I watched my father investing for growth during 1972 and well remember my bewilderment as prolonged falling share prices continued from May 1972 right through to January
1975. If that situation recurred during the first decade of the next century,
many equity investors will suffer a similar reduction in their net worth. The
alarming long-term crisis of confidence presently affecting Japan is an
example of how this horror story unfolds.

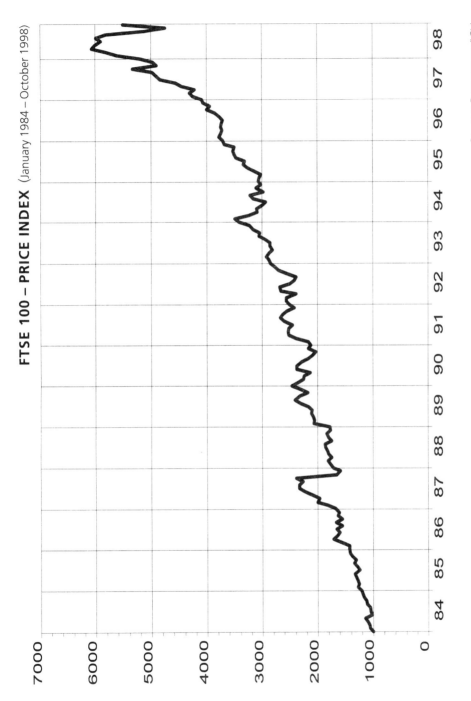

FTSE 100 – PRICE INDEX (January 1984 – October 1998)

Source: Datastream/ICV

The key **Nikkei** index benchmark for the Tokyo stock market fell from a peak of 38,915 in December 1989 to 13,916 on 11 September 1998, a fall of 64 per cent. This has wrecked the financial plans of millions of Japanese people in their fifties, saving for retirement.

The annual Equity-Gilt Study produced by Barclays Capital compares the performance of these two classes of assets over long and short periods. From 1947 to 1997, the annualised total return (which measures income plus capital gain) on equities was 13.8 per cent compared with 6.8 per cent for gilts. As inflation averaged 6.3 per cent over this period, equities produced a real return of about 7.5 per cent, after taking account of inflation (13.8 − 6.3 = 7.5), while gilts produced a minuscule real return of 0.5 per cent (6.8 − 6.3 = 0.5). Figures show that consistently reinvesting the dividends provided two-thirds of the returns from share ownership since 1918. A sum of £1,000 invested in gilts in 1947 rose to around £1,250 by 1997, (ignoring the costs of purchase and taxes) whereas that £1,000 invested in a diverse spread of equities would have grown to £30,400.

> *'How would I feel if I put my family's net worth in it?'*
> Warren Buffett

The traumatic October 1987 stock market crash occurred during this fifty-year period, and in the long-term result it is little more than a sudden blip. Stock market crashes are a complete red herring for the long-term performance of investments in equities.

Better Information Allays Misplaced Fears

When you compare this performance of equities versus gilts, it is clear most people have totally misunderstood the idea of financial risk. Equities are seen as 'risky' while fixed investments, like gilts or cash in a deposit account are 'safe'. This is obviously untrue when the statistics are seen in perspective. People are misled by short-term evidence and completely ignore the long-term facts. This misconception occurs with other 'risky' pursuits, like air travel. Many people worry air travel is 'unsafe' after reading of horrendous crashes. Yet statistics on fatal casualty numbers show air travel is safer than crossing the road. Nervous people will never be convinced by the statistical evidence: they are more influenced by the occasional one-off disaster and ignore the proven safe long-term trends. This faulty reasoning is used to decry stock market investments. Dramatic crashes in October 1929 or 1987 are fixed in folk memory, falsely suggesting shares are ultra-risky.

However, for those who look, there are some warning signs when stock markets become over-optimistic. If you have investments it is dangerous to put them on 'automatic pilot' for years. You can see these warning signs for yourself, but only if you follow the news and watch the markets more closely than you do now.

The Japanese market, for example fell steadily over nine years, with periodic rallies or rises through the 1990s. By reading about the market and making your own decisions, if you had invested in a Japanese unit trust, it would have made sense to take a loss during 1991 or 1992. If you had then waited for definite signs of recovery before going back into that market, you would still be waiting. However, you could instead have put your money to work elsewhere because by 1998, the Japanese economy was still in a deep recession with little sign of recovery. Yet in late 1990, most experts were advising investors to hold on to their Japanese investments. In hindsight, this was poor advice. If you did this with your Japanese unit trusts, make sure you learn the lessons and avoid this mistake another time. The better plan is to weigh up the possibilities of making your money grow in terms of your whole portfolio and to make your own decisions. After all, it is *your* money you are managing.

Insurance and pension institutions buy fixed interest investments to build a balanced portfolio. Their investment families consist of gilts, property, cash and equities, so their investments match their commitments to policyholders. Similarly, small investors need to match their investments to their expected retirement lifespan. If they thought like this they would invest in equities for the long term.

For example, had you bought shares in a representative group of major UK companies, like ICI, General Electric Company or Marks & Spencer, and held them from 1947 to 1997, you would have been investing in some of the best, most successful British companies, which have weathered all the ups and downs of the real economy through fifty turbulent years. Over that period, they grew into multi-billion pound businesses, multiplying their shareholders' wealth several times over.

The important message here is that whatever your age, keep your long-term targets in view. Don't get panicked into rash financial decisions by phoney one-off shocks.

A $1,000 investment in shares of General Motors early in the 1920s would have grown to $40,000 within a decade
A $1,000 investment in Bill Gates' Microsoft in the mid-1980s, would have seen it grow to $80,000 over a decade

You have to see the two 'risk' factors in the right perspective for your future: the inflation risk that erodes your capital sitting in the bank and the stock market risk that a one-off collapse in prices will decimate your capital. You ignore the ravages of inflation at your peril. An entirely new approach to risk is needed if your retirement is not to descend into nightmare poverty during

Collect a family of investments to prepare for all eventualities and provide a growing income and capital sum, right through your retirement

your eighties. This may sound melodramatic, but the figures are stark! I have met many pensioners in their eighties who, due to inadequate planning, are condemned to live out this miserable fate. We shall look soon at Albert's plight, (see page 104) as he is typical of this financial disaster.

Ways to Manage Risk

The records show that markets not only recover but that they do eventually go on to higher levels, so you must have the right approach to avoid being overwhelmed by false fears. Learning how to successfully manage your money means building the confidence to handle your financial affairs successfully. You can learn how to manage financial risks to avoid making the common mistakes most novice investors make. No matter what type of investor you decide you are, learning to manage risk is a top priority. So how can you control the risks of losing money?

Step 3
Learn to manage risk: avoid common mistakes

There are numerous ways to increase the chances of preserving your precious money. Any method you use that has this beneficial result is a tool for managing risk. It has been covered in my earlier books, but is so important, I have to include it here:

1. *The first essential is to start very slowly.* Think through the consequences, both good and bad, before making a firm commitment. Losing capital in your fifties and sixties is clearly a more serious setback than losing money earlier in life.

2. *Buy your investments step by step.* To avoid making poor decisions, use a monthly investment scheme. If you use a tracker fund with existing capital, buy blocks of units at three or six month intervals, to spread the risk of buying at a peak. This also applies if you build a portfolio of company shares directly. Buy your shares in two or three blocks at intervals of some months apart to reduce the risks of poor timing. If you have made a mistake after a few months, you will not have invested all the money you had initially planned. Staged investing is a safety measure.

3. *Never put all your money into just one scheme.* Build a family of investments, to gain a broad spread. This is the most crucial advice for beginners. It reduces risk because you are diversifying your assets: if one choice proves unsuccessful, the others may compensate. If you use a tracker fund, this automatically includes many companies; 100 in the FTSE 100 tracker or over 830 in the FTSE All-Share tracker. To ensure you have a balanced portfolio, do not put all your funds into equity-based areas. Cash funds help diversify the risks of being over-exposed to equities during a long decline in prices.

4. *Reading is an excellent way to reduce risk.* More knowledge enables you to make better financial decisions. Books for beginners and newsletters are listed at the

end of the book (see pages 213–5). When I give talks, people ask me if the reading is boring. I prefer to be positive, treating my investment family as a hobby, a challenge to keep me one step ahead. Reading is the best way to do this. Become immersed in your hobby and it is never boring.

5. *Join forces with other investors.* When you buy units in a unit trust or shares in an investment trust, you share the risk with the other investors. If you have 1,000 units in a unit trust, they are combined with millions of other units from thousands of like-minded investors, to buy hundreds of shareholdings. The value of your 1,000 units alone is too small to buy one fraction of this wide range of holdings.

6. *You can attend classes, conferences, seminars or money shows, or join an investment club.* Although less popular than in America, over two thousand clubs have now been set up in Britain. Books on how to start a club appear in the bibliography.

THE BEARDSTOWN LADIES – AN INSPIRATION TO MILLIONS

The success of an investment club run by fourteen ladies, thirteen of them over sixty, illustrates what retired people can achieve. They put this sleepy mid-American town on the investment map, (although it is already on the tourist trail as the town where the young attorney, Abraham Lincoln, achieved his first success, defending a youth falsely accused of murder). The consistently high returns the Beardstown Ladies' funds achieved seemed to have the professionals totally beaten. They wrote personal investment books and undertook public engagements; talks, tours and television appearances. Unfortunately, the figures for their reported gains over fourteen years, were incorrectly calculated. Their funds only grew by a modest 9 per cent a year, not 23 per cent as was previously thought. However, their efforts inspired millions of American and British investment hopefuls and helped to swell the numbers of investment clubs in America by many thousands.

---

7. *Try to follow the market where your money is invested, so you are not caught out by sudden major changes which adversely affect your investments.* We covered this point earlier, but I feel it holds the inner secret of success.

If you follow the market, you can avoid the sad experience of investing at a market peak. Figures show that novice investors repeatedly do this. Be sure you are not among them. At the peak, prices are very high and due for a drop. If you buy before the fall, it could be months, perhaps years, before the price of your investment recovers to where it was when you started. This sorry fate probably awaited many thousands of investors in Japanese unit trusts in the 1990s. It is particularly bad news for retired people not wanting to wait for years to see a positive return on their funds. There have been several major downturns in the British economy over the past thirty years, to justify keeping a watchful eye on the markets. When you follow the markets, you gain expertise and learn to see when prices are too high, a warning sign, or when they have fallen and it is appropriate to invest.

8. *Monitor your investments regularly, to ensure you reach the target you set yourself.* This is an excellent way to manage risk and should involve a routine yearly review.

9. *Periodically, have a portfolio 'spring-clean', to get rid of doubtful holdings.* If one of your investments is not working out as planned, you can sell it to reinvest the proceeds, hoping for a better result. Investment spring–cleans are essential because when you have limited resources, you cannot allow too much cash to be tied up in losing situations.

Again if you are not meeting your targets, a portfolio spring-clean can remove those investments that are not pulling their weight.

If the economy moves into recession, more frequent monitoring is sensible, perhaps with a bolder spring-clean. Treat the members of your investment family like your real family; take a concerned interest in how they are getting on to make sure they don't let you down. You cannot easily abandon a difficult member of your true family, but there are no such qualms with your portfolio family.

'This year we are going to take a step back in order to take a gigantic step forward.'

Richard Greenbury, chairman and chief executive, Marks & Spencer

10. *Not all your selections will be successful.* Sometimes it is better to sell the losers and re-invest the proceeds in other, more promising opportunities.

MR HUNTER BEQUEATHED HIS WIFE – NOTHING

I met Mrs Hunter at a talk I gave for the over-sixties. Her story shows how easy it is to confuse the risks of stock-market investing with the failure to properly manage those risks.

During the talk I told the audience, as I am telling you, that stock-market related investments are the best route to providing a rising income plus capital growth. In the question session, Mrs Hunter described her husband's experience. He worked in the building industry and one of his friends worked for Trafalgar House, a huge publicly quoted company with large engineering and construction interests around the world. In the 1980s, his friend bought shares in Trafalgar House and Mr Hunter decided to invest most of his capital in it as well.

Unfortunately, the company ran up debts, profits fell and the share price began falling. Despite this bad news, Mr Hunter did not sell the shares and they were still falling when he died. His wife had no idea what to do about this investment, so she did nothing, but continued to watch as the price collapsed to a few pence per share. In 1995, a Norwegian industrial company, Kvaerner, made a **takeover** offer for Trafalgar House. However, the shareholders received only a minute pay-out as Trafalgar House had few assets left and it was heavily burdened with debt. Over the course of just a few years, the capital Mrs Hunter inherited from her husband had shrunk to virtually nothing. She saw this as a powerful case for avoiding the risky stock market.

I told her that investing in shares was not the big disaster she thought. She had not recognised her husband's two mistakes: Mr Hunter went seriously wrong on two key points.

1. He tied up almost all his free capital in one investment. This is incredibly risky. If for any reason, it went wrong, he would lose everything, which in his case, is what happened.

2. Of even more importance, he failed to monitor his investment. When the Trafalgar House share price began falling, he should have read the newspapers or the company's annual report to see if he could discover reasons for this. As a general rule, companies, like individuals who acquire big debts face financial problems. He could have talked to the friend who first tempted him to buy the shares, to see if his friend still held his shares. The answers might have helped him decide what to do. Many investors buy company shares and then neglect to follow the fortunes of those companies. By doing nothing, as signs of disaster for Trafalgar House were emerging, Mr Hunter let his whole investment virtually disappear, leaving nothing to his widow.

Ignoring inflation, neglecting to monitor an investment or putting too much money at risk in one area are just a few of the mistakes private investors make. Here is a list of the ten most common mistakes. They indicate how careless people can be when making major financial decisions.

> *'An investor who has all the answers doesn't even understand the questions.'*
>
> Sir John Templeton, investment guru

Ten Common Mistakes Made by Novice Investors

1. Not understanding the difference between inflation risk and investment risk.

2. Failing to read about financial matters in order to ensure their finances will cope well in the future.

3. Relying on one expert without checking on that person's track record or credentials.

4. Thinking they can achieve financial prosperity if someone else takes control.

5. Buying a financial product from the first person (salesman) who approaches them.

6. Never reading the legal documentation that comes with the product they are buying – even though they are about to sign a legally binding contract.

7. Rarely monitoring how their investments are performing.

8. Putting all their money into one investment scheme.

9. Drifting into poor investments with little thought of 'shopping around'.

10. Taking tips on financial issues from friends, colleagues or newspapers completely on trust – indeed, often without a second thought!

Where is Britain's Wealth?

Most people make mistakes because they do not know how to manage financial risk. These two aspects of successful money management are inseparable. Partly, the problem stems from apathy or ignorance about personal finance. Surveys on this topic reveal the great depth of widespread ignorance, especially on the issue of financial risk. Inflation was relatively low in the 1990s, but this might not continue indefinitely. If rampant inflation returned, it could wipe out your savings. The danger is most acute for pensioners with too large a portion of their money in fixed interest savings, like bonds or deposit accounts. This may sound alarmist, but a look at how Britain's wealth is distributed suggests it is no empty threat. The figures reveal how poorly informed British people are and how widespread is the fear of investing in stock market-related assets.

Step 4
Calculate your wealth distribution

'Growth requires a sacrifice of current profits to lay the foundations for worthwhile future improvement.'

Philip Fisher, financial author

In 1998, HSBC Markets (the broker) calculated that over 45 per cent of wealth is tied up in housing, explaining why elderly people use home income plans, to obtain a larger retirement income. Almost 30 per cent is held in pension and insurance funds, within which are holdings of company shares and unit trusts. Most of the directly held equities are owned by families with above average incomes. Finally, over 25 per cent of total household wealth, is in deposit accounts. This alone amounts to over £500 billion, which is wonderful news for risk-averse Britons if we experience a period of deflation or falling prices. Cash will then be king. However, the long-term record shows these savings rarely keep pace with inflation. Adding the cash deposits (25 per cent) to the wealth locked in housing gives the startling figure of about 70 per cent of household wealth that is not invested for flexible retirement plans. These figures reveal the extent of the learning process future retirees face, if they are not to be overwhelmed by serious financial problems.

ALBERT'S RETIREMENT POVERTY

A letter I spotted in the financial section of a newspaper, illustrates a typical wealth distribution for a confused seventy-six-year old pensioner. He did not understand the tax allowances he was entitled to. We will call him Albert. Tax affairs for pensioners can be complicated, so he set out his savings portfolio to obtain an answer to his query. We can compare Albert's savings with the average statistics listed above.

Albert's Financial Situation in 1998:
Albert's single person pension was £66.26 a week, a yearly income of £3,445.52

This rises to £75 a week from April 1999, but only for certain pensioners – Albert would not qualify, as he had capital of £25,000

This consisted of:
• a Cheltenham & Gloucester (C&G) 30-day deposit account of £10,000.
• a Cheltenham & Gloucester postal account (pays a higher interest rate) of £3,000. (On these two accounts, tax was deducted at the basic rate of 23 per cent with no tax rebates).
• National Savings income bonds worth £12,000. (The bonds pay 7 per cent gross, to top up Albert's state pension. They give him income of £840 a year).

The income bonds give a monthly income paid gross, so he does not have to apply for tax rebates. With these details we can calculate his income and see how his capital is distributed. Albert's wealth distribution is typical of millions of elderly pensioners. He owns only savings deposits, which puts him in the category of a cautious saver.

Whatever Albert decides to do to improve his retirement income, his most costly outcome could be to do nothing

Wealth Distribution for Albert

Item	Income per year £	Capital £
State Pension	3,445.52	(increases in line with inflation)
C&G 30-day account	550 (approx)	10,000
C&G postal account	165 (approx)	3,000
National Savings		
Income Bonds	840	12,000
Total income	**5,000.52**	**Total capital 25,000**

(Tax-allowable income for pensioners over seventy-five, £5,400 per week in the tax year ending 5 April 1998)

Albert has capital of £25,000, but his income position is not good. His total income is only £5,000 a year, or £96.16 a week, which is below the poverty line of £110 a week and below the income support level of £110 per week in 1998. He does not reclaim tax rebates on his two C&G savings accounts, even though he could have a tax-free income of £5,400 for the 1997–1998 financial year. He is sadly, among more than 1.3 million pensioners living in poverty while ironically, having capital of £25,000. Too few people realize how much capital is needed to secure an acceptable retirement income.

Albert's capital shortfall
To lift his income from £5,000 to *£7,000*
He needs extra income of *£2,000*
For this he needs additional capital of *£40,000*
(£40,000 × 5% interest per year = £2,000)

Albert's income situation
Albert was asking for advice on his tax position. Many pensioners of his age feel too proud to seek help. Others do not know they are entitled to income support to bring their weekly income up to the minimum of £110 a week. Like millions of people in his generation, Albert probably paid taxes all his working life but still feels asking for state benefits is begging. With the welfare state over fifty years old, there will be fewer pensioners who think like Albert in future. Most of us know our taxes, paid throughout a working life, pay for these benefits.

Too Late For Albert?
Albert needs advice on claiming his tax rebates and exploring his entitlement to income support. However, if he sought advice from an independent financial adviser or examined some options for himself, he could improve his income. He could:
1. Increase his holdings in an instant access account (paying 7.5% gross in autumn 1998).
2. Buy a fixed-interest bond. They were offering 7.75 per cent in 1998.
3. If he owns his house, he could take out a home income plan.

Whatever he decides to do, the most costly outcome could be to do nothing.

WEALTH DISTRIBUTION FOR THE BLAKES

As an exercise, we can look at what percentage of George and Freda Blakes' wealth is tied up in their housing and bank deposit account.

The Blakes' Wealth Distribution

Item	Value in 1999 (£)	% of total
House (minus mortgage)	140,000	73.97
Pension	33,700	17.80
Life assurance	5,000	2.64
Bank deposit account	4,500	2.38
Car	5,000	2.64
Abbey National shares	1,000	0.57
Total assets	**189,200**	**100**

'No one can be sure what the returns will be on any form of savings over the next forty years. If inflation stays low and economic growth stays subdued, today's relatively low long-term interest rates and high share prices point to far lower returns on securities than over the past twenty-three years.'

Graham Searjeant, *The Times*

The Blakes' Main Wealth Distribution in Percentages

Item	%
House plus deposit account	76.37
Indirectly held equities & bonds (through policies)	20.45
Total equities & bonds (includes Abbey National)	20.98

For the Blakes' 1999 wealth distribution, we must add in George's pension fund of £33,700, as it is a source of capital for Freda if he dies before buying his annuity at sixty. The value of their home at £160,000, minus the mortgage of £20,000 is £140,000. The value of their home plus bank deposit account is £144,500 or 76.34 per cent of their total wealth of £189,200.

The Blakes have money invested in the stock market with indirect equity and bond holdings through their life assurance and pension fund, amounting to £38,700, or 20.45 per cent of their total wealth. Adding in 100 Abbey National shares worth £1,000, gives total equity holdings (both direct and indirect) of £39,700 or 20.98 per cent of their wealth. The Blakes are fairly typical UK savers: they have 76 per cent of their capital tied up in housing and deposit accounts. However, their wealth distribution is lopsided, with far more than 45 per cent in their home and less than 25 per cent in bank deposits. They also have 21 per cent in equities.

'I can give you anything – except time.'

Napoleon Bonaparte

What Type of Investor are You?

Step 5
What type of investor
are you?

When you compile your wealth distribution, you immediately see whether your savings make a balanced investment family. Are you like Albert and the Blakes with most of your assets in either your home or deposit accounts? Your wealth distribution is an instant snap-shot of your investor type. As the majority of British people are wary of equity-related investments, they are mostly nervous investors. But this is due to inadequate information and can be changed.

To devise a sound investment family you must know what type of investor you are – nervous, prepared to take a balanced view, an active risk-taker or some mixture in between. In general, novice investors should begin cautiously, to reduce the chance of making costly mistakes. Most retired people should be cautious or balanced investors. The aggressive route is only suitable for those willing to devote much time and effort to their investments and the markets. The purpose of knowing what type of investor you are, is to find a group of financial products for retirement which suit that type.

For example, you may appreciate the role equities or unit trusts play in achieving financial freedom, but if you are terrified by the thought of market collapses, that route is obviously not for you – at least until you overcome your fears.

Your investment personality is closely linked to the level of commitment you want to make. Despite the wonderful benefits that flow from being an active investor, there are clearly millions of people unwilling to devote the time or effort to securing their financial prosperity. As life is unpredictable, if you can regard building financial security as a life-long hobby, you will reap huge dividends, especially if your personal story changes unexpectedly. We saw how relevant this was for Mary Clarke, when her husband died, and for Mrs Hunter whose Trafalgar House legacy became a pittance. Think back to the sad tale of Bruce and Margery White. As their retirement began, they anticipated a long and happy future. Everything fell apart with Margery's sudden death.

When you think about retirement planning, therefore, you should couple the type of investor you are with your attitude towards taking a passive or active role in arriving at a successful outcome. This coupling is the underlying logic for why tracker funds are ideal for passive investors.

Get Ready to Go

Some people will relish the challenge of getting the best possible financial start to retirement. To others, this regime may seem tedious. Getting started often helps you clarify what type of investor you are and how bothered you want to be with delving into the mountain of literature on available products. If you start out with the best intentions but find your enthusiasm waning, you are getting a strong signal from your inner self that you may not stay the course if you adopt a super-active approach to finding the best investment options. A signal like that should not discourage you: listen to your inner self and opt for a spread of investments that will need no more than yearly monitoring. Most people facing retirement will probably opt for this approach.

However, if you have a dominant need to boost your income or increase your free capital, tilt your choice of investments to suit your special situation. Whatever type of investor you are, aim to match the wide range of savings products and equity-based investments to your particular profile, so you can be comfortable with plans to grow your capital. You must decide how much money to put into each investment. Again, this decision rests on what type of investor you think you are. If you simply want to set up your investment plan and rely on annual monitoring to ensure you stay on track, plan your portfolio accordingly. However, building a family of investments is right for all investor types, so aim to buy at least three or four different investments for your family. The details of how to do this form *Steps 6,* 7 and *8* covered on pages 111–20.

Investor Types

While there are obviously many shades of investor type, here is a short description of three main groups. Do you recognise yourself amongst them?

Nervous investors are easily recognisable.
1. Forever worried that things will go wrong and money will be lost.
2. They rely on 'safe' products and are natural savers.
3. They prefer 'capital secure' products, and ignore inflation.
4. They rely on interest earned on a fixed amount of capital.
5. They are usually passive about how their money grows.
6. Their savings options will not need much monitoring.

Once their product decisions are made, keeping a watchful eye on them, say, once or twice a year, will suffice unless circumstances change drastically. Nervous savers should ignore the risky avenues for growing their wealth until they acquire more skill in managing their finances, through reading. However, they should remember Albert's story. Low risk products rarely bring good rewards. They are safe and boring, but do not provide a growing income or create capital growth.

Savings Options

Advantages with saving products	Disadvantages with saving products
1. Low risk of capital loss.	1. Purchasing loss occurs with inflation.
2. Interest may be more reliable than fluctuating levels of dividends.	2. Low income linked to interest rates in the economy.
3. Interest is unlikely to be totally lost, but can fall to minute levels during deflation.	3. No capital growth.
4. Does not need much monitoring.	4. Does not provide a rising income.

'You don't go into equities for three months or six months, you go in for the long haul, and if you are in for the long haul, this sort of protection [guarantee on bonds] may not be worth it.'

Don Clark, Toquil Clark

Balanced investors will have less doubts than nervous types.
1. They realise some risks are unavoidable but want to keep them to a minimum.
2. They are willing to learn and will quickly improve when they know how to manage risk.
3. They will take a seven to ten year view to allow their capital to grow.
4. They are likely to take an active interest in building capital for retirement.
5. They want to rely on a rising income.

Outright risktakers are prepared to improve their finances.
1. They are bound to be active investors.
2. They are keen to achieve better financial security during retirement.
3. They know this can be risky but are willing to learn how to reduce the risks.
   I now recognise myself in this category, although I did not do an investor type profile on myself when I began to build up capital. I was driven to succeed by the need to escape from debt, rebuild the family finances and com-

pensate quickly for a lot of lost money. Most of the best options for this type of investor were fully covered in *The Armchair Investor*, which is based on the investment system I devised as I progressed. Learning how to build a portfolio of company shares is undoubtedly the most effective way to increase your wealth.

'In the stock market the only way to get a bargain is to buy what most investors are selling.'
Sir John Templeton

Equity Options

Advantages with equity products	Disadvantages with equity products
1. Good prospects for capital growth to outpace inflation.	1. Higher risk of capital loss.
2. Rising income as dividends grow with growth in the economy.	2. Dividends may be unreliable and can fluctuate or be withheld.
3. It is possible to build real and rising wealth.	3. The portfolio needs watching.
4. Purchasing power keeps pace, or outpaces inflation.	4. Requires more monitoring.

Create an Investment Plan

Having decided broadly what type of investor you think you are, the next step, *Step 6*, is to devise your own investment plan. This is the third block of your financial pyramid: building a capital fund, although it clearly depends on the state of your other two blocks – your home and pension arrangements. Your investment plan is uniquely tailor-made to satisfy your personal needs, as everyone starts their planning from a slightly different position, depending on age, whether you are single or a couple, and what your present and future wealth checks look like. However, all the steps to establish an effective investment plan apply to everyone.

Step 6
Devise your investment plan

Buying units in a tracker fund and leaving them to grow, year after year after year sounds boring, but it could be one of the surest routes to long-term wealth

Key Points in Devising Your Investment Plan
1. Refer back to your two wealth checks which identified your special needs and set your targets.
2. Learn how to manage the real risks before selecting your investment choices.
3. Calculate your current wealth distribution.
4. Decide what type of investor you are and what your level of commitment is:

111

passive or active.

5. Decide which financial products will match your needs and investor personality.

6. Build your family of investments.

Many changes occur during retirement, depending on your health and that of your partner, but the broad-brush outline of your plan, if properly designed, should withstand them all, seeing you safely through each phase, to the next one you might face. Not knowing how long retirement will last, one priority is to ensure you own a good spread of assets: at least four, to cope with any situation.

Spread of Investments for Retirement

1. An emergency cash fund.

2. A capital secure fund – to maintain its value during periods of deflation.

3. A fund to provide a reasonable income at the outset of retirement (perhaps in addition to your pension fund). It can be in equity-based investments.

4. A fund to provide a rising income plus the prospect of capital growth (through equity-based investments) to cope with future inflation. This includes some real financial assets, such as unit or investment trusts and company shares.

The Asset Spread for Retirement

Asset type	Uses in retirement
1. Emergency cash fund.	1. For unforeseen events.
2. Additional cash fund.	2. Extra cash for luxuries.
3. Cash or equity-based fund.	3. To supplement your income.
4. Equity-based investments.	4. For a rising future income and future capital growth.

If you create a portfolio of these four asset types you can cover all possibilities including unforeseen emergencies, extra cash for luxuries and to supplement your pension, plus some real financial assets to provide a rising income and capital growth during a long retirement. If your income and capital keep growing, you can maintain your standard of living over time. If you achieve this result, these growing assets should eventually outlive you.

After almost eighty years of inflation, people are conditioned to expect it to continue. We cannot know if the future will be like the past, but for retirement planning, you should be prepared for price stability or even price **deflation**, when prices and the values of real assets, such as houses and company shares, fall. This may seem unlikely, but throughout the 1990s it has been a reality in Japan. People there described price deflation as price destruction, indicating its detrimental effects: interest rates were a minute 0.025 per cent and equities underperformed government bonds in the 1990s by 16 per cent a year on average with inflation of −2 per cent in December 1998.

To prepare for either inflation or deflation during retirement, it is best to create a family of investments, a portfolio to cover both eventualities: have some cash and low risk investments in addition to owning some real financial assets.

To devise your investment plan, focus on your long-term goal to become financially secure: avoid getting too bogged down in a welter of confusing detail. This is advice I have taken for myself, so I know it can work. When I began investing, we relied on my husband's annual income, so I focused on building capital as swiftly but safely as possible. I began as an active stock market watcher, spending long hours reading and researching how to make my funds grow as fast as seemed safe. But as I became more financially secure, the burning urge to be active was replaced by a desire to leave my portfolio on hold and occupy more of my retirement life with hobbies and activities that I preferred to pursue.

> *'I think money that sits in the bank is just dead. If you are not taking risks your life grinds to a halt.'*
>
> Howard Jones, songwriter who wrote the hit *Things Can Only Get Better*

> *'The secret to success in the market lies not in discovering some incredible indicator or elaborate theory: rather, it lies within each individual.'*
>
> *The New Market Wizards*, Jack D. Schwager

THE BLAKES' INVESTMENT PLAN

From the Blakes' wealth distribution, it is clear they should make a determined effort to reorganise their existing assets. They need a better balance and more free cash. They should consider investing for growth but first they must devise their investment plan.

Their target
They need a group of financial products to provide them with a growing income and a rising capital sum, right through retirement.

Their 1999 situation
In Stage 2, they established their own special needs after compiling their

wealth checks. We found that they have an income shortfall of at least £2,600 a year. However, after examining their pension prospects, in Stage 3, we clearly saw that in 1999, the Blakes do not have enough free capital.

Correcting this forms the basis of their investment plan.

Their 1999 wealth distribution

They can see, from their lopsided wealth distribution with so little cash, that they are nervous investors. The decision of what type of investors they are is clear from their existing asset distribution. With so little cash in the bank, it is clear they never seriously attempted to build up their capital in the past. They will probably be nervous at the thought of plunging into investments they know nothing about. They will need to learn about stock-market related investments. Trackers could be a good solution because they have at least nine years before retirement.

Whatever they decide, the Blakes can begin to plan a small family of investments to own.

Choices to Suit Investor Types

Step 7
Investigate the products

There is a wide range of financial products to cater for the variability in investor types but this becomes part of the problem. For people in retirement, the best course is to settle on a small and simple group of investments. Selecting a few choice investments keeps your investment strategy manageable and under your control.

Tax-Free Choices For All

Everyone can benefit by using tax-free schemes. While not valuable to savers who pay no tax, it is a mistake to dismiss them. If you build up capital, you might find after seven or eight years, that you have saved enough money to make using tax-free funds efficient.

'The bottom line is that you need an edge. One of the ways you can get an edge is to find a successful system.'

Monroe Trout, futures trader

When I began investing, paying **capital gains tax** was not a problem. I still invested the full allowable amounts in **Peps** (Personal equity plans). After seven years, constantly growing funds meant this tax might indeed have become an issue had all the funds been held completely outside tax-free plans. If you use tax-free plans, optimistically, when your funds have grown, you will save on capital gains tax if you sell securities. Fees charged on tax-free plans are modest, compared to the tax that may be payable as capital builds up over several years. The problem for most people is that they do not think like long-term investors. This is a grave mistake as you enter a twenty-year retirement period. Start to think like a long-term investor and very soon you will find you are behaving like one.

The two popular tax-free schemes, **Tessas** (Tax-exempt special savings accounts) and Peps will be replaced in April 1999 by a single, more modest tax-aided savings scheme, the Individual savings account (Isa). All existing Peps will then be ring-fenced, meaning no further cash can be added, but existing funds will continue to grow tax-free. However, the concession to add a 10 per cent tax credit on the dividends ends in 2004. New Tessas opened before April 1999 will be allowed to run for the duration of the full five year tax-free period. Tessa and Pep holders, together with new savers, will be able to invest money in Isas, up to the legal limits.

At the time of writing the outlook for Isas is cloudy. While they may be less generous, they might be more flexible than the two tax-free products they replace. Nervous investors can focus on the cash element of Isas until they feel more comfortable about investing in unit or investment trusts primarily through trackers.

'People struggling to understand how to save for retirement must look enviously at the simplicity of products such as Peps.'

Peter Davies, Chief Executive, Prudential Corporation

When Isas come on the market, investors should read all the relevant information and weigh up their advantages. The judgement on whether they will be attractive savings plans will have to be made then.

Low Risk Products

Several other low risk products are suitable for cautious and balanced investor types; the difference rests in the proportions of each allocated within the investment family. National Savings products are firm favourites with savers. They are relatively low risk, although money might be tied up for five years. Some National Savings products are tax-free. Other suitable options include fixed-rate bonds, offering high rates of interest with no risk to capital or guaranteed bonds which, although your money is invested in equities, guarantee to return all or most of your capital plus part of the growth. More details on these products are given in Stage 7, on pages 187–8.

Higher Risk Products

Cautious and balanced investors should look carefully at the tracker option for some of their capital, as discussed in Stage 3, on pages 81–3, especially if they want to be passive investors. It is imperative to achieve some growth in your capital, so you should be willing to put at least part of your cash resources into an Isa, using a FTSE All-Share index tracker. Risk-taking investors who are absolute novices should also begin by investing in either the FTSE All-Share or FTSE 100 tracker, again through an Isa plan.

Although trackers need only a low level of commitment and monitoring once you have made a choice, you must appreciate in advance that your funds will follow the market both up and down. This could be a problem if the markets entered a lengthy decline after the prolonged rises of the 1980s and 1990s. However, on a thirty-year retirement span, history suggests they should grow over long periods.

While very little effort is needed for a tracker holding, two points are important:

1. Be willing to leave your funds to grow for at least ten years.
2. Use a monthly savings plan to iron out stock market fluctuations. There may be extra charges for making monthly payments, but not all companies impose a charge.

The Case for Trackers

Advantages	Disadvantages
1. Offer a wide spread of holdings for a small investment: 100 in a FTSE 100 tracker and over 830 in a FTSE All-Share tracker.	1. Slavishly follow the market, therefore rarely outperform it.
2. There is investment certainty, if the market falls, you know your tracker investment will follow it down.	2. When the market falls 20 per cent, so will the tracker.
3. Trackers are ideal for long-term investors because the long-term history for equities shows they rise over any ten-year period.	3. If the market suffered a prolonged downturn, as in Japan from 1990 to 1998, investors would lose a lot of their savings.
4. They rarely need to be monitored, so are ideal for long-term passive investors. They will not underperform the market.	4. For pension saving, funds can face a big fall in the last year if the market suffers a collapse.
5. Over the long term, holding a tracker investment ensures you enjoy every rise in the market.	

Balanced investors who want to be passive can happily rely on tracker funds or a small group of unit and investment trusts, as I described in *The Money Maze*. Within the existing legal limits, tracker, unit and investment trusts can be held inside a tax-free Isa if these plans prove effective in operation. Investment and unit trusts aim to outperform the market so they need more frequent checking to ensure the fund is performing as expected. Performance figures for these funds feature regularly in the financial sections of broadsheet newspapers. As you gain in confidence, you can progress on to buying unit and investment trusts aiming to outperform the market and then, on again to direct shareholdings. Small holdings of all these investments can be held within the Isas. But these final steps should only be taken if and when novices feel confident that they know how to invest safely for profit, having mastered the skill of managing risk. This applies especially to risk-taking investors. They should treat their hobby like a full time occupation, as I did, to avoid the risk of serious loss.

Another option for balanced investors seeking a reasonably high starting income would be to use insurance-based with-profits bonds. These offer the prospect of some future growth but are less risky than direct equity-based investments, which trackers undoubtedly are. Most insurance companies offer these investment bonds. They went out of fashion during the 1980s, but have become popular again, due to tax changes introduced in 1999. These bonds have always been popular with higher rate tax-payers because they provide a tax-free income to be taken over a period of twenty years. If the end of the term occurs after retirement, the policyholder might be in a lower tax band. However, as with all insurance products, there are commissions to pay to advisers, which, for these bonds can be as much as 5 per cent of your investment. Negotiate a reduction if you are investing over £10,000 as the commission could exceed £500.

Where to Start

When I began investing in 1990, I was a complete investment greenhorn and started by using collective funds, that is, investment and unit trusts, again within Peps, as appropriate. I used collective funds for safety, to build my confidence and experience in the early stages. In 1990, I had never heard of tracker funds as they were an insignificant part of the market and not well advertised.

If I were setting out now, as a complete novice in my early fifties, even though I know I am a risk-taker, I would most certainly utilise the trackers in combination with selected international unit or investment trusts for the first year or eighteen months, again putting them into a tax-free vehicle if possible, which inevitably means Isas now. At the same time I would run a paper portfolio for company shares, as described in *The Armchair Investor*. Then, feeling I was ready to start investing directly in company shares, I would begin slowly, researching one share at a time, and taking my own advice on which companies to invest in. I would do the necessary reading for this by following my FASTER GAINS formula, as outlined in *The Armchair Investor*. Attention to sensible risk management,

'An investment is simply a gamble in which you have managed to tilt the odds in your favour.'

One Up On Wall Street, Peter Lynch

as we described earlier, is important to all investors, but it is doubly vital to people close to or already in, retirement. The starting routine, listed below, is for guidance for active investors who begin as novices but want to progress to holding their own equities within a portfolio.

The Starting Routine

1. Begin by using collective funds.
2. Obtain information on suitable unit or investment funds. Choose trackers or international funds.
3. Read, in order to build your expertise.
4. Use monthly instalments to spread the risk.
5. Progress to direct share holdings when:
    i) you feel sufficiently confident
    ii) you have run a successful paper portfolio for about six to nine months – it must be showing a profit though!
    iii) you have saved at least £10,000 in capital.
6. Divide your capital into five equal blocks, one for each shareholding, reserving a small balance in cash. Start slowly, with one share holding at a time, leaving the balance of cash on deposit.
7. Make no further investments until what you have bought is making a profit.

Progressing on to High Risk Products

I set out with this starting routine slowly progressing as outlined above. Aiming for the best results, I used tax-free Peps for the maximum amounts available. For a risk-taking investor, this course produces the best of all worlds. I was able to grow my capital five times over in around six years, simply because I made several large gains in company shares I bought and held within these Peps.

Start to think like a long-term investor and very soon you will find you are behaving like one

I believe anyone determined to succeed and learn the necessary skills, can repeat the growth in portfolio values I achieved, and probably comfortably exceed it, because when I began I did not even know where to find recent investment books for beginners. By the late 1990s the choice had expanded considerably and there are additional aids to ensure good results. Planning financial security by directly investing in stock-market related investments can be one of the most rewarding hobbies you can cultivate in the last decade before your retirement, or even when you have retired, whether you are physically fit or not.

Your Investment Family

Having examined the range of possible products, we are ready for *Step 8*, to create an investment family, for all three investor types. As individual circumstances vary, so will the goals people set. Some, perhaps those already retired, may want to achieve a large and steadily rising income, while those with several years of planning ahead of them, might prefer to first build up capital. When you devise your own investment plan, you can produce the end result you want.

Step 8
Create your
investment family

What will this end result look like? It takes the form of a collection of financial products or investments, all working in harmony to produce your financial security. The group, in total, form a family of investments. Aim to build a small family of investments to protect your funds from inflation or deflation, while choosing those that match your underlying attitude to risk. The select group of investments form-ing your investment family become your total portfolio or fund, of which you are now the manager. Ask advice from professionals on what you should buy, but be willing to learn how to make your own decisions so that you are in con-trol, running your own investments.

So here is the nub of your investment target process:

1. Build an emergency cash fund, plus extra cash for special items.

2. Choose some investments to provide both a rising income and capital growth.

Schemes to use in Your Investment Plan to Create a Family of Investments

Products	No of years	Risk level
Emergency cash	Indefinite	Inflation risk
National Savings	1 or 5 years	Low
Tessas (can run to 2004)	5 years	Low
Guaranteed Products: i) fixed interest bonds ii) equity-based guaranteed bonds	1 to 10 years plus 5 years	Low Medium
Isas	5 to 10 years	Low for cash and life policies. Medium for trusts. High for shares
Unit/Investment Trusts i.e. Trackers	5 to 10 years plus	Medium
International unit or investment trusts	3 to 10 years plus but only if the growth story holds	Medium
Company Shares	5 to 10 years	High

3. Focus on a small group, to reduce the monitoring time involved.

4. Ensure the products you choose offer a wide spread, to reduce the risks of loss.

From this list, surprisingly, several products can be used by all investor types, but the proportions will vary. Trackers can play a part in everyone's retirement investment plans, as well as for pension planning, as we saw in Stage 3. Buying units in a tracker fund and leaving them to grow, year after year after year sounds boring, but judging from the past it would have been one of the surest routes to long-term wealth, over ten, twenty, fifty or eighty years. Trackers within a tax-free fund could be a useful addition to everyone's retirement investment family.

Most people are usually too busy earning money to make money

Nervous investors can be cautious, but should aim to dip a careful toe in the stock market, by investing perhaps, 10 per cent of their funds in trackers. The role of trackers is more positive for balanced types. Even for active risk-takers, especially if they are novices, there is a place for trackers while they build up their knowledge, experience and investment skills.

Choices to Suit Investor Types

Investment	Investor types	Risk level
Deposit account in an Isa (emergency fund)	Nervous/balanced/risk-takers	Low
National Savings	Nervous/balanced	Low
Guaranteed income bonds	Nervous/balanced	Low
Guaranteed fixed-interest bonds – for income	Nervous/balanced	Low
Trackers in an Isa – for rising income and capital growth	Nervous/balanced/risk-takers	Medium
Unit & investment trusts – for income and capital growth	Balanced/risk-takers	Medium
Insurance-based bonds – for income and capital growth	Nervous/balanced	Medium
Company shares – for rising income and capital growth	Balanced/risk-takers	High

BUILDING CAPITAL FOR THE BLAKES

When we last looked at the Blakes' retirement plans, we discovered their wealth distribution was very one-sided in favour of home ownership. They need to cover an income shortfall of £2,600 and generate more free cash in retirement. However, their future finances could be transformed before George retires, because they have two streams of income that could be reallocated to invest in something with a better chance of growing faster than inflation before their retirement date arrives. A fund that achieved this result would give them the capital sum now missing from their plans and on their current programme will remain missing, even on retirement. The fund needs to be watched carefully, as the rising stock market of the 1990s means the timing of when they should begin to invest will be important. Investing at a peak would be detrimental to the ultimate size of their capital fund. Although they may be nervous, with nine years to retirement, this is the time to invest for growth. After George retires, beginning to save for growth will be risky.

Selecting the Right Route

To decide which of several routes they might take, now is the time for more paper exercises. Charting their progress on paper will help them clarify which of these options to take.

'I'm from Yorkshire and so is my wife. We've put it [£3 million from shares sold in Games Workshop] in the building society, though we might buy a small cottage by the sea.'

Tom Kirby, chairman, Games Workshop Group

1. Reroute Bank Savings

The first, most obvious stream of income is the £60 per month (£720 a year) they save in the bank.

i) This money could be invested into a monthly tracker fund within an Isa plan, one for George and a second for Freda, so the cash grows tax-free. However, this savings pot can only be used once: should they opt for a tax-free fund or invest it in George's pension fund?

ii) Increase George's pension contributions, discussed in Stage 3 on pages 67–9.

After working out the possibilities on paper, their final decision will depend on their attitudes to creating a larger secure income or a bigger capital fund with flexibility to cope with future unforeseen needs.

2. Reroute Car Loan Money after May 2002

On its own, £720 a year would not make a great impact, but they could boost it by saving another £2,000 each year, by diverting £2,000 from the car loan repayments after May 2002, when the car is fully paid off. Saving £2,720 each year in a tracker fund within an Isa plan over five years would make a significant improvement to their capital situation. Saving in a monthly scheme is a proven way of reducing risk, as some months the tracker units will be cheaper than others, depending on the state of the market. This means they can average out the costs of buying their units over every year they save.

a. If they are nervous, they might consider spreading the money by:
i) putting half their funds into a tracker, using the FTSE All-Share index and
ii) putting the other half in a guaranteed income bond or a higher rate deposit account.

b. If they feel more confident, they could invest all their funds in a tracker, using the FTSE 100, but this route would need careful monitoring to ensure they stay on target to build their funds as planned.

c. Another option, with the tracker route, is to split their savings, so that they invest £1,360 every year in each of these two tracker types, the FTSE 100 and FTSE All-Share index.

Many major fund management groups and insurance companies run large tracker funds. They advertise in the financial sections of the weekend newspapers so you can write for information. Although during the 1990s the trackers achieved excellent growth records because the stock market rose strongly, it would be unwise to expect the continuation of such good returns in future.

If the tracker grew by around a cautious 7 per cent each year over five years, by 2007 the Blakes' fund might be £23,283.

Without adding £720 a year to the bank deposit account, it will not reach the £15,300 they were expecting. But by 2007, their savings of £4,500 might grow to around £7,000. This deposit fund could serve as their emergency cash fund. If Isas prove useful, they might consider building up this emergency cash in an Isa, as the money can be withdrawn at any time without penalties, but earns a tax-free rate of interest, after charges imposed by the provider. However, until investor compensation schemes become effective in 2000, investors' cash will be at risk if they place it with unlicensed deposit takers such as fund management groups. Their total capital would rise to £30,283 (£23,283 + £7,000 = £30,283).

If the tracker achieved a 9 per cent growth rate, their tracker fund would reach £25,217. By 2007, their total funds would be £32,217.

3. Move to a Smaller House
A third source of funds to consider is the money tied up in their home. Here, they have several choices, but if they decided to move, they could buy a smaller property in 1999 when their home was worth £160,000 or in any year up to or after George retires. We looked at the figures for the move in 1999, in Stage 2, on page 51, when we saw they could save over £72,000 by 2007.

Similar calculations would apply to any year they chose to move, but here we will look at a move in 2007.

Move in 2007

If the value of their home grew to £176,000 by 2007 and they sold it to buy a smaller house for about £126,000 without a mortgage, they would release around £50,000 from the sale. This could be added to their tracker funds of £23,283 that they had saved from 1999 to 2007, to give a total fund of £73,283.

Perhaps they want to split their funds 50/50 with a National Savings or a guaranteed bond. Again, it is impossible to predict whether either house prices, or the UK stock market will actually rise or possibly fall from 1999 to 2007, or by what amount they will change. Charting your progress on paper

> *'Do you remember what you learned in those early days?'*
>
> Jack Schwager
>
> *'I learned how quickly you can lose money if you don't know what you're doing.'*
>
> Munroe Trout

Savings Options for the Blakes

Cash to reroute	Option for that cash
1. Bank savings (£720 per year for 8 years) £5,040	• Monthly payments into a tracker fund.
2. Bank savings + car loan cash (£720 per year for 8 years + £2,000 per year for 5½ years) = £17,040	• All money into a monthly FTSE All-Share tracker. • Half into a tracker and half into guaranteed income bond.
3. Mortgage money (£4,320 for 8 years) £34,560 + £20,000 from sale of house in 1999	• All money in a FTSE 100 tracker fund. • Half in a FTSE 100 and half in a FTSE All-Share tracker. • Half in a FTSE 100 tracker and half in a guaranteed income bond.
4. Free cash £50,000 from sale of house in 2007	• All money in FTSE All-Share tracker. • Half in a FTSE 100 tracker and half in a FTSE All-Share tracker. • Half in FTSE trackers and half in a) National Savings b) guaranteed income bonds c) with-profits bonds.

is all about exploring the possible options. If you do this, you are well on the way to outsmarting the future as you will be far better prepared for whatever happens than if you simply sail into retirement without a second thought. Some guesswork is clearly involved. This exercise will help the Blakes to think more positively about their various options. They must try to stay flexible and monitor their progress as they go along.

Investment Choices for the Blakes

Available cash to reroute	Investment choice	Amount saved each year (£)	Total saved by 2007 (£)
Bank account savings	FTSE All-Share tracker	720	9,228
Bank account savings + car loan money	FTSE All-Share tracker	720 + 2,000 (from May 2002)	23,283 (7%) 25,219 (9%)
Move in 1999	FTSE All-Share tracker	20,000 lump sum + 4,320 each year	81,789 (7%)
Move in 2007	FTSE All-Share tracker	23,283 + 50,000 lump sum	73,283

The best antidote to changing conditions is to own a capital fund that allows plenty of flexibility

Stay on Target

Forecasting how your finances will look in ten years time is probably as far as exercises on paper can go. Many imponderables may be overlooked. However, if you have a capital sum of around £50,000 to £100,000 as you start your retirement, estimating how it will grow with or without drawing an income can help you with your long-term planning. You can follow the routine we have used for the Blakes to see how your finances will look over a ten-year period to provide capital on which you can then draw an income from your accumulated funds.

Although building up a capital fund prior to retirement may sound like the ideal solution, fine on paper, but elusive in reality, it is perfectly possible to achieve this kind of result. I know, because I did it using direct investments in company shares, rather than trackers. But I did have the great **bull market** behind me, right through the 1990s. Moreover, I treated building up my cash as a full time job, always reading or checking to see if I was still on target. In my case, this proved to be a seven year occupation which has given my family a true sense of financial freedom with time and energy now to pursue other activities.

Sadly, predicting the future is a mug's game. With the best will imaginable, it may not work out as you estimated on paper. To keep yourself on target, especially if your finances are as unbalanced as the Blakes, you should be willing to monitor your progress each year. You might need to watch your investment family even more regularly, perhaps on a six or even three-monthly basis if the economy or global stock

'Basically, when you get down to it, to make money, you need to have an edge (a system) and employ good money management (risk control).'
Monroe Trout

markets become turbulent, as occurred in the 1970s and in August and September 1998. By monitoring your investments in this way, you can make appropriate changes or improvements as you go along. If you follow the progress of your investment family as closely as you watch your real family, your diligence should be well rewarded.

You gain a substantial advantage if you have several years before retirement in which to build your capital. Learning to manage money is undoubtedly a skill. It takes time and some effort to acquire. But, given time, when you retire, you should be able to confidently invest your pension lump sum, along the same successful lines as your earlier investments. The pension lump sum is an add-on extra fund to bolt into place within your investment portfolio of growing assets. If I were fifty-five again and newly retired, I would be ready and happy to repeat my earlier experience on learning how to look after my own capital, especially since today small investors enjoy more support and research services than were available in 1990, when I started.

ANNE SCHEIBER'S BRILLIANT RESULT

The story of Anne Scheiber illustrates how successful small private investors can be if they take the trouble to grow their money. Her example is inspirational for people making retirement plans. She was a spinster living in a shabby apartment in a run-down district of New York. She spent her whole career with the American tax authorities, the Internal Revenue Service in a clerical role checking the tax affairs of wealthy Americans. As a woman working in a man's world before the second world war, no opportunities for promotion occurred. She spent over forty years with this one employer but never achieved a salary increase or advancement. Being good at her job, she held it until she retired in 1947. Her capital on retirement was $5,000 and she received a small pension from the Internal Revenue Service. This pension was just enough to live on if she was frugal, which is how she managed to survive through her retirement years.

When she retired, she had lost contact with her family of nephews and nieces. She had no friends, took no interest in moving to a better apartment, never bought new clothes or went to theatres and concerts. But she did take up one hobby that became her all-consuming passion: she taught herself how to invest in the American stock market.

During her working life she realised that most of the wealthy people she had to investigate made their money investing on Wall Street. She decided that was where big money could be made. Throughout her retirement, she studied the market, developed a system of buying shares in America's most successful growth companies, like Coca-Cola and Gillette, and rarely sold any of her holdings. By the time of her death she was receiving enormous dividend cheques on the shares she had bought, all of which were reinvested in the market. The only two men she had any contact with throughout her retirement were her **stockbroker** and lawyer.

When she died her portfolio had grown from $5,000 to an astounding $14 million. She was the ultimate self-taught long-term investor: she never sold any of her holdings and lived to be a hundred. This gave her investments forty years to grow to this superb size because she kept reinvesting her dividends. When I told this story to a group of retired people, a lady in the audience interrupted to ask, 'What was the point of making all that money, when she never enjoyed spending any of it and had no one to leave it to?'

Well, for me, the real punchline in this marvellous success story is what she chose to do with her money. She left it as an endowment to a small college for women, so that students there could achieve degrees by studying to make better careers for themselves than she had been allowed to do. But because endowments in America are free of state taxes, her stingy employer, the American Internal Revenue Service, never received a penny of her investment nest egg. It went entirely to the people she wanted to benefit from it.

We can't all live to be a hundred and make such a wonderful success of our investment talents, but Anne Scheiber's is a truly inspirational tale of what retired people can achieve. Moreover, there are some interesting records relating to the fifty year period during which she amassed her fortune. They illustrate that the erratic nature of short-term trends should never deter the long-term investor. According to Victor Sperandeo, a successful American options trader, anyone who bought American shares between the 1962 low and the 1974 low would have lost money. Whatever new investments she was buying, Anne Scheiber would probably have been regularly reinvesting her dividends during this twelve year period. Between 1973 and 1974, Wall Street declined more than 75 per cent and her investments had to survive this collapse plus two October crashes, in 1987 and 1989. Despite these adverse events, her wealth continued to accumulate right until her death in the early 1990s.

The final piece of advice comes from Victor Sperandeo!

'The key to building wealth is to preserve capital and wait patiently for the right opportunity to make the extraordinary gains.'

Victor Sperandeo

Key Points To Remember

STAGE 4: CREATE A LUMP SUM FOR CAPITAL

1. To supplement your pension, especially if it is fixed and will not rise every year.
2. To create emergency cash for large or unexpected outlays.
3. To keep pace with inflation so you can maintain your standard of living, right through your retirement.
4. To achieve flexibility for future needs.
5. To leave money to your family or favourite charities.
6. Schemes to consider for your Investment Plan:

    i) emergency cash fund: low risk

    ii) National Savings: low risk

    iii) guaranteed bonds: low risk

    iv) Isas: five to ten years: medium to low risk (can hold a cash element)

    v) Unit or investment trusts trackers (within or outside Isas): five to ten years: medium risk

    vi) With-profit insurance bonds: five to twenty years: medium risk

    vii) Company shares: three years at least: high risk
7. Build a family of investments.

'The general idea is that what works most of the time is nearly the opposite of what works in the long run.'

William Eckhardt, trader

STAGE 5 PREPARE FOR LIFE – LONG OR SHORT

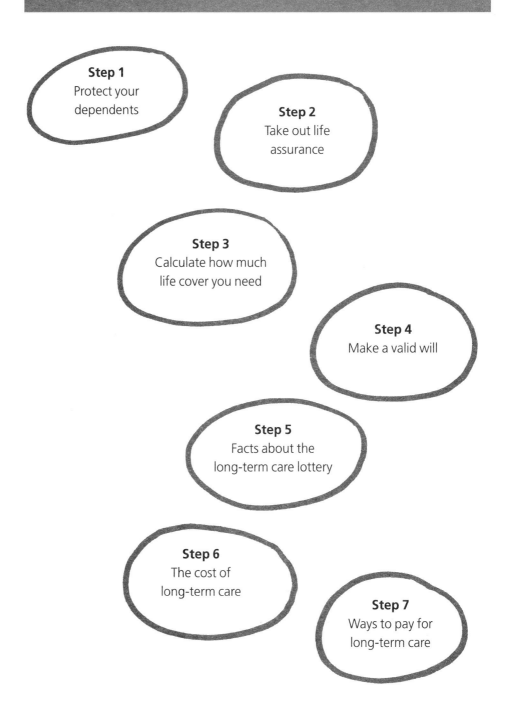

Step 1
Protect your
dependents

Step 2
Take out life
assurance

Step 3
Calculate how much
life cover you need

Step 4
Make a valid will

Step 5
Facts about the
long-term care lottery

Step 6
The cost of
long-term care

Step 7
Ways to pay for
long-term care

MOVE TO **STAGE 6**

Prepare for Life – Long or Short

'The financial complications that go with death could not come at a worse time, because nobody is in a state to deal with probate and sorting out the deceased's money affairs.'

Deborah Moggach

In life, Howard Johnson, Mr Hunter and Gordon Clarke probably had nothing in common. Their paths never crossed and they lived separate lives. But they were joined in death by a common thread: they left their widows a miserable financial headache. Would they have been shocked to know that this was one of their most enduring legacies? The distress suffered by these widows pales somewhat, when set beside the tragic story told to me by a taxi-driver ferrying me to a meeting.

A MOTHER TO RELY ON

Mrs Hamilton's son, Nigel, was experiencing a family crisis. His first marriage had broken down and he was separated from his wife and two teenage daughters. He had moved in with his best friend's sister, who was seven months pregnant with his baby. Nigel went to Mexico for a major sporting event but he died suddenly from a ruptured artery in his brain. Although Nigel had such complicated family commitments, he had no life assurance, had not taken out holiday insurance and had not made a will.

Mrs Hamilton was distraught by the thought of her son being buried in Mexico, thousands of miles away. As a sixty-year old widow, she had little spare cash yet she was willing to spend £6,000 to fly Nigel's body back to Britain and arrange his burial. She lived frugally, so this crisis outlay involved a huge sacrifice.

Nigel was only forty. His death was totally unexpected but to add to this sudden shock, it left six members of his family in a nasty mess. His two daughters and unborn child were not provided for; he left no financial support for his wife or newly pregnant partner and his mother had lost a son and £6,000 through his thoughtless irresponsibility.

Taking care of those you leave behind is like learning to swim: learn to swim and no one need ever lose their life trying to save you from drowning. With the typical nuclear family in decline, millions of people need to reconsider their life assurance protection. Not only are there more single parent families, but many divorced people enter a second marriage or a steady relationship with another partner and start another family in their forties or later. In consequence, there are thousands of children at risk of financial hardship from a parent's premature death before they become independent.

Insurance is underrated in financial planning, but it can provide invaluable assistance if you have the misfortune to die young. Many people would see long life as a great asset, but it can become burdensome if you have ignored the careful planning required to keep life sweet.

Insurance-based solutions can help for both living too long or dying before your time, so we will follow a logical sequence to examine ways to prepare for life, either long or short. The route takes you along the planning path on page 128. *Step 1* describes different types of life assurance policies you can use to protect your dependents. In *Step 2*, we discuss how these policies might be used for this important role. *Step 3* considers the issue of how much life cover you need. *Step 4* briefly covers the need to make a valid will. *Step 4* is closely linked to inheritance tax planning which is discussed in Stage 6, suggesting Stage 6 is really the logical place to cover making a will. Your paths could diverge here, as making your will might be more important for you personally than exploring inheritance tax plans. However, using a logical route, preparing for life means worrying about the consequences of both dying too soon or living too long, so the two aspects belong together. We move on to *Step 5*, to consider the complicated background to long-term care. *Step 6* discusses protecting your assets within the law, before going on to *Step 7* to investigate long-term care policies.

Types of Protection

Some life assurance is expensive, but there are cheap options.

1. **Term assurance** is widely used by people to cover an outstanding debt, like a mortgage, or to provide a lump sum for their dependents. This might include a widow without a pension, or children of a single parent or those starting a second family in later years.

Step 1
Protect your
dependents

Term cover has no investment element and only has a value when a claim is made during the term while the policy is running. Term assurance is like house or car insurance, only paying out on a claim. It provides a fixed amount of money, often several thousand pounds, to be paid out if the insured person dies within the policy term. The policy is pure protection, in case disaster strikes.

2. A **whole-of-life** policy can be used to avoid the life cover gap which arises at the end of a term policy. As long as you continue paying the premiums, the policy will pay out on your death, even if you live to a hundred. A whole-of-life plan includes investment, so it acquires a surrender value if you decide to discontinue the premiums. However, as with any other insurance policy that is surrendered, the value will be less than its value on the assumption it continues to full term. By providing protection throughout life, it is a useful tool for **inheritance tax planning (IHT)**, designed to cover taxes payable on an **estate** consisting of all the financial assets on the death of the owner of those assets, so we will consider it in Stage 6, on pages 153–61.

If you look upon your life assurance as a back-up plan in the event of disaster, the case for arranging it becomes overwhelming

3. **Family income benefit** is another form of term assurance. It acts as a replacement income paying out the agreed amount on a death for every year until the term expires. The income can be indexed to take account of inflation.

4. An endowment policy is a savings plan, not strictly a life policy but it usually has an insurance element written into it and can make a useful contribution to providing protection. If your endowment is for £30,000 over twenty-five years, the policy will pay out £30,000 on the death of the policyholder during that twenty-five year term.

5. Single premium insurance bonds, which are popular with people approaching or in retirement, also contain assurance. These bonds, often called investment bonds, provide a regular income while hoping for some capital growth. The level of assurance is, therefore, rather low.

Types of Life Protection

Policy	With investment	Income or lump sum	Cover for
Term – single life	No	Lump sum	Children and elderly
Term – joint life	No	Lump sum	Children
Term – family income benefit	No	Income	Children
Family income benefit – joint life	No	Income	Children
Whole-of-life	Yes	Lump sum	Children and elderly and IHT
Endowment	Yes	Lump sum	For a major item
Pension	Yes	Lump sum or income as annuity	Surviving spouse

6. Finally, as we saw in Stage 2, a pension policy usually contains a death clause to pay out a certain amount if death occurs before the pension is drawn. The amount payable varies with the type of superannuation or pension plan. Occupational final salary schemes are the most generous, while traditional with-profits pensions may not return the fund built up.

Who Needs Protection?

Regardless of age, everyone with young or old dependents needs life assurance. This may sound surprising, but widows with only the modest state pension to rely on may be just as vulnerable to financial hardship when a partner dies in retirement as young children who lose a wage-earning parent. Life assurance for people in their fifties is especially important if they remarry and have second families late in life. It becomes a sound back-up plan as Roy Hanson's story explains.

LIFE ASSURANCE – YOUR BACK-UP PLAN

Roy Hanson was in his fifties and married to his second wife, Jennifer who was thirty-five. They had one son, Michael, aged ten. Roy was one of three partners in a small manufacturing company. Jennifer kept all the household accounts because Roy worked long hours at the factory. She was a well organised person. All the important documents relating to the family's affairs were locked tidily in a safety box, which she produced when we began our interview on their personal finances. The Hansons had a comfortable income, so she did not work, although on odd occasions she helped out at the factory.

Step 2
Take out life assurance

Examining their insurance plans, I realised there was inadequate life assurance to provide a replacement income if Roy died before Michael became independent. Jennifer was almost twenty years younger than Roy, so I pointed out to her the dangers of this lack of life assurance, which she quickly recognised. Roy agreed to take out life cover, because he left all these financial decisions to Jennifer. However, I could not persuade his two partners at the factory to take out key man insurance. In the event of one death, the other two partners could buy out the widow's share with the insurance money. Without that cover, the widow becomes the third part-owner of the business. As a profit-sharing partner she would be entitled to participate in all their plans and financial decisions, even if the remaining two male partners did not want her to do so. Within a year, Roy developed a malignant tumour. Although it was surgically excised, it continued to spread. Roy died within three months of his illness being diagnosed.

Jennifer collected the insurance money but it was far short of providing a full replacement income, because Roy was unwilling to buy the full amount of life assurance I recommended. As for Roy's two partners, perhaps they adjusted well to Jennifer's right to be involved in their affairs. She seemed competent enough to play a positive role, even though they had no choice in her participation.

'He always had money. When he died, they found £10,000 in his boxes and money scattered about everywhere, a great deal of gold. There were above five hundred pocketbooks, of different dates, and in every one money — guineas, one pound notes, one, two, or three in each . . . He had never given away or parted with anything.'

Blood Royal, Christopher Sinclair-Stevenson, comment on George IV

Term assurance

This is one of the cheapest, most focused forms of protection, as it can precisely cover whatever risk you face. The premiums are fixed at the outset.

1. It is especially practical for working parents of young families who have high running expenses.

2. Life cover for mothers is important even if they have no paid employment. Think about who will help bring up the children if their mother dies. Paid nannies are expensive.

3. Older people with substantial business debts or an outstanding mortgage should take out term assurance to cover the entire debt for as long as it is estimated to remain outstanding. This ensures you do not leave a large legacy of debt to a surviving partner.

Don't Gamble with Term Assurance

With term assurance, if the policyholder survives beyond the term, the policy expires worthless. This may sound like a gamble because with a term of twenty years, if you die twenty-one years after your policy began, there will be no payout. However, the greatest value of term assurance is as a short-term solution to cover the monetary shortfall arising from premature death when dependents or outstanding financial liabilities need to be protected. To reap the greatest benefit from a term life assurance policy, during the period it is in force, aim to build up a capital sum, as described in Stage 4, to replace the life cover. By the time the policy expires worthless, your capital resources will hopefully have increased to fill the gap. George and Freda Blake were doing just that; saving £60 every month in a bank deposit account to build up cash to replace the £5,000 of term assurance life cover on George's life. This cover will end in 2017 on his seventieth birthday.

Whole-of-Life Policies

These eliminate the gamble inherent in term assurance. If you think you will be unable to build up capital to replace your term assurance when it ends, consider buying whole-of-life assurance while you are young and healthy. As it has a surrender value you can cash it in later, perhaps to pay for your child's university fees if you decide further life cover is not needed.

Family Income Benefit

This is a solution for protecting a young family. It should be considered by both mothers and fathers with dependent children, since increasingly, more women are wage earners. If a 'stay-at-home' mother dies, a father has to employ a replacement, unless he can rely on an accommodating grandparent who is suitably capable and willing to accept the burden. The cost of professional help for looking after children could range from between £6,000 to £12,000 a year, plus national insurance contributions. The number of years the policy should run are calculated from the age of the youngest child. In a family of three children aged from three to ten, the term would need to run for fifteen years, until the youngest reaches eighteen. Where both parents make a financial contribution which would be difficult to replace, a joint family income benefit is a good option, set up to pay out on the first, not the second death. As the total amount of life cover over ten to twenty years may be considerable, a medical examination might be needed before the insurer accepts the deal. As this policy pays out an annual income, it will only pay out the balance of the last year's income if you die during that final year of the term. Here, again, if further life cover is unexpectedly needed, trying to save to replace the expiring policy as you go along, may avoid the need to buy more expensive policies later in life. Saving ahead of that later need could, therefore obviate buying another policy when you are older and the premiums higher.

Alternative Protection

Widows and widowers may be vulnerable to the adverse effects of a spouse's death. If they rely on a source of income that will cease on the death of a partner, they need to calculate how their finances will cope with the loss of that income. Mrs Hunter's plight when her husband's Trafalgar House investment went so disastrously wrong, illustrates how widows can be left financially insecure on the death of the partner who always made the main financial decisions in the relationship. However, premiums for life assurance grow progressively more expensive with age. Moreover, people in their late forties or older, may have contracted one of a number of serious ailments which incur excess loading on insurance premiums. Or, you may be a heavy smoker or drinker or have an occupation rated more risky by insurance companies. All these situations, therefore, require some policy alternatives, although they may not provide ideal solutions. Some options are:

1. Joint Protection. If you are in this difficult situation, consider a joint life policy where premiums will be lower because they cover a normal (your spouse) plus your own impaired risk. This benefit will also apply if one partner is ten, or more years older than the other, as the combined ages usually make the premium on a joint policy cheaper than for separate cover. Although separate life assurance for both partners might be more beneficial and better value for money, if it is not affordable for one partner, through age or infirmity or lifestyle, the joint route covers the deficit.

2. Use term assurance, as a less expensive option instead of a whole-of-life plan, which is more open-ended.

3. Endowments. These policies provide protection against premature death, but are also a form of compulsory saving, to cover expensive future events that can be planned in advance. These might include school or university fees, a family wedding, paying off a mortgage or providing a lump sum for retirement. The premiums will be designed to allow for growth to pay out the lump sum on maturity, usually through guaranteed annual bonuses and a large but not guaranteed terminal bonus. Cautious people use endowments for major planned events because the guarantees make them less risky than directly held equity-based investments, such as holdings of unit or investment trusts and company shares.

Clearly when considering a very long-term savings plan, you should explore the details carefully before you sign the contract. However, if circumstances change and you cannot afford to continue to the maturity date of your policy, a good second-hand market exists for investors willing to buy them from you at prices well above the surrender values offered by insurance companies. These policies attract good second-hand prices because they are useful products for financial planning. The names of specialist companies who buy endowments and other with-profits policies to sell them on for you are listed in Stage 7 on page 190.

Compromise is Better Than Nothing

Life assurance becomes more expensive for older lives but there are some cheap alternatives and the most important message when planning protection for dependents is to not spurn the compromises because they are not ideal. Doing this can create enormous hardship for survivors.

INSURANCE IS PEANUTS

It is far better to settle for a lower compromise than to dismiss the entire project of arranging some life cover out of hand once you realise you cannot afford the total amount you think you need. *Widow*, was written by an American mother who was left with a teenage son when her lawyer husband died of cancer. After his death, with her income grossly depleted and no life assurance, she worked as a waitress. Her standard of living fell drastically and she agonised that her son was deprived of so many things other boys take for granted. Before he became ill, she had failed to persuade her husband to buy life assurance. He scoffed at the amount of cover it would provide, 'It's peanuts.' Sadly, the peanuts would have been better than nothing but now even peanut butter, a firm favourite with American children, was no longer affordable.

How Much Life Assurance Do You Need?

When you do a replacement income exercise, you will be astonished at how much capital is needed as a lump sum to replace your income over ten or twenty years. We saw this for Brenda Johnson; her husband, Howard, was in his fifties and could not afford the premiums on life assurance to provide £80,000 as a lump sum if he died before drawing his pension. To provide an income of £4,000 meant putting a lump sum on deposit to pay out £4,000 from interest alone, leaving the capital intact. At 5 per cent interest a year after tax, £4,000 as income needs a lump sum of £80,000.

Step 3
Calculate how much life cover you need

However, this is just an estimate or a guide, as in some periods the interest paid might exceed 5 per cent, while during other periods it may be lower. When the interest paid is lower, the temptation to withdraw an amount higher than the interest must be resisted. If you cash in your capital you lose all its future income-earning ability.

To discover how much life assurance you need, you should rework the budgets we drew up in Stage 2, but instead of using a prospective forecast retirement date, the second budget has to estimate what amount of income each year will be needed to cover the loss of the parent who has died for as many years as there are children under age eighteen to be provided for. The start date for this exercise is always the present. If you have two children under age ten and want to provide for them to go to university, you may need to consider an annual income of around £8,000 each year for at least fifteen years, plus an additional amount for inflation. As a minimum, you need to think about life assurance for around £160,000, and £200,000 if you want to provide an income for a surviving spouse facing the financial burdens of bringing up your children alone.

'A bad decision is when you know what to do and you don't do it.'

Duncan Goodhew, Olympic gold medalist for Britain in 1980

If you cannot afford the high cost of the amount of life cover you think you need, be ready to compromise.

In the case of Nigel Hamilton, with two teenage daughters and an unborn baby to provide for, if he had taken out term assurance to age sixty, when the baby would be twenty, he would have needed at least £150,000 life cover. This amount kept on deposit at 5 per cent a year, would provide an annual income of £7,500, around £2,500 to each child. As this is only £48 per week, it is almost irrelevant how much income Nigel was earning during his life. It would be increasingly difficult to care for any of his three children for less than this each week, unless the state benefit of income support was available.

As his teenage daughters reached eighteen, the whole £7,500 could have been transferred for the benefit of the child of his second partnership, but as two different mothers were involved, this might have proved contentious. We will look at this incident again in Stage 6, as Nigel Hamilton did not leave a will, so his affairs would be even more difficult to unravel. If the £7,500 continued to be paid to all three children, it could contribute towards university finance or even a wedding for one of his daughters.

LIFE ASSURANCE FOR THE BLAKES

When people think about protecting vulnerable dependents they automatically think of children; they rarely consider their non-working spouses. However, elderly widows or widowers relying on a partner's pension, can face financial difficulties because they will have problems finding part-time work to compensate. Unless proper arrangements are in place the pension dies with the pensioner it belonged to.

As we saw in Stage 2, Freda Blake would lose the benefit of the whole of George's regular income if he died before reaching sixty. Suppose he died in 1999, she would receive his full pension fund, valued then at £33,700, plus the term life cover of £5,000.

In addition, there was £4,500 in bank deposits.

The total funds amount to £43,200 but the outstanding mortgage debt is still £20,000.

If Freda repaid the mortgage outright, she would be left with a lump sum of £23,200 (£43,200 − £20,000 = £23,200).

As her annual income is only £6,500, she needs to rework her annual budget to see how she would manage. She will have her income, plus her Abbey National dividends and about £1,160 in interest she will earn by putting her lump sum of £23,200 on deposit at about 5 per cent a year. When these calculations are worked through, George and Freda may discover that if George dies, Freda cannot afford to stay in their family home; and we haven't even considered how her finances would cope if she wanted to stop work at sixty in 2009.

Life Cover for Freda Blake

Item	Amount £
Pension fund	33,700
Life cover	5,000
Total	**38,700**
Deduct outstanding mortgage	20,000
Balance of funds	18,700
Cash on deposit	4,500
Total capital	**23,200**

The Insurance Shortfall

In Britain, although we have a highly sophisticated and competitive industry to cater for our various life assurance needs, millions of families are inadequately insured to protect vulnerable dependents from financial hardship if a bread winner dies prematurely. This is not just a social tragedy, it stems from ignorance about the vital role insurance plays in personal finance. I did not properly appreciate the reassuring protection life cover provides as my father had a low opinion of insurance policies. My attitude was transformed when I joined a national brokerage company in 1980 and realised that I and my young family would have to leave our family home if my husband died. The cost to Nigel Hamilton of providing £150,000 for his family through insurance is a fraction of the cost he would face if he chose to borrow the sum from a bank, assuming that a bank would lend it to him. If you look upon your insurance plan as a back-up in the event of disaster, the case for arranging it becomes overwhelming.

Affordable Health Insurance

Many over-sixties who had never thought about private health insurance to cover medical costs, were encouraged to do so when the government offered tax relief on premiums for them. Unfortunately, that sensible concession was rapidly withdrawn in 1997. However, to avoid excessive queues and possible delays for medical treatment it can still make sense to investigate private health insurance costs.

As a compromise the premiums are more affordable for a policy covering only hospital costs, the most expensive part of any treatment. You can then plan for major operations at a time that suits you, rather than join an indefinite queue and suffer pain and uncertainty while you wait. Applying for cover only for stays in hospital is cheaper than taking out comprehensive private health insurance.

The policy covers consultants fees, theatre and medicine costs, your stay in hospital and some ancillary services, such as physiotherapy. There may be time constraints on allowable payments for claims made on surgical or medical conditions that you already have when your policy begins, but these will finally be covered after a period free of treatment. This trouble-free period differs for each policy, but as so many major companies now offer medical health insurance, investigating a plan to suit you could prove worthwhile.

Make a Will

Step 4
Make a valid will

The statistics on longevity for the twentieth century are astonishing, but one of the most incredible statistics for personal finance is the fact that the majority of adults, (around 70 per cent) do not make a will. It seems amazing that so many people ignore this vital and relatively simple service they should perform for the close family they loved so much in life.

The problems for a family are infinitely more complicated when no will has been made. Although this important topic is certainly part of preparing for life, whether long or short, I have linked it to inheritance tax planning in Stage 6, because it belongs naturally there. However, it is one aspect of retirement planning that should be firmly dealt with either at this Stage or when you reach Stage 6.

Outliving Your Resources

Step 5
Facts about the long-term care lottery

As the number of pensioners grows, the problems of outliving one's financial assets will become more serious for millions of people; firstly, for those who could not or did not make adequate preparations during their working lives, but secondly, for every tax-payer who must now pick up the financial burdens of caring for growing numbers who cannot support themselves. The problems for long-term care (LTC) can only increase, since it it estimated that the number of people over seventy-five will rise from around 4 million in 1998 to about 7 million by 2031 when there will be around 700,000 people over ninety. In the late 1990s, people aged sixty owned around 4 million homes, while an estimated 6 million elderly people were being looked after in their own homes, with an equal number of unpaid carers. Over three hundred people every day need LTC for the first time. The Royal Commission on LTC,

'People are stranded in inappropriate conditions — at home or in hospital — because authorities are not providing help when assets meet the statutory £16,000 mark.'

Gail Elkington, Help the Aged

139

is now due to report in 1999, with no certainty on how fast or how many of its recommendations will be implemented.

The Lottery of Long-Term Care

At present, care for the elderly is a faceless, 'uncaring' lottery run by local authority bureaucrats. It was covered in one of the Channel 4 television programmes, *Mrs Cohen's Money*, and I was shocked by the facts I learned about it then. Relying on the state is now a demoralising experience for thousands of elderly people who thought the welfare state would care properly for them. Many pensioners eligible for financial help are forced to pay their own costs because councils are not paying their share of care-home fees. Increasing numbers are depleting their savings or staying for months in hospital beds because local councils avoid their legal obligations to meet long-term care costs.

The Department of Health has guidelines for local councils to provide help with long-term care when an eligible person's capital falls below £16,000 and his income is not enough to meet the weekly costs of care. These can amount to anywhere between £200 to £400. When assets fall below £10,000 people are legally eligible for full assistance. A sliding scale of benefits operates for asset levels between £16,000 and £10,000. Although a national system should apply, councils adopt different criteria in deciding on eligibility; and may take a variety of different assets into account, depending on where in the country you live. In some areas, the council might pursue you ruthlessly to discover when (and to whom) you disposed of your family home, assuming you did this to avoid paying your care costs. In other areas, they may disregard this element of your financial situation entirely.

By law, councils should include all a person's assets when arriving at the £16,000 to £10,000 capital levels: savings in bank and building society accounts plus investments in bonds and company shares, income from pensions and the value of your property, if owned outright. Around an estimated 40,000 homes are sold each year to fund nursing home costs. Under the present system a rough justice means test is applied for which the people involved were totally unprepared.

The system seems completely arbitrary on asset calculations; the only link between different localities appears to be whether or not the local authority is adequately funded to meet its total commitment to the numbers requiring care in the area. If your home is worth more than £16,000, you may be required to sell it to fund your own care, unless you have dependent relatives over the age of sixty living in the house. An elderly child, brother or sister, in addition to a spouse, would qualify, but family members less close than this or partners outside of marriage may not be eligible for protection again depending where you live.

Many people, incensed by the lottery aspects of LTC provision, have sought ways to avoid the loss of assets to fund their care. If you decide to transfer some or all of your assets so you can qualify for full assistance under the social services means test, the scrutiny you undergo will vary by nothing more elaborate than your postal address. Some councils investigate gifts made within six months of entering care, while others check back over the past year, or longer. You might be taken to court to enable the council to claw back the assets you gave away. This harrowing experience faced Colin Roach when his wife Christine went into care.

> *'The problem at the moment is that people do not know their rights, which lets councils get away with too much. With a bit of knowledge behind them we find people have a better chance of getting a fair deal.'*
>
> Evelyn McEwen, Age Concern

THE NIGHTMARE SCENARIO

Colin and Christine Roach were in their late seventies when Christine's health deteriorated so far Colin could no longer look after her adequately at home. The council assessed Christine and she moved into a nursing home but they could not force the sale of the family home to pay for the care because it was jointly owned and Colin was still resident there. The couple owned a joint with-profits insurance bond for £30,000, and Colin thought the same protection would apply. It had run for ten years, and they drew a yearly income of £1,500, 5 per cent, from it. The bond was equity-based and its capital value had grown in addition to the income they had withdrawn; it was worth around £40,000.

After some delay, the council investigated the Roachs' asset position and learned about the bond. They issued an invoice to Colin to pay £8,000 in back fees for the care Christine had received. During the time it took the council to establish this claim, Christine's condition had deteriorated further. She was no longer able to sign a form for the insurance company to release part of the bond funds to meet the council's demand. As the policy was written in joint names, Colin needed an enduring power of attorney to enable him to withdraw money from the bond. Unfortunately, he had not organised this legal document while Christine could still sign her name. The council refused to accept this as a valid reason for non-payment of back fees. They threatened Colin with legal action as his debt to them on Christine's behalf continued growing. He had to seek a legal remedy to enable him to alter the signatories to the bond. It took six months for the judicial process to grind its way to this conclusion, so Colin could withdraw the necessary funds. He now had to encash over £14,000 to meet the outstanding nursing home costs.

As the bond was jointly owned, the council could only demand half its

141

capital value plus half the income it provided, but as the stock market continued to rise, the amount the council could claim would also rise. Moreover, it is currently disputable whether Colin could demand a refund if the value of the bond were to fall on a major stock market set-back. He might have to take the council to court, which in financial terms, would negate the purpose of that whole exercise, since litigation against a huge institution like his local authority would be impossibly expensive.

'We are becoming increasingly concerned about the quality of our future lives as we are about the lives of those who follow us, including the members of the Royal Commission.'

David Hobman, Director of Age Concern

Assessments For Care

In addition to the wide national variation in applying the guidelines, there is confusion among the public on the procedures involved in obtaining care provision. In deciding on your right to help, your local authority holds all the cards: it will undertake two separate assessments. Your right to appeal against the judgements made will rarely succeed, as it will be made to other council officials who share the same financial constraints as those who initially refused your case.

1. The first assessment is made on medical grounds, namely: are you entitled to professional care by the state and how this should be provided.

2. The second assessment is the means test that the social services apply to your asset situation: are you within the legal limits eligible for state funding?

If you are judged a suitable medical case for care, the council decides whether you should receive support in your own home or in a residential or nursing home. Various home services can be provided, depending on your level of need, including meals, home help with cleaning and shopping and even nursing help through your general practitioner.

If your case is judged too difficult or unsuitable for support in your home, a move to a nursing home may still not be forthcoming, as many councils do not have adequate funding to provide places, even for those considered eligible. This invariably results in a system of queuing and waiting lists of elderly patients with no idea when they will be transferred from hospital beds to residential or nursing beds.

In August 1998, The Community Care (Residential Accommodation) Act came into force. This exactly sets out the legal terms of what local authorities must do in long-term care cases. The guidelines also clarify when a council is allowed to include your home as part of your assets.

The Cost of Care

If you have assets worth over £16,000 you will not be eligible for any state help. In 1998, the costs for private care averaged at around £16,000 to £18,000 per year for nursing care. The sum of £17,836 was the 1998 average quoted but care costs are labour-intensive and invariably rise faster than inflation. The average stay in a home is around eighteen months to two years. The state pension contributes to care, amounting to around £7,500 over that period, so on 1998 fees, care costs could swallow up around £20,000 of your capital, depending on the fees charged in the home you enter. However, many residents stay in homes for much longer; four years spent in a residential home could deplete your capital by about £52,000, ignoring inflation, and after including your state pension resources. This is a vast drain on capital. According to the British Nursing Association, four hours of private daily nursing support at home can cost about £14,600 a year.

Step 6
The cost of long-term care

'If people don't take out some form of plan, even the most astute investors could see a lifetime of savings whittled away within a few years on private nursing care.'

Liz Bigmore, Windward Investments

In 1998 there were around 500,000 people in long-term care, but figures suggest that on current estimates, 20 per cent of today's elderly will need care. Before rushing out to buy expensive protection, therefore, it might be worth considering other ways to protect your assets, since on these statistics, only one in five people will need professional care. However, this figure rises to one in every three over the age of eighty-five, when people have become more frail and increasingly dependent on others.

There are methods of financing a possible requirement for long-term care:
1. Investigate buying immediate care or impaired life annuities.
2. Home income plans might cover the costs.
3. Perhaps renting out your home to retain your ownership of it.
4. Insurance policies, covered below.
We discussed home income plans in Stage 2 on page 48, while different types of annuities were covered in Stage 3 on page 86–7.

Policies to Protect Your Assets

Several UK and foreign companies offer pre-funded policies. You can use monthly, yearly or one-off payments until you make a claim. On average, insurance premiums cost around £1,000, depending on the company, your age and the level of benefits you want to secure. The level of benefits can range from £2,500 a month to £30,000 a year. However, insurance policies covering LTC

143

Step 7

Ways to pay for long-term care

are relatively new in Britain; they do not yet have a proven history of paying out valid claims. By 1998, about 20,000 people aged between sixty-five and seventy-five have taken out (LTC) insurance and savings plans. Most of the plans on offer are complicated, expensive and may be open-ended to allow for subsequent premium revisions. Currently, insufficient data has been collected to show whether premiums will get dearer. The policies that include review clauses allow the levels of payments made under the policy to be altered after you have been paying for a period of several years, often five or more. It is impossible to know whether premiums will rise, as this depends essentially on how long it takes the companies to obtain a larger data bank of claims figures. When these become available, companies will be able to more accurately assess the insurable risks they are exposed to. With a longer sequence of claim histories, the premiums should become more firmly based and reflect the on-going risks.

Seek Help Before You Buy

Another major defect currently is that although several UK companies offer policies, this market has no strict regulation so there is inadequate protection and compensation for policyholders when disputes arise between them and the providers. The long litany of mis-selling scandals by the insurance industry suggest prospective purchasers remain cautious.

With so many possible snags, seek out specialist advice before you buy. One company, IFACare, (details in Stage 7 on page 196) comprises a group of independent advisers offering expertise on both the financial and legal aspects of LTC. It provides names of specialists in your area.

If you decide to buy a policy, investigate the field thoroughly with the help of an independent adviser as there are several variations to methods of paying and levels of cover available. IFACare suggests those considering insurance should choose a flexible policy which includes care counselling. This is doubly important for elderly people who no longer have close relatives alive or whose children live considerable distances away. A care counsellor will visit the home and assess the level of needs at first hand. In general, as with most insurance products, the younger you start paying, the cheaper the premiums.

Key Points to Remember

STAGE 5: PREPARE FOR LIFE – LONG OR SHORT

1. Protect your dependents, children and the vulnerable elderly.

2. It is better to have some life assurance than none at all, if you cannot afford the full amount you need.

3. Opt for compromise alternatives if you are a high insurance risk due to age, illness, occupation or social habits.

4. Rework your retirement forecast budget to calculate how much life cover your dependents will need following a premature death.

5. Learn about your legal rights to LTC.

6. Explore the various alternatives to paying for LTC provision.

7. Seek professional help before you buy a LTC insurance policy.

'Start paying into a plan while still in good health and while you can still afford it.'

Penny O'Nions, IFA

STAGE 6 PASS DOWN YOUR NEST EGGS

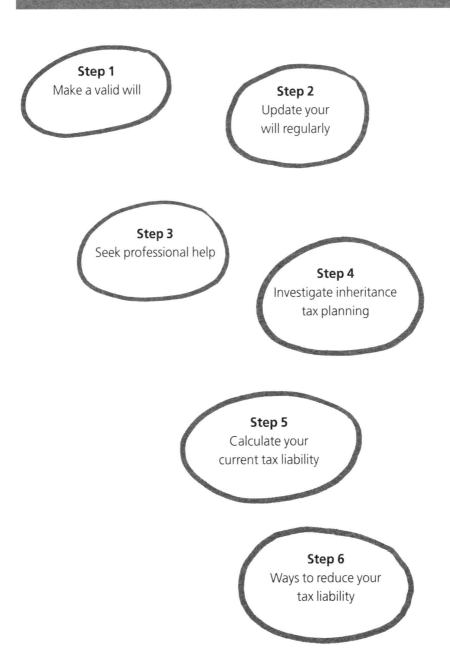

Step 1
Make a valid will

Step 2
Update your
will regularly

Step 3
Seek professional help

Step 4
Investigate inheritance
tax planning

Step 5
Calculate your
current tax liability

Step 6
Ways to reduce your
tax liability

MOVE TO STAGE 7

STAGE 6

Pass Down Your Nest Eggs

'Bill [Gates] and I both have a similar philosophy on giving back to our communities. I know in my case that 99-plus per cent of my wealth [currently about $36 billion] will go back to society, because we have been treated extraordinarily well by society.'

Warren Buffett

We saw in Stage 5, how crucial it can be to have life assurance to protect dependents in the event of an untimely death. And if the deceased person failed to make a will, which applies to about two-thirds of adults in Britain, the problems for the surviving spouse can be far more complicated and invariably, more distressing. We have glimpsed the tip of the unhappiness caused by this oversight in many of the lives of people mentioned in earlier stages. Although I have given these people fictitious names, their stories are true.

Step 1
Make a valid will

Make Your Will

Why do so few people bother to make a will? Although society has become far more open and liberally-minded about some seamier aspects of life, death is one subject that still carries a social taboo. And if contemplating the deaths of those we love makes us feel morbid, then for most people the thought of confronting their own mortality seems even more difficult to handle. Making a will invokes gloomy thoughts, so it is easy to put off the day when you do it. Time passes, the urgency fades and the will never gets made or changed to reflect altered circumstances.

Although you can buy a standard proprietary will form from large newsagents where you simply follow the instructions to produce a do-it-yourself version, if you have not made your will as yet, it might be better to employ a solicitor. The fees are not prohibitive, unless your affairs are complicated or your circumstances have changed, perhaps by impending marriage or divorce. In such situations, the reasons for using a solicitor are even more valid. When you use the services of a professional, you have the peace of mind that comes with knowing your financial affairs are in order with virtually no possibility that your will is invalid. This eventuality can arise from errors if you inadvertently fail to make your will according to the strictly laid down rules. It might also occur if you accidentally use ambiguous wording or ask a **beneficiary** (a person who inherits under a will) or the spouse of a beneficiary to witness your will; making your gift void. Failing to revoke your previous will can also cause later difficulties. Fortunately, the court has wide powers of discretion to decide on what proportion of the estate, if any, is to be paid out in the event of a valid claim being at risk by invalidation of your will. Your estate consists of all your assets, property, valuables and household effects at the time of your death.

Young people often imagine they have plenty of time to make their will, but accidents do happen and even young parents should take this responsibility seriously, to protect their children. Another reason why people fail to make a will is because they mistakenly believe their immediate next of kin, usually a wife or husband will inherit all their assets when they die. Unfortunately, as we shall shortly see, this is a serious misconception. If you do not make a will, you have died **intestate** and the **laws of intestacy** will be rigidly applied to your estate.

If there is one thing worse than having no money, it is having too much

Most people would be shocked to know the consequences of dying intestate and the problems it can cause for loved ones.

Who Will Benefit?

In Britain, over 60 per cent of people own a house, even if there is some outstanding debt on it. A jointly owned asset, like the family home, normally passes to the survivor, so it is not an asset which comes under the terms of a will until the second death occurs. It is famously known that Shakespeare's bed featured as one of the **bequests**, or gifts, he made in his will. These days, most homes contain expensive goods; televisions, computers, fitted carpets, furniture for lounge, kitchen and bedroom, not to mention one or two family cars.

Many British homes are so well endowed with these items, we treat them as everyday possessions. Moreover, millions of people now own bank and building society accounts or shares, plus insurance policies, Tessas and Peps. In legal terms the total value of your possessions, including your assets and all household effects, even money in the bank, comprise your estate. But you may be pleasantly surprised to learn the true worth of your estate, if you add up all the values of your treasured possessions. Perhaps you have already done this as a paper exercise for your net worth, as suggested in Stage 2. Once you have tackled this simple exercise, it surely makes sense to at least think about who is going to receive these goods following your death.

You Choose or Let the Law Decide?

If you do not make a will, you have forfeited your last free choice. All the decisions regarding your assets will have been taken from you. A stranger, working to a rigid legal formula, will decide who will inherit the valuable goods you leave. The people who inherit your effects may be the very ones you wanted to exclude, if you had made your wishes known. You 'make' rather than write a will, because it gives you the right to personally direct exactly who will benefit from your assets and who will not. Properly made, a will is a legally binding document to carry out all your last wishes after your death. Literally, your will is your last word on the subject of who gets your valuables.

It is not only in murder thrillers that people go to extreme lengths to ensure their final wishes are observed, often excluding certain people from benefiting at all. This also happens in actual families. A surprising number of bitter disputes arise from **legacies**, that is, gifts bequeathed or omitted in a will, even when relatively small sums of money are involved.

If you die without leaving a will, the laws of intestacy apply. A government official will take control of directing what happens to all your assets, including your personal possessions. The Probate office has two duties to perform:
1. It appoints a personal representative, an **administrator**, to administer these effects in accordance with strict rules of priority.
2. These effects will then be distributed according to strict guidelines on who among your relatives will benefit and how much they get. Personal friends, unmarried partners, colleagues and favourite charities are all excluded.

For appointing an administrator, in order of priority, a surviving spouse or the children of the deceased may be appointed to act. If they are unwilling, administering the estate can fall to other close relatives; parents, brothers or sisters, nephews and nieces. Occasionally, a close friend may be appointed attorney to the person entitled to act, or even to serve as administrator.

'I made it on my own and as a commoner. I am not going to leave behind a mess.'

Suliman Olayan, 78 year old Saudi financier

The administrator's duty, where necessary, is to see that the assets are sold at the best possible price and that all debts and expenses are paid off, including burial costs. Once completed, distrib-ution occurs in accordance with the Administration of Estates Act and the order of priority among your kin for the distribution plus stipulated amounts of money that can be passed to beneficiaries up to a statutory level.

The order of inheritance for relatives of an intestate person are as follows:

1. Spouse.
2. Children or other issue (grandchildren).
3. Parents.
4. Brothers and sisters of the 'whole blood' or, if deceased, their issue (off-spring). Such issue will divide their deceased parent's share between them.
5. Brothers and sisters of the 'half blood' (having one common parent with the deceased) or, if deceased, their issue.
6. Grandparents
7. Uncles and aunts of the 'whole blood' or, if deceased, their issue.
8. Uncles and aunts of the 'half blood' or, if deceased, their issue.
9. If there are none of the above then the estate goes to the Crown: in fact, the Inland Revenue.

There is a time limit for tracing relatives of the deceased but following an extensive search, if no close living relatives are found, your assets go to the Crown. Intestacy rules are made in broad terms and cannot take account of personal wishes, so it is possible that close relatives will benefit, even though you may have preferred friends to receive a legacy. There is no place in the intestacy rules for a cohabiting partner, close friend or a relative by marriage to be included.

NIGEL HAMILTON DIED INTESTATE

Although I never learned from my taxi driver if Nigel Hamilton left a valuable estate when he died unexpectedly on holiday in Mexico, we can look at his complicated family situation to see who, if anyone, will benefit from his estate if he died intestate.

Sonya, the partner carrying his unborn child is not entitled to any part of his estate, although in due course her baby could benefit. As he was only separated from his wife, with no legal divorce, his estranged wife would receive the full legacy to which she was entitled under the intestacy laws. This may not have been what Nigel intended, had he known how the intestacy law operates. Even if his divorce was underway but not final, his wife is still the first beneficiary. His two legitimate daughters would also benefit, but with a modest estate, his mother might not have been able to recoup the costs of returning the body to Britain, as this expense might need the consent of the administrator, possibly Nigel's estranged wife. The point is surely made, and we need not pursue the complications that arise in such uncharted situations.

Update Your Will

Once your will is made, keep it in a safe place, where it can easily be found in a sudden emergency. Ensure that your **executors** (persons appointed in the will to deal with the estate) know where it is lodged. Leave a copy with your solicitor or at your bank. Update it regularly as your financial circumstances change or as it becomes necessary to change **guardians**, appointed to look after minors under the age of eighteen, executors, or **trustees**, nominated to deal with a **trust**, either mentioned in your will or set up as a separate legal document. A trust is a portion of an estate, or the whole estate, to be administered by trustees for the benefit of the named person in accordance with the trust document. Over a normal adult lifespan, three or four changes in these various representatives might be necessary.

If you have young children you might want to appoint your parents or a close friend as guardians, but check with them to ensure they are willing to act. Always ask the people you want to act as trustees or executors whether they are willing to take on the task. As your children grow up, you can appoint them as executors in conjunction with a surviving spouse. By using a solicitor who keeps a copy of your will, your children will have a professional contact to rely on in case problems arise after the second death. This is particularly important if couples travel together on long air flights.

Step 2
Update your will regularly

'When people get too old to set a bad example, they start to give really good advice.'
Melissa David

Always make sure your will is updated before going abroad or on any trip where accidents might happen, and also prior to undergoing any surgery which requires a general anaesthetic. At such times, make sure your finances are completely up-to-date. This sounds like a chore, but in fact, if you are thinking positively about your money, it is a tremendous help for doing regular reviews of your personal finance; one of the most important routines retired people should constantly do. Finally, write a letter outlining the various details relating to your will, so that bequeathing your estate is simplified as far as possible for executors, trustees, relatives and beneficiaries. You will probably be thoroughly acquainted with all the special details of your finances, but imagine how an executor will feel if this information is in a mess. We saw in Stage 2, how tough it was for Mary Clarke, who had to spend months sifting through the muddle of her husband's papers after he died.

The letter should set out all the useful names, addresses and telephone numbers that your executors might need: bank, solicitor, business partners, your boss, if he owes you salary payments, your agent (if he collects fees for you), an auctioneer, if you have a collection of books, stamps, collectables or antiques which your beneficiaries might want advice on before selling. If you have made funeral arrangements, as some people do in advance, ensure all the documents are with this letter or that it states precisely where these documents are. Make sure at least one member of your close family knows where this letter lives, especially before you go away, leave the country, or go into hospital.

Keep important keys with this letter. You may have policy documents or valuables in a bank safety deposit box, or a safe at home. Keys for these or any other locked up places should be easily available to your executors.

A change in personal circumstances can often change the validity of your will. This applies especially to divorce or if you marry after making your will. A divorced spouse is not entitled to any part of your estate; divorce renders all gifts to an ex-spouse void. It is therefore important to act, or the application of the law may affect other persons in your will. Your will is revoked if you marry after making it, unless the will states that it is being made 'in contemplation' of that forthcoming marriage and it is to remain in force after the marriage.

Using Professionals

Solicitors are experts at drawing up wills and creating trust funds. They will also act as executors of an estate. Banks provide an advisory service on preparing wills and dealing with **probate**, the process of proving your will. However, where professionals are engaged, the fees will not be cheap. If you elect a bank or solicitor to act as an executor for you, payment provision for probate should be included in your will. Professional fees used to be based on the value of an estate, but are now more often based on the time taken in handling your affairs, onto which expenses and VAT are added. A solicitor is the ideal person to prepare a power of attorney document if you are going abroad and want your spouse or a parent to be able to deal with any important financial matters arising while you are away. An enduring power of attorney can be invaluable for an elderly couple where many assets are jointly held. We saw in Stage 5 the problems Colin Roach faced when dealing with his wife's nursing home bills, once she could no longer sign her name.

Step 3
Seek professional help

Another good reason for consulting a solicitor is that you may not know the up-to-date situation on legal aspects regarding inherited wealth. Major changes to finance legislation on this issue may be brought in which have a significant bearing on the plans you want to make. The solicitor is well versed in the exact state of every aspect of the law at the time you make your will.

If your affairs are complicated or involved or you have a large estate to leave, it is sensible to seek professional advice, to prevent subsequent difficulties. You might borrow a book on wills from your local library to read up on the topic before you go to the solicitor. If you have some idea of what you want to achieve, it could save on his expensive professional time. It makes sense to write out your current net worth, described in Stage 2, so he has a full picture of your present financial situation. Your net worth list reveals the current value of all your assets, but your estate also includes all your personal and household effects.

Throughout *Financial Freedom* we have looked at ways for you to gain control over your financial situation. This is important in order for you to become your own fund manager in charge of making your money work for you in retirement. However, this does not mean you lose control by taking advice from specialists; you are simply acknowledging that for certain aspects of financial security you need expert help. Rather than seeing this as relinquishing your responsibilities, it is yet another form of insurance: protection against things not working out as you planned. You are simply using an expert who helps to ensure you avoid the likely pitfalls ahead. This attitude towards professional help applies just as much to financial advisers when deciding which products you should acquire as it does to solicitors for preparing your will and helping you reorganise your estate, if necessary, to avoid paying too much **inheritance tax**. This is the tax you or your beneficiaries, will have to pay if you have built up a valuable estate during your working life but have omitted to make adjustments to reduce or eliminate the tax liability.

'Well, I am glad you are such friends with the duke [of Queensbury]. I hope you can continue so to his life's end, for, depend on it. Whoever is most in favour then will have the Largest Legacy.'

Mrs Susanna Bolton (sister to Horatio Nelson) to Lady Emma Hamilton

Learn About Inheritance Tax

If there were no laws on inheritance tax, we could simply pass on any wealth we accumulate during life to those we wish to benefit from it. And that would literally, be that. This is the situation that currently applies between husband and wife provided the recipient lives permanently in the United Kingdom. The transfer of assets between spouses upon death is exempt from inheritance tax.

Step 4
Investigate inheritance tax planning

For all other transfers, however, the government has imposed laws to tax wealth. Without this wealth tax on death, making a will would be more straightforward. Since there are ways to avoid overpayment of tax or even reduce it to zero, the whole subject has mushroomed to cater for the complicated rules the government imposes to levy this tax.

Inheritance tax and the planning that goes with it are pretty dry topics for most people and certainly not exciting bedtime reading. If you want to become your own inheritance tax expert, you will need to grapple with the minute details. But here we will look at the broad principles of how it operates in England (the law in Scotland is slightly different). We will look at the main topics only for two reasons.

1. Everyone preparing for retirement should view inheritance tax planning as a special area within that planning. In 1998, inheritance tax was set at a level of 40 per cent on an estate worth in excess of £223,000, but the rates and levels could be changed by Parliament. Most people with more valuable estates should consult books on this issue or seek specialist advice from a solicitor.

2. Many financial advisers suspect that new legislation will be brought in within the next few years to totally revise this area of taxation or tighten up the existing rules. The objective would surely be to raise more revenue because the government wants to reform the welfare state without increasing income taxes. Increasing inheritance taxes could be a sleight-of-hand solution.

It is a sad thing if a rich man has no heir to his property

Therefore if you think you might face an inheritance tax problem, address it soon, before new legislation takes effect.

The Government – An Unexpected Beneficiary

Inheritance tax is the current name for estate duty, first levied in the 1880s. It is a tax on property passing to your heirs when you die and applies whenever you make **capital transfers**, that is, pass on assets, to someone other than your spouse. However, it is only payable over the statutory limit or **nil-rate band**. The flat rate at 40 per cent is much higher than the average top rate of 28 per cent in Europe. With the tax so high and wealth more widely spread, it makes sense to explore ways to legally pay the lowest tax bill, or avoid it altogether. Ignore this issue and a major beneficiary of your estate could be the Inland Revenue. This clearly will not worry some people as a wide range of attitudes exists to leaving money for dependents.

JUST ONE PENNY IN THE BANK

Although I have met many people who have a cavalier attitude to passing on their wealth, one of the most decisive characters I met was a self-employed plumber who ran his own business. He told me proudly he had six children and ten grandchildren and his wife was active in the local community doing voluntary work with handicapped children. He said, with some passion, that he wanted to die with just one penny in the bank, even though he was fifteen years older than his wife, so she could outlive him. Moreover, despite his pride in his large family he had no care in his head to leave them any money or mementos at all. Of course, everyone can plan their finances as their whims dictate, but I personally have never thought like this.

Pass On Your Wealth

Wealth in Britain has risen astonishingly over the last thirty years. Today, it is not just a few privileged aristocrats who have expensive assets to leave to their families and friends. When you add together all your possessions you may find you have far exceeded the legal limit above which your beneficiaries must pay tax. Many taxpayers seem unruffled by the prospect of paying tax at the highest rate – 40 per cent – on wealth they leave at death, even if they accumulated it by working. Many would be surprised to know how hard this tax bites on those left behind if no evasive action is taken. This tax now applies to quite modest estates, since, as we have seen, wealth in Britain is spreading through a much wider percentage of the population.

> *'In case of anything happening to me . . . I have given you £500 sterling a year out of the [Bronte] estate, but I hope we shall live many years. The moment I get home, I shall put it out of your power to spend dear Horatia's [Nelson's natural daughter] money; I shall settle it in trustees hands and leave nothing to chance.'*
>
> Horatio Nelson to Lady Emma Hamilton, August 1804

INHERITANCE TAX FOR THE BLAKES

Inheritance tax is payable on estates where assets exceed the nil-rate band, currently £223,000 for the financial year beginning 6 April 1998. The nil-rate band rises in most years, to take account of inflation, but that cannot be taken for granted. In the 1980s, when my husband and I first started making wills, mainly to appoint guardians to care for our children, the nil-rate band was around a lowly £125,000. If it had kept pace with inflation, we would now be allowed to protect well over £500,000 of assets within the nil-rate band. As the level of tax is set at 40 per cent, people who were basic rate tax payers throughout their working lives, like George and Freda Blake, may face tax bills levied at 40 per cent if they do not make special arrangements to reduce the inheritance tax due when they pass on their wealth to their son, Henry and daughter Alice. The problem will be increased if they build their capital to fund retirement.

Step 5
Calculate your current tax liability

We can do some exercises on paper to see how inheritance tax would affect the Blakes. As there are no taxes payable on transfers of assets between spouses upon death, we need only consider the situation which arises after the second death, when the whole jointly owned estate inherited by the last spouse will pass to the children. However, as an illustration, we can look at how their assets would be treated if George died first in 1999. We saw in Stage 2 that the Blakes had a combined net worth in 1999 estimated at around £182,550. This calculation was made to help them plan for their income and capital needs in retirement. It adds together the value of all their assets and deducts all their debts or loans. The same net worth exercise with some modifications, can be used to estimate their inheritance tax liability. For probate, all possessions must be listed and valued prior to selling or distributing them.

List all valuables for probate
For the inheritance tax exercise, the Blakes must add to their net worth lists all their combined personal household effects, including valuable personal items that we ignored for retirement planning. Apart from their house contents, including furniture, paintings and books, Freda might have an engagement ring worth £500 and a pearl necklace inherited from her mother, worth £300. George might have a computer worth £750 plus a hi-fi system valued at £400. In reality, their personal effects would probably be far more numerous and therefore more valuable. One way to calculate these is by referring to your latest home contents insurance policy. There, you list valuables which exceed a certain sum, so the insurance company knows how many such valuables you possess.

However, although the Blakes own some of their assets jointly, including their house and the bank account, for estimating inheritance tax due, their estates are not equal. George alone owns the car and the bank loan on it. He also owns his pension fund valued at around £33,700 in 1999, while Freda owns 100 Abbey National shares. George is the policyholder of the life assurance policy. He is the legal owner and pays the premiums, but the **sum assured** of £5,000 was arranged for Freda's benefit in case George dies before his seventieth birthday.

For retirement planning, the Blakes focused only on their main financial assets, but everything valuable must be included for probate. The executors must file certain documents in order to establish their right to deal with the property of the deceased, called 'obtaining grant of probate'. The probate valuation of the estate becomes the basis for the inheritance tax due. Financial problems can arise because no distribution of the estate is allowed until probate is granted, but the tax falls due before that. If insufficient cash is available, executors can borrow on evidence that the estate can repay the loan, but this incurs interest charges.

For both estates, the totals figure is well below the nil-rate band of £223,000 allowable per individual. As neither estate would attract inheritance tax, they need take no action. However, to see how inheritance tax

George's Assets in 1999 (Assumes house is worth £160,000)

Assets	Value in 1999 £
House (jointly owned)	80,000 (½ £160,000)
Mortgage (jointly owed)	-10,000 (½ £20,000)
House value in 1999	**70,000**
Car	5,000
Car loan	-5,400
Pension fund	33,700
Life assurance	5,000
Bank account (jointly owned)	2,250 (½ £4,500)
Credit card debt	-625
Personal effects	1,150
Totals	**£111,075**

works, let us suppose they own a house worth £275,000 with the mortgage fully repaid, that George's pension fund was worth £80,000, his life cover was for £50,000, and he owned a second-hand Rolls Royce car worth £15,000 with no debt. Although transfers of assets between spouses upon death are exempt from inheritance tax, the situation on the second death will look very different. We can rework the sums to see first what assets Freda will inherit.

George's Assets in 1999 (Assumes house is worth £275,000)

Assets	Value in 1999 £
House (jointly owned)	137,500 (½ £275,000)
Car	15,000
Car loan	Nil
Pension fund	80,000
Life assurance	50,000
Bank account (jointly owned)	2,250 (½ £4,500)
Credit card debt	-625
Personal effects	1,150
Totals	**£285,275**

Assets After the Second Death

If George's estate is valued at £285,275 and all his assets pass to Freda, there will still be no tax to pay. However, her estate is now quite substantial. It includes the whole value of the house at £275,000 and £130,000 for George's pension fund on death plus £50,000 in life cover. She would still have her Abbey National shares, worth £1,000 and her own jewellery but she now also owns all the money in the bank account plus George's Rolls Royce worth £15,000, his computer and his hi-fi system. There is no car loan, but if we assume the credit card debt of £1,250 is still outstanding, we can calculate the value of her entire estate. The total would now amount to £426,200.

If Freda died within six months of George's death in 1999, we can look at their childrens' inheritance after her death. After deducting the nil-rate band, the inheritance tax due on her estate will be 40 per cent of £203,200, that is, £81,280. If Freda had given Alice £213,100 three months before she died and left £213,100 to Henry in her will, her intention to treat each child equally would have been thwarted because of the way in which inheritance tax is charged. Henry would be liable for no tax at all, because the nil-rate band of £223,000 applies, but Alice would have to pay £85,240 which is 40 per cent on her lifetime gift. Alice would only receive £127,860, while Henry would receive £213,100. This would not be what Freda had intended.

'Passing along a lot of money can be bad for the people who receive it.'

Bill Gates, founder of Microsoft and the world's richest man

Freda's Assets in 1999

Assets	Value in 1999 £
House	275,000
Car	15,000
Car loan	Nil
Pension fund	80,000
Life assurance	50,000
Bank account	4,500
Credit card debt	-1,250
Abbey National shares	1,000
George's personal effects	1,150
Freda's personal effects	800
Totals	**£426,200**

Before she died, Freda could have chosen to set aside the lump sum of £130,000 from George's pension fund and life policy, writing it in trust for the children so it would pass directly to them on her death. This one act alone would have taken £130,000 out of her estate leaving a total of £296,200. But if, in addition, she had made a gift of the current nil-rate band of £223,000 to her children in her will, tax would only be due on £73,200 (£296,200 − £223,000 = £73,200). At 40 per cent the children would incur a tax liability of £29,280. This is a big reduction on the initial tax bill of £81,280 that would fall due if neither of these actions were taken.

The Value of Trusts

Until he retires and buys his annuity, the value of George's pension fund is the return of the fund on death. To ensure it does not add to the value of his estate it should be written in trust for his children. If this is done, the pension fund will lie outside George's estate. The same situation would apply if George writes his life assurance policy in trust for Freda. Both items would no longer count as part of his estate. Many hundreds of thousands of pensions and life policies are taken out every year. They are valuable assets which can play a role in protecting vulnerable family members. Yet if they are not written in trust, they remain in the estate of the policyholder and may add to the tax bill due on his death. This would have been even more relevant if George had outlived Freda because their estates are uneven with more assets belonging to George. Taking valuable assets out of the estate reduces the amount of tax that may fall due.

Step 6
Ways to reduce your tax liability

Many people think trusts are obscure legal documents, designed to help millionaires organise their assets, but certain trusts are extremely useful even if your estate is modest. Trusts allow you to arrange your affairs exactly as you want. In this respect, trusts are similar to wills. A trust is a legal document or documents, that allow you to dispose of your property in accordance with your strictly defined wishes. Clearly, if George dies before age sixty, his pension fund and life cover will only be of benefit to Freda or his children. But there are several situations where you do not want to lose control over a possession during your lifetime, even though you want a beneficiary to obtain that property when you die. Trusts can be effective in giving an asset away while retaining control at the same time. However, there is specific legislation to prevent you giving possessions away but retaining the benefit. For example, listing yourself among a group of possible beneficiaries, so you can alter the beneficiary at a later date. An arrangement like this might not qualify for inheritance tax exemption.

> *'Her quarterly allowance from England – £8,000 – was totally inadequate to meet the extra expenses in which she had involved herself: she was naturally generous, and had little or no idea of managing her money.'*
>
> Caroline: A biography of Caroline of Brunswick, Thea Holme
>
> (Caroline was Princess of Wales 1795–1821)

There are some disadvantages to setting up a trust. It can be rigid and inflexible when circumstances change, it can be expensive to set up or administer, especially in the hands of professional advisers; solicitors, bankers or accountants, and there are different kinds of trust, to cover various options, so it is vital to establish the appropriate trust initially. If you want to set up a valid trust where trustees will hold property or an asset for the benefit of clearly identified beneficiaries, it is advisable to consult a solicitor.

Equalisation Of Estates

Returning to the Blakes' possible inheritance tax liability, if George alone was the owner of their house, valued at £275,000 with no mortgage, this asset on its own would exceed the nil-rate band. Even taking £130,000 for his pension fund and life policy out of his estate would leave his children facing a large tax bill if Freda died first and he had not made full use of his nil-rate band. As a general principle it is sensible to share out assets so both partners have an estate of roughly equal size, since you do not know which partner will die first. By equalising the estates, both partners can make better use of the nil-rate band gift. To utilise this fully, George should transfer half the house into Freda's name. This process is called **equalisation of assets** and is a frequently adopted routine to avoid paying excessive amounts of inheritance tax when one partner in a marriage owns more of the family wealth than the other. This process can be effected for business interests, company shares or large holdings of bank or building society deposits. No tax liability arises by transferring assets between partners within a marriage, even upon the death of one spouse, but after the second death, the combined estate could be valuable, and therefore avoiding actions are useful to mitigate the tax liability.

House ownership can give rise to inheritance tax problems for many people, as so much of British wealth is tied up in houses. People try to split the ownership to utilise the nil-rate band on the first death. Joint ownership exists where two people legally own a property jointly. When one dies, full ownership normally accrues to the survivor. We have assumed George and Freda are joint owners for their house and bank account.

If the property is held as tenancy in common, each person separately can dispose of their interest in the property. If your house is held as tenancy in common, ownership does not automatically pass to the survivor when one of the joint owners dies. Couples often think that holding the family home as tenants in common will avoid some inheritance tax, if each partner gifts their share of the home to the children in order to utilise the nil-rate band. On the first death, however, if half the house has been gifted to the children, the house might have to be sold to pay them out. I call this the 'King Lear effect' because when he gifted his kingdom to his daughters, they threw him out. If you use a tenancy in common agreement for your property, you might be evicted from your home if the children want to realise their share of the property when your spouse dies.

One way around this is to use a 'deed of family variation'. This is a legal agreement entered into after a person has died under which the beneficiaries of the will rewrite its provisions. If you want to alter the tenants in common arrangement after a death, but have children like King Lear's daughters, this could end with serious recriminations. There is a possibility that deeds of family arrangement will be eliminated by government legislation. Attempts to do this have been made, but so far, it has survived.

Lifetime Gifts

Some cash gifts made during a person's lifetime are exempt from inheritance tax. Everyone is allowed an annual exemption of £3,000 against capital gifts, making £6,000 for a married couple. If this is not used in any year, you can carry it forward for the next twelve months only. Other exemptions exist, including gifts on marriage, small outright gifts to any one person or expenditure which can be considered 'out of income'. Charitable gifts or those to the public's benefit or national interest are equally exempt. If you make lifetime gifts of this nature, keep lists of the date and the amounts gifted with your documents, so that the details will be easily available to your executors. All other lifetime gifts are subject to inheritance tax only if the person making the gift dies within a seven-year period from the time of making the gift. The tax reduces on a sliding scale depending on how many years have elapsed before the donor's death. The time scale is shown below. This is another concession that experts think may soon be eliminated.

Potentially Exempt Transfers Subject to Inheritance Tax

Years before death	Percentage of death rate (%)
0–3	100
3–4	80
4–5	60
5–6	40
6–7	20

In this Stage, we have looked at several ways to conserve wealth and ensure it passes to the people we want to benefit. However, little of this may happen unless we have made the right moves to provide for financial freedom in retirement. Now it is time to move on to Stage 7, and turn all the ideas we have covered during the previous six Stages into actions.

Key Points to Remember
STAGE 6: PASS DOWN YOUR NEST EGGS

1. If you have heirs or a favourite charity, be sure to make a will.
2. If you do not make a will, the laws of intestacy will apply to your estate.
3. Use a solicitor for making your will, setting up trusts, helping you reduce an inheritance tax liability.
4. Keep your will in a safe place and update it regularly.
5. Make use of lifetime gifts to reduce your inheritance tax liability.
6. Use trusts to take valuable assets out of your estate.
7. Use the nil-rate band to gift property to your heirs.

'We (my brothers and I) grew up in what we thought was a poor home, but we grew up in a very rich home, because what our parents did for us was give us values. And that's the legacy – not money.'

Morton Mandel, chief executive, Premier Farnell

STAGE 7

Tackle the Detail

'When friends ask me if I missed dentistry when I retired,
I always answer, "Yes – for one minute." '

A friend from my college days of 1955 to 1960

Having now read Stages 1 to 6 of *Financial Freedom*, you have a lot of the background detail you need to prepare your own financial pyramid using your tailor-made investment plan. The layout of Stage 7 will help you convert this information into a manageable programme of action. It provides a step-by-step guide on how to put your plans into action, taking you once again through all the previous stages covered throughout the book.

'The devil is in the detail' is a popular saying among financial professionals. Perhaps it is the thought of all those mind-blowing details in money matters that puts most people off: they lack the enthusiasm even to get started. I hope however, that now you have progressed through the first six stages, you feel more optimistic that managing the detail will not pose insoluble problems. You have seen how constructive it can be to explore all the possible options for increasing either your income or capital or both, as you head towards retirement. Success in this endeavour might mean the difference between a comfortable, prosperous future and a miserable, penny-pinching old age.

However, personal finance is a minefield through which you should tread with care. New products emerge and old products evolve with every change in government policy. These never-ending changes shift the focus, first in one direction and then in another. Although we are only laying out the framework here, *Financial Freedom* should give you greater confidence in your ability to acquire more skill and experience. Then you will be equipped to take these constant changes in your stride.

At the time this book was written, the outcomes for Isas, stakeholder pensions and inheritance tax changes were still unclear. Annuity rates were plunging so that the paper exercises to calculate the Blakes' annuity were over optimistic. By the time the book is published, even if these issues are clarified, there are almost certain to be others that are undergoing a major review. The markets might suffer a sudden collapse or carry on soaring. But although the book faces an inevitable cut-off date, you should remain optimistic. Continue expanding your new-found knowledge, through reading. Newspapers and personal financial magazines, listed in the bibliography will help you. The reading should not be a chore, but some reading is essential. The alternative – stumbling blindly into retirement – may be a recipe for financial hardship.

'Not one of these people said they truly regretted anything they had actually done – what they regretted was what they hadn't done.'

Charles Faulkner, Neuro Linguistic Programming trainer, on his conversations with hundreds of elderly patients

Keep your notes together. I use a manual personal organiser system as I find it a simpler method than using computer spreadsheets. Keep all your records in one place and above all, treat your reading positively; it is the passport to insider knowledge that will keep you on the road to achieving your primary goal of financial freedom throughout retirement.

We begin with a brief overview of the key principles involved, which we discussed in Stage 1, followed by working through some of the detailed routines for each of the stages.

STAGE 1: STEP INTO RETIREMENT

Statistically, on reaching fifty, your chances of living another thirty years are better than they have ever been. Without careful preparation, the loss of your regular income alone is bound to make a big change in your financial fortunes, unless you have a truly superb pension package, or win the National Lottery! Without these bonanzas, you should take control of your finances to ensure your retirement years are happy and comfortable.

Be resolved to face the apathy, fear and ignorance that may have prevented you from handling your financial affairs successfully in the past. Start by stepping firmly into retirement with my list of useful tips to help you overcome the inertia so frequently linked to coping with money matters.

1. Avoid drifting into retirement, by focusing on your key objective: to become financially secure. You need a blueprint plan designed to take account of your own special circumstances; this master plan forms the seven stages of *Financial Freedom*. It maps the route ahead for you. Using it, you turn this problem into a solution by preparing your campaign using these seven stages, putting it into action and then monitoring your progress to keep yourself on track.

2. Turn the negatives into positives by stating your goals in positive terms, as money targets. They must be your personal goals and they should be specific; vague goals are rarely reached. For example, tell yourself, 'I have capital of

£8,000 now which I will double to £16,000 within 8 years.' This goal becomes a target, far more likely to be reached than if you say, 'I would like to have more money in the future.' If you set yourself realistic money targets within a reasonable time frame, you will gain the confidence to know you are capable of reaching or even beating them.

3. Break up your goals into manageable blocks. This is the underlying basis for the seven stages in your retirement planning. Work through each stage in turn before starting on the next.

4. Focus on each task one by one. Each stage consists of several steps and you should concentrate on every step in turn until you are ready to move on to the next stage. This approach will prevent you being overwhelmed by the elusiveness or sheer size of your long-term goal.

5. Involve yourself and your partner in achieving your goals. Making money is a skill, like any other, and can be learned. Try to depend more on yourself. By all means use experts or professional advisers to sort out the difficult areas where their advice will be invaluable, but make your own decisions. Don't be deterred by thinking you might be wrong. No one gets every major decision right. The actions of thousands of professionals in mis-selling scandals illustrates that. Instead, keep an open mind, so you can reverse a decision that turns out badly without feeling you have failed. Knowing a course of action is wrong but persisting can lead to greater problems later. This is especially true in financial matters.

6. Judge your success by your own progress. It is more constructive to gauge your success by comparisons with your past record rather than with the progress of the market or of other people you know in similar situations. Setbacks are a normal part of life. Treat them positively by thinking through how you can overcome them, rather than negatively comparing your mistakes with friends who seem to have avoided them. Pace your progress so you are regularly moving forward to achieve your pre-set targets. Avoid the temptation to take short cuts which may prove expensive: use *Financial Freedom* as a get-rich-slowly plan of action.

7. Try to stay focused and motivated at all times. If you do this, you can achieve the targets you have set. Devise your plan, start putting it into action and monitor it regularly to ensure you reach the good result you have planned.

'Think like a man of action, act like a man of thought.'
Henri Bergson

Financial Freedom Through a Master Plan

If your only long-term plan is to achieve financial security, what does that mean to you? You will know when you have found financial security for yourself when you stop worrying about your future cash problems and whether or not you have enough money to do the things you want to do. The capital you personally need to become financially secure becomes one of your financial targets: calculate it as shown in Stage 2 below.

To achieve financial security you need your own unique master plan central to which is your financial pyramid, a necessary financial planning tool for every stage of life but indispensable for retirement. As you approach retirement your pyramid needs a sharper focus.

Seven Stages Form Your Master Plan

The heart of the master plan is your financial pyramid, which rests on three main foundations:

1. Your home. This is a valuable asset if you own it. If necessary it can be a source of cash.

2. Your pension will be a reliable replacement income.

3. Your free capital will supplement that pension. To help you build this capital according to your pre-set targets, you devise your own unique *investment plan*. It contains your investment family.

You should aim to achieve an evenly balanced financial pyramid to cover unforeseen eventualities; it is the basis of financial freedom in retirement.

Become Your Own Adviser

Faced with a dismal catalogue of scandals, how should prospective investors proceed? The prolific available choice of financial products requires some guidance.

Here Are Some Useful Rules:

1. If you seek financial advice from a professional, be sure you make your own decisions.

2. Only *buy* the financial product you think you need: do now allow an expert to *sell* you the product he is selling.

3. Use a major UK company with a household name, especially for companies with a tied agency salesforce, (selling only its products exclusively). In a mis-selling scandal, pressure exerted on famous names should ensure a swift resolution. This might not apply to foreign companies. If your company faced bankruptcy, a major UK company would probably be taken over by a similar company. (This happened to the victims of the Barings collapse, in 1991. But note: Barings continued to operate within the Dutch bank, ING, but UK holders of its **bearer bonds** were not compensated for their loss!)

How to Choose an IFA (Independent Financial Adviser)

All IFAs are covered by the Personal Investment Authority (PIA) and regulated by the Financial Services Authority (FSA).

To find an IFA in your area contact IFAP Ltd, 17–19 Emery Road, Brislington, Bristol BS4 5PF. Tel: 0117 971 1177.

They will send an information pack with a voucher for a free consultation with no obligation, plus the names of three IFAs local to you.

If a relative or friend can confidently recommend an adviser, this can be the best route. Ask your friend the following questions about their adviser before deciding to use their recommendation. If you go to an adviser you do not know, ask the following questions before allowing them to arrange your financial affairs.

1. Will he give you references from satisfied clients to vouch for his/her quality and reliability?

2. Has his/her company a speciality, say on pension planning, or does it cover all insurance and investment products?

3. Does the company offer a fee-paying service or commission-based advice?

4. If you opt for fees, what is the scale of charges?

5. How will paying by fee compare with paying by commission on the product you want? Fees have to be paid in advance and incur VAT.

6. If you opt for commission, will he share it with you, especially if you have done your own research and know exactly what you want to buy (termed '**execution-only**' for share purchases.)

Some IFAs now use this term for selling insurance products. If you know exactly what you want, they will spend less time on selling you your policy and will be more willing to share the commission, perhaps returning up to 50 per cent to you.

Notes

1. Check the IFA has complied with the disclosure rules. These ensure that all charges are fully explained to consumers during the sales process.

2. If the adviser agrees to rebate almost all his commission, say 90 per cent, if you know exactly what you want, traditional companies will be more competitive than the new (direct) providers, but you must reinvest all the commission rebate to achieve this cost benefit. Discuss how to do this with your IFA.

3. Some products generate substantial commission levels, so a fee-paying basis will be more effective. Among the high-commission products are single premium bonds, with-profits bonds, traditional long-term policies set up to run for twenty or more years, including pensions, endowments and whole of life assurance.

4. You cannot save money by buying direct from the insurance companies. Even if they will deal with you instead of your adviser as intermediary, the commission will not be deducted and returned to you. This also applies to unit trust commission.

Dealing With Complaints

1. Always file every piece of promotional and factual documentation relating

to each investment product you buy. Store it in a safe place, preferably with the policy in case queries or disagreements arise later.

2. If you are not satisfied, write to your adviser or their company before taking your complaint to the regulatory body he or she is covered by.

STAGE 2: PUT YOUR HOUSE IN ORDER

' "OK," says my wife, "you've been retired for three months now. What are you going to do for the next twenty years?" '

Tom Rayfield, *Financial Times* (1 April, 1998)

However many years in the future your retirement lies, the planning process will be roughly the same. Before making any binding decisions, examine the full picture of your current financial position and how retirement (or perhaps, the next ten years of your retirement) might change it.

Put Your Financial House in Order

Prepare Your Forecast Financial Needs
Begin by preparing a complete financial overview for two dates: today and your expected retirement date.

Five Steps to Prepare Your Forecast Financial Needs
i) now
ii) at retirement

---

i) Now

Compile today's budget	i. Collect all bills, salary and bank statements for a full year
	ii. List (a) all income items and (b) all expenses
	iii. Total (a) all income items and (b) all expenses
	iv. Deduct total expenses from total income to find the balance
	Positive balance = you are living within your income.
	Action: try to save more money.
	Negative balance = your spending is too high.
	Action: budget to restore a positive balance.

| Compile today's net worth | i. Total all your valuables and assets
ii. Total all your debts and loans
iii. Deduct the total debts from the total assets

Negative balance = negative net worth.
Positive balance = positive net worth. |

CURRENT BUDGET + NET WORTH = WEALTH CHECK

ii) At retirement

Compile your estimated retirement date budget	i. Estimate retirement income ii. Estimate expenses plus a percentage increase iii. Deduct items which cease at retirement iv. Total income and expenses v. Deduct total expenses from total income **Positive balance** = you can live on your retirement income. **Negative balance** = there is an income shortfall.
Compile estimated net worth for retirement date	i. Total up your valuables and assets plus a percentage increase ii. Total up all your estimated debts and loans at retirement iii. Deduct the total debts from the total assets **Positive balance** = negative net worth. **Negative balance** = positive net worth.
Compile a gains and losses list for two dates: now and at retirement.	List the evident gains plus the obvious losses in your financial situation

RETIREMENT BUDGET + NET WORTH = RETIREMENT WEALTH CHECK

Financial mistakes are invariably costly

Set Your Retirement Targets for Income and Capital

1. Compare the two schedules, for today and your forecast retirement date.
2. Prepare your gains and losses list:
    i) Do you have too much wealth tied up in your home?
    ii) Will you still have an outstanding mortgage debt on your retirement date?
    iii) Will you still have outstanding loans at your retirement date?
    iv) Will your forecast pension be large enough to cover your expected expenses in retirement?
    v) Is there an estimated income shortfall?
    vi) By your forecast retirement date will you have accumulated a large enough capital fund to provide some flexibility for future needs?

vii) Is there a capital shortfall?

viii) Will your forecast capital cover any shortfalls arising from the termination of life assurance policies at retirement?

Budget For i) Today
ii) Retirement

Items	Today			Retirement		
	Monthly *Husband*	Monthly *Wife*	Annual	Monthly *Husband*	Monthly *Wife*	Annual
Income						
Interest						
Dividends						
Bonuses						
TOTALS						
Expenses						
Mortgage						
Food						
Household						
Car/transport						
Holidays						
Entertainment						
Clothes						
House						
Insurance						
Extras						
Tax/NI						
Savings						
Pension						
TOTALS						

Do You Need More Cash?

Ideas to improve your income or save money:

1. Budget to find some cash to save.
2. Rearrange existing assets.
   i) move some cash from a large deposit in a bank or building society into equity-based investments
   ii) move some cash into an account paying a higher rate of interest
   iii) move to a smaller house

iv) take on a part-time job, for pleasure; this will broaden your social contacts plus provide extra cash to save

3. If you decide to move, try to reduce costs where possible.

i) ask the builders on a new development site about sales details. Buying early can save money as developers are happy to secure a few advance sales

ii) buy your house at auction, but don't get carried away with the bidding

iii) buy a run-down property and organise the improvements yourself, either by hiring builders or by using relatives to undertake the work for you

iv) rearrange your existing mortgage, either through your current lender, or switch to another lender, or investigate the new current account mortgages introduced that allow you to pay off your mortgage at your own pace

v) pay off your mortgage early

vi) sell your home directly without the use of estate agents

4. Switch to a cheaper credit card to save high interest rate bills.

5. Shop around for a new car. Prices vary widely, especially outside major towns. Car prices in Europe are much lower than in Britain, but they may be left hand drive.

6. Shop around for insurance renewals, especially on car, travel and home cover to get the cheapest deals. High competition is driving prices down, so ask around for quotes or use a professional broker. His fee is paid by the insurance company, so it does not cost you extra to use the broker.

Retirement Targets

Assets	Estimated value at retirement date £	Shortfall £	Target for retirement date £
Annual income			
Net worth			
Capital fund			

Should You Rearrange Your Assets?

1. Is there too much wealth tied up in your home? See Stage 2 and item below.

2. Will you have an income shortfall on retirement? See Stage 3 and item below.

3. Is there a capital shortfall? See Stage 4 and item on pages 186–94.

4. Do you need more life assurance? See Stage 5.

Put Your Real House in Order

1. Take on another mortgage?

2. Buy a second or holiday home as a transition phase?

3. Pay off your mortgage early?

4. Take out a home income plan?

5. Move to a smaller house?

6. Move to sheltered accommodation?

'You build up years of debt, which acts as a depressant on the economy until it gets worked off over a long period of time. A debt liquidation tends to last for years.'

Stanley Druckenmiller, active manager of the Quantum Fund

Take on Another Mortgage?

Taking out a mortgage at retirement could make sense if you are expecting to receive a pension large enough to support a UK mortgage during retirement. Intense competition among lenders means credit-worthy sixty-year-olds can now obtain a twenty-year mortgage.

Advantages in following this route:

1. Tax relief at 10 per cent applies up to £30,000 on first mortgages on your main residence.

2. A mortgage still outstanding on death can reduce an inheritance tax liability.

3. If inflation continues in Britain, the value of your home will rise while the real cost of the debt falls. (See Stage 4 on pages 93–6).

Buy a Second or Holiday Home?

Purchasing a second home, as a transition phase, is an option used by many people nearing retirement. There are advantages, but problems with a second foreign home are possible:

Advantages

1. Allows you to adjust to the smaller property over a period of years, before the major move is ultimately made.

2. Benefit from high levels of sterling against foreign currencies, e.g. the Euro, which makes buying property in Europe cheaper.

3. Lower levels of interest rates apply in Europe for countries tied to the D-Mark (Holland, France, Belgium, Italy and Germany). A difference of around 3 per cent lower than UK interest rates makes buying a European property on a mortgage cheaper than buying in Britain. However, until the issue of Britain joining the single currency is resolved, the levels of British versus European interest rates could remain volatile.

172   4. British banks will lend against overseas properties, but mortgage offers vary

widely. Terms range between seven and twenty years and cover both fixed-rate and variable-rate loans. Your credit worthiness will be assessed by the UK lender as for a British house purchase, but many lenders take prospective rental income into account when judging your ability to maintain repayments. European banks may be willing to lend, but in France, for example, they rarely lend more than 60 per cent of the property's value.

5. Currency factors can work in your favour. If the pound is low when you decide to sell, you will make a larger profit: you will get *more* pounds back in exchange for the foreign currency.

Disadvantages

1. Uncertainties exist due to the advent of the single European currency in January 1999. Britain was not part of the first wave of entrants, but Europe has had lower inflation levels over prolonged periods since the 1950s. This could affect future house prices in Europe.

2. Expensive on upkeep and decoration.

3. Emergency repairs might be needed in your absence.

4. There are currency and interest rate risks attached to buying a foreign property with a foreign currency mortgage.

    i) Exchange rate risks arise if sterling values alter against the Euro if Britain stays out of the single currency for longer than currently expected. For example, if sterling *falls*, your mortgage payments will *rise* (you will get *fewer* lira, francs or D-Marks to the pound).

    ii) Interest rate risks arise because rates in Britain have traditionally been higher than in Europe: if interest rates *rise* in Europe, so will your mortgage repayments.

5. You will need cash of around 10 per cent of the purchase price of your property, to cover expenses, including estate agents' fees, legal and surveyor's fees and removal costs.

6. You must put down a deposit on a property purchased overseas.

7. There may be alterations or redecorations to pay for in addition to the costs of upkeep and repairs.

8. There will be further costs for the agent looking after the property during your absence and collecting rent from tenants on your behalf if the second home is let out while you are not using it.

9. Tax will be payable on rental income you earn.

10. There may be capital gains tax to pay on profits if you decide to sell the overseas property and remain in your British home.

11. On recent trends, profits on foreign cottages or small properties may not be as large as might be expected for British properties.

12. Properties in unstable political regimes may be confiscated or damaged during local war situations.

Ways to Pay for a Second Home (abroad)

1. Pay cash.

2. Take out a mortgage on your existing British property, if it is unencumbered.

3. If you are still repaying the mortgage on your UK home and there is adequate equity in your home to support paying for the second home, take a **second mortgage** on that to enable you to buy the overseas property outright for cash.

4. Take out a UK loan secured on the property abroad. This can be effected through a number of British banks many of whom offer lower variable rates on French, Spanish and Italian properties than on British homes.

> *'I firmly believe that for every good thing in life, there's a price you have to pay.'*
>
> Monroe Trout

Pay off Your Mortgage Early

The debate about paying the whole balance of the mortgage off early presents an immediate problem for many people at retirement. Like many planning details, take your special circumstances into account as there are advantages and disadvantages.

Advantages

1. Save interest – it can amount to thousands of pounds.

2. Eliminate debt – years earlier than you had planned.

3. Increase income – no further monthly interest or capital repayments due.

Disadvantages

1. Mortgage interest rates are cheap – the cheapest on the high street.

2. For inheritance tax planning – keep the debt to reduce tax due on death.

3. Inflation reduces the real value of your debt. You lose this bonus by paying the mortgage off early. An inflation rate of 3 per cent a year reduces the real value of your debt by half within twenty-five years, the normal span of a mortgage.

> *'Japanese consumers have in the last decade, seen home values fall by two-thirds and share values fall by 60 per cent. In Japan, cash is king.'*
>
> Allen Meltzer, economics professor at Carnegie Mellon University

Take Out a Home Income Plan

After the 1980s scandal on home income plans that unlock cash tied up in the value of your home, improved versions have been devised.

Available Types of Home Income Plan:

1. Reversionary schemes involve selling off part or all of your property to the company providing the cash. In return, you receive a lease for your life, or that

of your surviving spouse. The amount of equity you sell to the company varies, from about 20 per cent up to the full current value.

2. Annuity-based schemes involve selling all, or a percentage, of the home equity in return for a joint life annuity, usually fixed at the outset, although it may be escalating, if you are willing to take a smaller initial income. A small 'peppercorn rent' may be deducted from the income.

3. Shared Appreciation Mortgages (SAMs). You sell all or part of your property to the company. On the death of the last survivor a percentage (usually around 25 per cent) of the capital appreciation in your property from the date you took out the plan, is returned to your estate, the remainder (often 75 per cent) goes to the company. Your family will enjoy part of the rise in the value of your property while you enjoy the benefits of a rising income.

Advantages

1. They provide extra income for people who do not want to sell their homes.
2. Use a Safe Home Income Plan, (Ship) provided by four specialist groups. Its members are Stalwart Assurance, Allchurches Life, Home & Capital Trust and Carlyle Life. Ship members offer two important guarantees:

 i) Complete security of tenure with the right to live in the property for life. If circumstances change, you can find an alternative property.

 ii) A guaranteed cash sum or regular income payment, with the assurance that the money will not be invested into high-risk areas. You can receive the money as a lump sum, so you can make your own investments, or as a regular income, payable for life for you and a surviving partner.

 iii) Your own solicitor must certify that the principal terms of the contract have been fully explained to you before your scheme is finalised.

3. Home income plans are flexible. If you sell 60 per cent of the equity in your home for a regular income linked to property prices or a fixed annuity-based income, you might increase your income again later by selling another 20 or 30 per cent of the value to the same company.

4. The tax treatment of home income plans was favourable in 1998. Mortgage interest relief at source, known as Miras, was available on the first £30,000, higher than for other taxpayers on Miras. The £30,000 is doubled for joint partners if both are over seventy-five and the Miras rate is 23 per cent rather than the 10 per cent available for mortgages for house purchase from April 6 1998. Pensioners who receive income support or council tax benefits may find these are reduced or lost with a home income plan.

Disadvantages

1. You will pass on less of your assets to your family on death.
2. Some schemes are complicated and legally binding. Examine the options with the help of an adviser, before making a firm decision.

'Focus on those things you want least to happen and on what your response should be.'
William Eckhardt, trader

3. Unless covered in your contract, problems may arise on moving to another property.
4. If house prices rise and you have taken out a shared equity plan, you may not own sufficient equity or value in your home to move.

Move to a Smaller House

Although you may not want to leave your large, comfortable home, there are several advantages in moving to a smaller property as you begin your retirement.

Advantages of Downsizing Your Home

1. Move while you are sill relatively fit and mobile to avoid the trauma of moving when your health is less robust.
2. Release some of the cash tied up in your house, to increase your available income during retirement.
3. A smaller home needs less upkeep and saves on expenses, redecorating and housework.
4. You can move to an area or a street, with better facilities for retired people; near to shops, a medical centre, public transport, the library, the park.
5. You can move to a property on one floor, i.e. a bungalow or flat, to avoid the problems of stairs, which can create difficulties for elderly people.
6. You can choose a property in an area without hills, which can create difficulties for walking.

Move to Sheltered Accommodation

Companies in This Market

1. Most sheltered accommodation schemes are run by specialist management groups.
2. They may be subsidiaries of house building companies, which own the freehold to the site and sell the properties on a long lease.
3. Generally, the organisations are private and run commercially to make profits.
4. Some schemes are run on a voluntary basis or by charities with no profit motives.

Advantages

1. Some schemes allow an ownership swap of your freehold home for a warden-protected leasehold property, which if newly built, will include modern facilities tailored for pensioners' needs.
2. The presence of a resident warden or manager.

3. An alarm system to link the resident to a communications centre for emergencies.

4. Communal areas include a residents' lounge, a laundry room and a flat for the use of residents' visitors in many purpose-built blocks of flats.

Disadvantages

1. There are costs associated with providing the warden.

2. There are costs for insuring the premises, cleaning and maintenance, for the buildings themselves and for communal areas (lifts, corridors, lounge, gardens, forecourts, etc).

3. Providing reserves to cover major repairs or redecorations. Payments towards this sinking fund may be part of the regular service charge or may be a lump sum deducted from the sale of the flat after the resident has moved out.

4. Charges for services vary but can range from £20 to £25 per week. Residents pay council tax, water rates and for their individual use of gas, electricity and telephone bills. The ground rent payable can vary between £50 and £300 a year, depending on the locality and type of residence.

5. Repairs within your flat will be your responsibility.

6. With such a large range of variability in service costs, it is most advisable that prospective buyers should seek legal advice before entering into any agreement. This is an additional expense.

Check the Company Credentials

The law has been strengthened recently for the rights of sheltered housing residents, but you should check how experienced the management group is and how often representatives meet the residents. The National House Building Council (NHBC) operates a code of practice, which protects sheltered housing buyers' rights, for both new and second-hand purchases effected since April 1990. Age Concern urges prospective buyers to check out the management company thoroughly before entering into any agreement and to use only a builder who is registered with the NHBC. Then your residents' rights will be fully protected through a legally binding agreement between the builder or freeholder and the management company.

A second code, introduced in 1996 by the Association of Retirement Housing Managers (ARHM), regulates management companies, including those in the private sector and covers services and charges. While not binding, it has been approved by the Environment Secretary, which means a court will consider the code provisions in disputes with a management company.

Ways to Buy Sheltered Accommodation

1. Buy at full market value as with any property purchase.

2. On new developments, some builders will agree a direct swap of your own mortgage-free home with a newly built warden-controlled property.

177

Other options are more complicated so legal advice should be sought before proceeding.

3. Shared ownership where you can buy part (30, 50 or 75 per cent) and rent the remaining part of your new property. This route is popular with some councils and housing associations. Details are available from the Elderly Accommodation Council, Tel: 0181 742 1182.

4. Some builders offer an equity share scheme, but on re-sale it may give back a smaller share than your original purchase.

5. Loan stock schemes are another variant. Here, the purchaser takes out an interest-only loan or a returnable deposit, to be paid back on termination of the tenancy. However, residents' rights may be less clear-cut than for lease-holders.

6. Housing associations often run leasehold schemes, where the buyer takes only 70 per cent of the lease. The balance is funded by a housing corporation subsidy which remains in the possession of the housing association.

7. Several building societies will consider an interest-only mortgage with special deals for over-sixties. You will be responsible for monthly repayments of interest on the mortgage, but the capital owing will be repaid on death or on selling the property. This arrangement is useful if you have a sizeable estate with inheritance tax implications. Deferring repayment of capital reduces your ultimate tax liability.

8. Put the ownership in the name of your children. However, ownership disputes may arise later, especially if large outlays for long-term-care payments become necessary.

STAGE 3: BUILD AN INCOME TO RELY ON

A pension is undoubtedly the best way to create a replacement retirement income. It is a form of deferred pay.

As we have seen, everyone should aim to build a pension as a reliable replacement income. It is a secure source of income to cover your daily living expenses.

Check the Value of Your State Pension

The value of your state pension benefits are based on your own (and possibly your spouse's) record of national insurance contributions. To establish its value, ask your local Department of Social Security for a pension forecast including your Serps entitlement, using form BR19. Stakeholder pensions to replace Serps are not due to be introduced until approximately 2001. They are intended to be cheaper options for lower-paid workers.

Calculate What Size Pension You Need at Retirement

i) As detailed in Stage 2, on pages 29–31, use the estimated income and expenses figures you have calculated for your forecast retirement date from your two budgets, for today and at your retirement to see if there will be an income shortfall. Your estimated expenses at retirement indicate your target pension size.

ii) Use a figure of at least two-thirds your estimated final salary to set a target for your future pension requirement.

iii) If neither of these methods gives an adequate result, work on a calculated best guess until you can use one of the two methods listed above to get what you believe will be a workable result.

Deal With the Shortfall

If your calculations suggest a possible shortfall, prepare a table as in Stage 3, page 67 to reveal its size.

Estimated Pension Shortfall

Salary at retirement £	Two-thirds final salary £	Pension shortfall £
a)		
b)		

Closing the Shortfall

Fund size at retirement	Total premiums to add	Increase in annual premiums	Extra annual cash to find
a)			
b)			

> *'Poverty is something like a bonsai tree. You get only this little base to grow from. You are a stunted little thing. Maybe you could be a giant thing, but you never find out – that's poverty.'*
>
> Muhammad Yunus, chief executive of Grameen Bank

Information on Your Private Pension Arrangements – How Good is Your Pension Scheme?

Final Salary Scheme
Seek out answers to the following questions from the trustees of the final salary scheme you are in.

i) What is the retirement age for your scheme? It is usually sixty-five for men and sixty for women.

ii) Will your pension be worth two-thirds of your final salary after forty years? There are limits for certain high earners.

iii) Is your pension based on full earnings? Some schemes exclude bonuses and overtime. Some include the state pension.

iv) What size lump sum will you receive on retirement? This varies according to the scheme rules.

v) If you retire on grounds of ill health, will you receive a disability pension equivalent to the pension you would have obtained if you had continued to work until retirement?

vi) What level of death benefits for dependents are provided? Are they four times annual salary as a tax-free lump sum? If not, what level of death-in-service benefit is offered?

vii) Will there be a pension for a surviving spouse and children under eighteen?

viii) If yes, what percentage of your salary will this pension be?

ix) Will there be death benefits and a pension payable to a surviving partner who is not a legal spouse?

x) Will your pension in retirement rise in line with inflation?

xi) If not, will there be any level of annual increase, (escalation) in the pension paid?

xii) What arrangements are made to the existing pension fund for employees who move to another job?

xiii) What penalties, if any, will be imposed on transferring to another employer's scheme if you move jobs?

Money Purchase Scheme

Check all the above queries with the trustees of the money purchase scheme you are in, together with those listed below:

i) What is the size of the joint employer/employee contribution? Ideally, it should be around 10 per cent and increase with age.

ii) Which fund manager is running the scheme? Look for a fund manager who is well established in the pensions industry and who has a good long-term performance record.

iii) If you have never heard of the manager, ask the pensions trustees for further information, preferably in written form.

iv) Is there an independent performance measurement service?

v) Are administration and sales charges paid by the employer or deducted from individual members?

vi) Is life assurance and disability insurance an option?

vii) If yes, what are the benefits and are they paid for by the employer?

viii) Is there a penalty-free transfer to a new employer's scheme if you move jobs?

ix) Will there be financial penalties for taking early retirement?

Your Personal Pension Scheme

i) Who is the pension provider? Ideally, it should be a well-known, long-established pension or insurance company.

ii) What is the long-term pension performance of this company? Aim for a company which is consistently above average in industry surveys, preferably those done by independent research or in magazines such as *Money Management* or *Pensions Management* or as reported periodically in journal supplements, as in *Investors Chronicle*.

iii) What is the charging structure of your plan? It should be below the average, preferably paid on a fee rather than commission basis.

iv) If commission fees are charged on your plan, are they taken up-front (termed front-end loaded) or evenly from each contribution over the lifetime of the policy? The latter is a less expensive arrangement for the policyholder and is therefore more beneficial for building your fund.

v) Is there flexibility to reduce, stop and resume, or increase contributions without incurring penalties?

vi) Can you apply for life assurance alongside your pension to gain the tax advantages for your life cover premiums?

vii) Can you take the pension penalty-free for early retirement?

viii) Is there a return of the whole accumulated fund on death before retirement?

ix) If not, what would be the return on death?

x) Can you write your policy in trust?

> '*My starting point is that all human beings are entrepreneurs. Some get a chance to express it. Those who never had the chance probably believe they are not entrepreneurs.*'
> Muhammad Yunus

Calculate the Current Value of Your Privately-Funded Pension

i) If you belong to an occupational pension scheme, ask the employer for details of the present value of your final pension, and an estimate, if possible, for your final pension benefits.

ii) If you have a personal pension, ask the salesman who sold it to you for an up-to-date valuation on the size of the fund now and for your due retirement date, estimated on current premiums.

iii) If you have lost contact with the salesman, write to the company which is your pension provider, for the same information sent to you in writing.

iv) Ask an independent financial adviser the same questions to assess your future benefits.

Additional Voluntary Contributions (AVCs)

Within an occupational pension scheme, every member is allowed to make contributions of up to 15 per cent of their income. If you are in a final salary or group personal pension scheme, ask the employer for details of the company's AVCs and whether you are eligible to contribute. This will depend on the shortfall if any, in your contribution record to date. Making additional voluntary contributions to your employer's pension scheme is a cheaper option than using another pensions company, as higher charges will be paid to the salesman who signs you up to the additional contributions arrangement. Use your existing scheme if possible.

Personal Pension Solutions for Late Starters – Cheap Options

i) Direct providers answer all your queries over the telephone and then set up your plan. You must do some preliminary investigating for yourself and know in general what you want your pension to achieve for you.

> *'Credit should be accepted as a human right. It is the beginning of economic life.'*
> Muhammad Yunus

ii) Mutual companies have more competitive charges as they do not pay dividends to shareholders.

iii) Annual recurring single premium pensions. Each one-off premium counts as a single contribution and incurs very low charges.

iv) Investment trust pensions have lower charging structures.

v) Tracker funds have low charges, either through direct providers, traditional companies or investment trusts. Paying by monthly contributions may carry extra costs.

Information on 1980s Mis-selling Scandal

In January 1999 phase two of the pensions mis-selling review began. It covers non-priority cases sold between April 1988 and 30 June 1994. Investors who fall within the scope of phase two will be invited by companies to put their case forward for review by 30 March 1999. However, firms can't begin to deal with phase two cases until their priority review is complete.

For advice and information on the pensions review, contact either
i) the Personal Investment Authority (PIA) Helpline – Tel: 0171 417 7001
ii) the Financial Services Authority (FSA) – Tel: 0845 606 1234.

Should You be In or Out of Serps?

Serps is the state earnings-related pension scheme.
To decide on whether to contract out or not depends on:
i) Your age; older investors get bigger rebates but only up to a certain age.
ii) Your sex; as women tend to live longer than men, they give up more by contracting out.
iii) High earners benefit more by contracting out, as small rebates get eroded by the high charges providers make.

iv) If you doubt the ability of a pension provider to make good returns, do not contract out. The July 1997 budget made it harder for providers to outdo Serps, due to the abolition of the right of pension funds to reclaim advance corporation tax on dividends.

v) Most financial advisers now think it would not be worthwhile opting out of Serps if you earn less than £12,000 a year.

vi) Experts suggest men over fifty-two and woman over forty-five, should contract back in because the investment made with your contributions does not have long enough to build up into a sizeable fund.

For more information:

vii) You can find out if you are a member of Serps and how much your pension might be worth by contacting the Benefits Agency, part of the Department of Social Security.

viii) If you cannot sort out the details of contracting in or out on your own, seek help from an independent financial adviser.

ix) If you don't have an IFA, refer back to the Stage 1 section in this chapter, on page 166 for information on finding the names of three IFAs in your area.

Allowable Percentage Limits for Personal Pension Contributions

Ages	Percentage limits
35 and under	17.5
36 to 45	20
46 to 50	25
51 to 55	30
56 to 60	35
61 to 74	40

Ways to Protect Your Fund Ahead of Retirement
Useful rules to follow:

1. Actively monitor the progress of your pension policy.

2. Five years before retirement, begin switching equity funds into a deposit fund.

3. By two years prior to retirement all your cash should be in a deposit, or fixed interest fund to protect it from a stock market collapse.

Work Your Way Through the Annuity Maze
1. Did your with-profits pension plan begin before 1988?
Yes: Check with the company to see if it has a guaranteed annuity rate and if

so, do not commute 25 per cent as a tax-free lump sum as you may not improve on the guarantee being offered. Go to 2.

No: Go to 2.

2. Do you need all the income from your pension right away?

Yes: Use 75 per cent of your fund to buy a pensions annuity now. Take the 25 per cent tax-free cash only if you are willing to build it up into a fund of capital or pay off debts. Go to 3.

No: Defer taking your annuity or consider using phased or income drawdown schemes. Think carefully before embarking on income drawdown. It can be a risky gamble, so treat these options with caution. They are only suitable if you fulfil certain essential criteria:

i) if you are still in your early sixties

ii) if your fund is larger then £250,000

iii) if you have other sources of income to rely on. Go to 3.

3. Are you in good health or a non-smoker?

Yes: Buy a standard annuity. Go to 4.

No: Buy an *impaired life* or an *immediate care annuity* if you are planning to go straight into a home. Go to 4.

4. Do you want to protect part of your pension for your spouse?

Yes: Choose a *joint* life annuity. Go to 5.

No: Choose a *single* life annuity. Go to 5.

5. Do you want the maximum possible pension right away?

Yes: Avoid all the following options as they eat into the initial value of your pension. Go to 9.

No: Consider all the following options in turn. Go to 6.

6. Do you want your pension guaranteed for a specific period?

Yes: Choose the guaranteed option of five or ten years. Go to 7.

No: Buy an annuity without a guarantee. Go to 7.

7. Do you want your pension to rise in value over the years?

Yes: Go to 8.

No: Go to 9.

8. Do you want a fixed increase for your pension?

Yes: Choose either 3 per cent, 5 per cent or index-linked escalations. Go to 9.

No: Consider with-profits annuities where increases depend on the growth achieved by the investment funds. Go to 9.

9. Have you got a preference for how you want your pension to be paid?

Yes: Choose from monthly, quarterly, half-yearly or annually. Go to 10.

No: You have to make a choice, as the pension has to be paid at set intervals as specified at the outset. Go to 10.

10. Do you want to get the maximum amount of pension available on the market?

Yes: Use a specialist annuity bureau to find the best **open market option** for your age, sex and size of fund. You should also consider taking your pension monthly, quarterly, half-yearly or annually *in arrears* as this increases the amount paid out, although not by much.

No: Settle for immediate payments on the specified period of your choice using the company you built up your pension fund with. However, this alternative will almost certainly not give you the best result.

> *'Tracking the index does not avoid risks of a market fall but removes the risk of a fund manager getting it wrong.'*
>
> Gordon Maw, Virgin Direct

Special companies for arranging annuities:
Annuity Direct Tel: 0171 684 5000
The Annuity Bureau Tel: 0171 620 4090

Is Income Drawdown Right for You?

1. What is the size of your pension fund? For safety it should be at least £250,000.
2. What is your age? You need at least twenty years to compulsory purchase at seventy-five, to give your funds a chance to recoup at least some of the income withdrawn.
3. Never withdraw the maximum possible income, as this can be detrimental to the growth prospects of the remaining fund.

Problems With Pensions

1. **Inflexible** – solution: buy more than one personal pension plan.
2. **No real growth** – even index-linking only keeps pace with inflation.
3. **Not transferable** – you must live at least ten years to recoup the full fund you built up while working.
4. **They die when you die** – nothing left to pass on to heirs – solution:
    i) buy a joint life annuity
    ii) always take the 25 per cent tax-free lump sum offered as commutation, unless your plan includes a high guaranteed annuity rate.
    iii) take out a tax-free savings plan, an Isa, in addition to your pension scheme, to supplement your pension income and pass money on.
5. **Tax deducted at source** – no help with cash flow to year end.

6. **Very high charges possible** on most personal pension plans.
High charges = poor performance = poor returns.

> To avoid high charges, consider these options:
> i) recurring annual single premium plans
> ii) direct tracker pensions
> iii) investment trust pensions with much lower charges.

7. **Constantly changing conditions**
   - **Falling annuity rates**
   i) people live longer, therefore more demand for annuities
   ii) more pensioners with baby boomers retiring soon
   iii) falling interest rates = lower annuity rates (1987–1998).
   - **Government tinkering**
   i) changes in Serps
   ii) state pensions were linked to inflation instead of average earnings, from 1981
   iii) Gordon Brown's pensions 'raid' (1997). No outcry then, so watch out for another 'raid'.

With so many problems surrounding pensions you should aim to build up a capital sum to overcome some of the worst problems.

STAGE 4: CREATE A LUMP SUM FOR CAPITAL

For long-term investors, any correction is likely to be merely a blip in the long-running history of growth creation within the economy. What pensioners must judge is, 'How long is long term?'

Build Your Capital Fund

A capital fund provides flexibility for retirement planning and has several important uses:

1. To supplement your pension, especially if that pension is fixed and will not rise every year to take account of inflation.
2. To provide emergency cash to pay for big items or expected outlays.
3. To keep pace with inflation so you can maintain your standard of living throughout retirement.
4. To achieve flexibility for future needs.
5. To leave money to your family or favourite charities.
6. More flexible than your home or pension.

Build Your Financial Pyramid

1. Own your own home.
2. Build up a pensions fund.
3. Build a capital fund for flexibility: create your investment family. Include:
   i) cash funds, national savings and guaranteed bonds
   ii) life assurance to protect vulnerable family members, see Stage 5, on pages 195–6
   iii) insurance-based products, such as endowments, for safer returns, to pay for school or university fees
   iv) equity-based funds (collective funds), company shares

Schemes to Consider for Your Investment Plan

1. Emergency cash fund: low risk.
2. National Savings: low risk, but uncompetitive interest rates applied from autumn 1998.
3. Guaranteed bonds: low risk.
4. Isas: 5–10 years: low to medium risk (can hold a cash element).
5. Unit or investment trusts trackers (within or outside Isas): 5–10 years: medium risk.
6. With-profit insurance bonds: 5 to 20 years: equity-based, therefore medium risk.
7. Company shares: 3 years at least: high risk.

1. Suggested Investment Family for Nervous Investors

Investment	Percentage	Risk level
Deposit account in an Isa	20–30	Low
National Savings	20	Low
Income bonds		
i) Guaranteed income bonds	20–30	Low
ii) Guaranteed equity-based bonds	10–15	Low
Tracker in an Isa	10–15	Medium

2. Suggested Investment Family for Balanced Investors

Investment	Percentage	Risk level
Deposit account in an Isa	10–20	Low
National Savings	10	Low
Guaranteed bonds	10–20	Low
Trackers in an Isa	20–40	Medium

3. Suggested Investment Family for Risk-takers

Investment	Percentage	Risk level
Deposit account in an Isa	10–20	Low
Guaranteed income bonds	10–15	Low
Trackers in an Isa	15–25	Medium
Unit & investment trusts	15–25	Medium
Company shares	20–35	High

'Her plans for saving by steering a middle course, out of fear of some remote contingency, enabled her to amass a fortune of 14 million francs, on which everyone tried to draw, when bad times came later.'

Madame Mère, Napoleon's Mother, Gilbert Martineau

Products to Consider for Your Capital Fund

1. Build an emergency fund.

The rates of interest paid on bank and building society accounts change constantly.

   i) You need to stay alert as providers may not update customers when cash languishes in a relatively poor-paying account.

   ii) Do not put more than £18,000 into an account run by a small savings institution. 90 per cent of this is the maximum compensation you will get back if the institution goes out of business.

   iii) Supermarkets and other new entrants to the savings market often offer high interest rates.

There is a large range of comparable products of low-risk, even ultra-low-risk savings vehicles for income-seekers which are worth considering. Some products are better suited to non-taxpayers, while others will appeal to basic rate or higher rate taxpayers.

2. National Savings.

National Savings products are popular with retirees but interest rates were reduced in autumn 1998. Most National Savings products then became uncompetitive and alternative options might give better returns.

3. Guaranteed income bonds are low risk. They run for fixed terms, from one to five years and are offered by insurance companies. Although interest rates are guaranteed throughout the term of the bond, early encashment can lead to some loss of capital. The bonds are suitable for money that will not be called upon short-term or in an emergency. A five year term will give you a reliable annual or monthly income, payable even in the event of your death.

The minimum purchase varies widely, depending on which company offers the bond. Interest rates paid tend to rise, the larger the investment made. The usual method of interest payment is annually, while monthly payments can be organised but with a lower rate of interest. The availability of these bonds varies considerably in line with changing levels of interest rates. You can buy them direct from the issuing company, but if you use a financial adviser he should know the entire range on offer and hopefully give you the best deal available at that time.

Tax Situation on Guaranteed Bonds:

i) there is no tax liability on the income paid to basic rate taxpayers

ii) higher rate taxpayers will face an additional tax payment

iii) non-taxpayers cannot claim a tax refund, so these bonds are not suitable for them.

Purchase Life Annuities

Consider increasing your monthly income with a purchase life annuity. As with all annuities, these can be purchased with a lump sum and the older you are when you buy it, the higher return you get. Once purchased, however, although the income continues until death, your capital is totally lost. Think through the consequences carefully before you act. Purchase life annuities differ from the compulsory annuities that are bought with a pension fund on retirement because with a purchase life annuity, part of the income is regarded as a return of your capital and is therefore free of tax.

There is a wide range of variations:

1. Income can be level or on an escalating basis.
2. They can be on a single or joint life.
3. Interest can be paid monthly, half-yearly or annually.

Once the conditions are arranged no alterations at all in the initial deal are possible and no money is refundable. Therefore, discuss the purchase in advance with members of your family or take professional advice. As with all annuities, interest rates rise or fall in line with medium-term gilt-edged stocks and throughout the 1990s as yields on these bonds have fallen, so have annuity rates.

Many leading insurance companies provide purchase life annuities and there are a number of specialist firms who will find the best deal on the market for you.

Specialist companies for arranging annuities are given on page 185.

'Personally, I have been in a constant financial crisis. What difference does it make for me if there is now one in Moscow?'

Lera, vegetable seller in Nizhny Novgorod, *Financial Times* August 17 1998

Forced Early Surrender of With-Profits Endowment Policies

A strong second-hand market has grown up during the 1990s to sell these policies to investors who want an investment return less volatile than holding equities directly. These policies are therefore more valuable to sell on directly to other investors to continue them to maturity than to surrender them back to the providing company. The policies must be in force. That is premiums must be up-to-date. Policies are not acceptable if they have lapsed. They should be around three to four years into the term.

> For details on second-hand sales of with-profits endowment policies, contact:
> Neville James, Tel: 01243 520000
> Beale Dobie, Tel: 01621 851113 Fax: 01621 850724
> IPTC, (The Insurance Policy Trading Company)
> Head office Tel: 01483 427575, Fax 01483 418866
> Midlands office Tel: 01952 884422, Fax 01952 884455.

How to Buy Gilts or Corporate Bonds

1. Investigate unit trust gilt or corporate bond funds by sending away for newspaper information.
2. Search for information on the Internet.
3. If you need professional help on buying gilt-edged stock, corporate bonds or fixed-interest funds, seek advice from an independent financial adviser or an accountant.
4. A free guide on investing in gilts is available from the Bank of England's Registrar Department. Tel: 0800 818 614. This guide explains how gilts work, how they are taxed, why prices move and how to buy and sell them.
5. A free 36-page guide to Bonds is available from M&G, Tel: 0800 210 222.

Information on Isas (Individual Savings Accounts) as at August 1998

1. UK residents aged eighteen or over will be able to open an Isa from 6 April 1999. Husbands and wives can each own an Isa. Investments held in an Isa will be completely tax-free. Company shares held within an Isa will receive a 10 per cent tax credit on all the dividends paid into the fund, for the first five years only, until April 2004.
2. There will be no minimum holding period and no minimum investment.
3. Upper limits on amounts put into your Isa are as follows:
    i) £7,000 in year 1 (1999–2000): this includes up to £3,000 in cash.
    ii) £5,000 each year thereafter, for a ten-year term. There will be a review after seven years.
    iii) Investments which are eligible will include: a) a cash element no more than £1,000 per year (£3,000 in the first year) b) life assurance – up to £1,000 each year. Many insurance companies have expressed doubts about being able to provide cost effective life assurance within an Isa c) stocks and shares, including units in collective funds.

iv) Any changes made to the Isa regime will not be implemented until after the initial ten-year term is complete.

Arrangements for Existing Tessas

1. Tax-exempt special savings accounts (Tessas) held on 5 April 1999 will be allowed to run to maturity (a five-year term).
2. Savers can continue subscribing under the existing rules.
3. When the Tessa matures they can transfer the original capital but not the interest earned, into an Isa. This transfer will not affect their normal Isa limits.

Arrangements for Existing Peps

1. Personal equity plans (Peps) held on 5 April 1999 will be allowed to continue in force.
2. After 5 April 1999, no additional cash can be entered into the plan.
3. Dividends on company shares held in the Pep can continue to be added.
4. Peps will enjoy the same tax treatment as ISAs, including the 10 per cent tax credit on dividends until April 2004.

   Full details of the Isa regulations are on the internet at www.open.gov.uk/inrev/isa.doc

> *'Trying to outguess the market in the short term is a punter's game.'*
>
> Mark Dampier, Churchill Investments

Take the Tracker

Tracking the market over the long term by buying units in a tracker fund on a monthly basis inside a tax-free fund, like an Isa, is a good route for novices to start building up a fund of capital.

Advantages

1. Passively managed funds are relatively cheap on charges.
2. Errors of judgement on the part of the managers are eliminated.
3. They remove the uncertainty of picking a poorly performing fund which underperforms the market.
4. During the long 1990s upswing in stock markets, they have performed well.
5. They compare favourably with actively managed funds which have the potential to fluctuate widely and only a small percentage of them outperform the market.
6. Investors avoid the problem of searching for funds that outperform the market.

Disadvantages

1. Some actively managed funds beat the index substantially. A few UK growth

191

funds rose by almost 200 per cent over five years while the FTSE All-Share index rose 120 per cent over the same period. The ten-year record is even better: some active UK growth funds returned over 400 per cent while the FTSE All-Share grew 319 per cent and the FTSE 100 index returned 288 per cent.
2. In a falling market active funds could outsmart the trackers by falling less far.

Pointers for Finding a Good Index-Tracker Fund
Although there is little to choose between trackers in performance terms, there are some useful pointers to finding a good fund:
1. Track the index that suits your investor type:
    i) FTSE All-Share for nervous investors. Covers over 830 companies.
    ii) FTSE 100 for balanced investor types. More risky as it only covers 100 companies.
2. Avoid tracker funds that impose extra fees, such as 6 per cent initial charges, or regular savings charges; £2 a month fee for regular savers is equivalent to a 4 per cent initial charge on a saving of £50 a month.
3. Pick a big fund. Small funds have trouble matching the index performance because dealing costs are large relative to the fund size.
4. Ask unit trust providers for a chart of their tracker fund's performance to check how closely it has followed the index in the past.

The Association of Unit Trusts and Investment Trusts (Autif) publishes a list of all unit trust index-tracker funds with their charges. Tel: 0181 207 1361.

How to Find Information on Collective Funds
1. Read investment journals in the public library or subscribe to:
    i) *Investors Chronicle* which has a weekly funds update listing the one-year and five-year return on funds for the UK, Europe, the US and Asia.
    ii) *Money Observer,* which gives monthly comparisons on a six-month, one-year, three-year and seven-year basis.
2. Cut coupons in the weekend newspapers' financial sections advertising well known fund managers. Phone their freephone numbers or send in the coupons for details of their funds. They will send an investor package of broad-based facts. Ask for the latest half-yearly managers' reports and accounts of individual funds you are interested in, which will give you more information.

'It's not whether you're right or wrong that's important, but how much money you make when you're right and how much you lose when you're wrong.'

George Soros, investment guru

3. Search for fund information on Internet web sites for the main fund managers.

Ways to Deal With a Recession
If you suspect the economy is about to go into recession, rearranging your

192

assets could be a timely move. You should know that the economy is facing problems by articles appearing in the broadsheet newspapers, particularly the *Financial Times*. Television news reports will be pessimistic, highlighting rising unemployment figures, company failures and perhaps increasing bad debt situations across the economy.

Adopt measures to improve your chances of retaining the value of your assets at such times.

Deal with high-interest debts

1. Pay off high-interest debts, including store and credit card debts. Most of these have APRs (annual percentage rates) in excess of 20 per cent.
2. If you cannot repay the whole debt, switch to a card charging a lower rate of interest.
3. Arrange loan insurance cover in case you lose your job and cannot repay these debts. Note that loan insurance often only pays out after twelve months for sickness and redundancy.

Deal with your Mortgage

1. Reduce your mortgage with a lump sum repayment to cut down the size of the monthly repayments due. This will also put you on course to clear the loan earlier than planned.
2. If you have cash on deposit and are not facing financial constraints, think about repaying the entire outstanding mortgage to eliminate the burden of monthly repayments.
3. If you have not previously arranged a discounted mortgage investigate a remortgage package, either with your existing lender or change to another. This may save hundreds of pounds a year. Ask about capped rates, which allow borrowers to benefit from expected falls in interest rates over the next few years, hopefully from 1999 on.
4. Arrange mortgage insurance through mortgage-payment protection policies. Such policies pay for your monthly repayments plus any associated costs, such as home contents and buildings insurance if you are off sick or made redundant. Mortgage insurance only pays out for between twelve and twenty-four months, depending on the level of cover you arrange. If your mortgage was taken out prior to 1 October 1995, you must wait two months before you get any help from the state. Rules applying to mortgages taken out after 1 October 1995 suggest you might have to wait up to nine months for help which will only cover £100,000 of mortgage debt.

Move to a smaller property

If you were planning to move house and now expect house prices to fall, try to sell your house before the recession really begins. Selling houses becomes far more difficult during a recession. After the sale, rent a property and put your cash on deposit until house prices have fallen. You can then buy your smaller property at a lower price while the recession is still affecting the property market.

Rearrange your investment family or portfolio of assets

1. At the approach of recession, interest rates will still be relatively high, as they were at the time of writing, in summer, 1998. Fixed interest bonds, such as gilt-edged stock or good quality corporate bonds, are sensible investments at such times, because their prices will rise as their yields fall once interest rates start falling. If you buy early, before the recession strikes, you lock in the high rate of interest and stand to make a capital gain as prices rise when the recession finally arrives.

To buy gilt-edged stock, corporate bonds or fixed-interest funds, seek advice from an independent financial adviser or an accountant, see page 190.

2. Bonds only offer this good double profits impact, a high return plus capital gain, before the recession takes hold. Then, interest rates have to be cut to try and revive the struggling economy. As interest rates fall, new bond investors will not be attracted to the lower yields on offer and will search elsewhere for better returns. Their favoured investment will be equities (shares), as they begin to anticipate a good economic recovery. When the recession arrives, professional fund managers move out of bonds and into the stock market. Rising demand for shares pushes prices higher and this trend is reinforced by improved company earnings as the recovery finally sets in.

3. Some companies fare less well than others during a recession. Amongst the worst hit will be banks, because they experience rising bad debt problems as customers go bankrupt. Entertainment, retail and leisure companies also suffer as consumers cut back on their spending. Other companies are in what the professionals call 'defensive industries'. Even during a recession, people must still eat, take medicines if they are ill and buy water, gas and electricity.

4. Start regular monthly saving in a tracker or mixed equity-bond fund, to take full advantage of the next upswing when it comes.

'The way to build long-term returns is through preservation of capital and home runs.'
George Soros

Delay big spending decisions

Defer buying large purchases, including carpets, kitchen appliances, expensive luxury items and high technology gadgets. The prices of most expensive goods fall during a recession, so your money goes further by waiting to buy.

STAGE 5: PREPARE FOR LIFE – LONG OR SHORT

Life Assurance

1. To protect dependent children, especially young children from second marriages.

2. A vulnerable spouse on the death of the partner.

3. To cover a debt.

4. To pay an inheritance tax liability.

Types of Protection

Without an Investment Element

1. Level term assurance – lasts for a specified number of years.
    i) single
    ii) joint life, first death (pays out on the first death)
2. Family benefit term assurance – provides an annual income for a specified number of years.
    i) single
    ii) joint life, first death (pays out on the first death)

With an Investment Element

(It will have a surrender value after you have paid in premiums for around two to three years).

3. Whole-of-life assurance – lasts for life.
    i) single
    ii) joint life – can be either first or second death. First death is to provide protection for a surviving spouse. Second death is for inheritance tax planning.
4. Endowment savings policy – a savings policy for a lump sum that runs over a specified number of years.
    i) single
    ii) joint life, first death
5. Pension fund – pays out a lump sum of a fixed size (final salary scheme) or a variable size (personal pensions) on death before retirement.
6. Insurance-based bonds – there is a very small insurance element, usually covering twenty years, or until the bond is cashed in.
    i) single
    ii) joint life, usually second death as it is a savings investment

'If you're worried, channel that energy into research.'

William Eckhardt, trader

How Much Life Assurance Do You Need?

1. Rework your forecast retirement budget from Stage 2 to calculate how

195

much income will be needed each year to cover the loss of a parent for each child under eighteen. This cover is necessary for both father and mother, even if one partner is not employed in work outside the home.

2. Multiply the annual income needed per child by the number of years, until the youngest child reaches eighteen.

3. Add in a yearly income for the spouse left to support the children.

4. If you cannot afford single term life assurance for the amount you need, settle on a compromise:

    i) consider joint life

    ii) a reduced amount for the sum assured

    iii) a savings plan with some life cover protection, e.g. an endowment policy.

Long-Term Care 'Means Test' Regulations

1. Above £16,000 in assets there will be no financial help from the state. The £16,000 level may or may not include your home, depending on:

    i) where in the country you live

    ii) if you have other dependents over sixty living in your home

    iii) if you have given away your home in order to qualify for state funding in an area where this is disallowed.

2. Below £10,000 in assets you are eligible for full help, but may not receive it, if the council in your area operates a waiting list for entry into a home.

3. For people with assets between £16,000 and £10,000 in value, a sliding scale operates but may not apply in the area where you live. You may be forced to use your own savings, even if they fall below the statutory level.

'Life expectancy in the UK has increased by up to fifteen years since the second world war. But this has not been matched by an equivalent increase in healthspan. Up to eleven of the extra years are years of illness and disability.'

Dr Game, head of genetics and biochemistry at the Biotechnology and Biological Sciences Research Council

Sources to turn to for help

1. For a free guide to long-term care call Help the Aged on 0171 253 0253.

2. IFACare Administration, Bridge House, Severn Bridge, Bewdley, Worcester DY12 1AB, is a group of independent advisers offering expert help with financial and legal aspects of LTC. Tel: 01299 405 285.

3. Age Concern publishes leaflets on residential and nursing homes. Astral House, 1268 London Road, London SW16 4ER Tel: 0181 679 8000.

STAGE 6: PASS DOWN YOUR NEST EGGS

Use a solicitor for:
1. Making your will.
2. Storing a copy of your will.
3. Setting up trusts.
4. Helping you reduce an inheritance tax liability.
5. Acting as an executor for your estate.
6. Preparing an enduring power of attorney.
7. Any other points of law arising on your financial affairs.

Steps to Take when a Close Relative Dies
1. Establish whether there is a will.
2. Identify who the executors are.
3. The executors must compile a list of all the deceased's assets and liabilities and value each item. This may involve writing to insurance companies to notify them of the death and request up-to-date information.
4. All property and personal possessions must be included in the list.
5. No assets can be realised until any inheritance tax is paid and probate is granted. Therefore, check if a loan may be required to pay the tax.
6. If inheritance tax is a possibility, the fine detail of assets and liabilities must be submitted to the Inland Revenue's capital taxes office.
7. All estates valued at over £5,000 require probate. Obtain the probate document from the local probate registrar. The address can be obtained from the Citizen's Advice Bureau, the local library, or the telephone directory.
8. Complete the forms and return to the probate office. The executor must attend a meeting with the registrar to swear that all the details are correct. Which? produces a guide to wills and probate. Tel: 0800 920 126.

The Costs of Administering an Estate
If possible, small estates should be administered by family members or close friends as professional administrators charge high fees for this service. Some banks level a fee of around 5 per cent on the first £10,000 with a descending scale for the remainder of the estate. For an estate of £100,000, the main high street banks charge around £3,800 to £5,000. Family solicitors often make smaller charges; an estate of £150,000 might cost £1,250 to £1,300. You can negotiate with a family solicitor. He might reduce the final fee if you discuss this with him. Professional advice also incurs VAT added to fees charged.

Check List for Making Your Will

1. Are you happy to use a standard proprietary form?
Yes: Follow the instructions carefully to ensure your will is not rendered invalid through accident or oversight. Go to next item on updating your will. (Page 199)
No: Use a solicitor. Go to 2.

2. Do you have a family solicitor?
Yes: Go to 4.
No: Go to 3.

3. To find a solicitor:
i) ask friends or colleagues for a recommendation, or
ii) phone the Law Society for a list of solicitors in your area or town. Tel: 0171 242 1222. Go to 4.

4. Do you have children under eighteen?
Yes: Go to 5.
No: Go to 7.

5. Do you need to appoint guardians to care for your children if you and your spouse both die before they reach eighteen?
Yes: Discuss appointing guardians with your spouse, with the person you want to appoint, and then with your solicitor. Go to 6.
No: Go to 7.

6. Do you need to appoint trustees to care for your children's assets if you and your spouse both die before they reach eighteen?
Yes: Discuss appointing trustees if they are to manage a trust for minors. Go to 7.
No: Go to 7.

7. Discuss appointing executors to manage your estate, first with your spouse, with the person you want to appoint and then with your solicitor. Go to 8.

8. Are your affairs complicated or do you think you will have an inheritance tax problem?
Yes: Go to 9.
No: Go to 10.

9. Prepare a list of your valuables, your net worth, plus all your personal and household effects so you can discuss inheritance tax planning with your solicitor if necessary. Go to 10.

10. If you hold some assets jointly with your partner, have you got authority to sign documents on their behalf?
Yes: Go to next item on updating your will.
No: Ask your accountant to arrange an enduring power of attorney that will covers both partners.

Keep Your Will Updated
1. Store it in a safe place.
2. Leave a copy with your solicitor.
3. Make sure guardians, executors and trustees are still alive and willing to act.
4. Update your will whenever there is a major event in your situation such as: i) marriage or divorce ii) going abroad for a period, perhaps to work iii) going into hospital.
5. Update your finances before going on holiday or into hospital so your affairs are in order.
6. Keep a letter outlining the important names, addresses and telephone numbers in a safe place.
7. Leave safety box and other important keys with these letters.

> *'The time of maximum pessimism is the best time to buy, and the time of maximum optimism is the best time to sell.'*
>
> Sir John Templeton

The Value of Trusts

If you think you may face an inheritance tax liability or have complicated financial affairs, setting up a trust to pass assets on to your heirs can be applicable. Discuss your financial situation with a solicitor before completing your will as some of the suggestions he makes should be incorporated in it. Employing a specialist lawyer will be expensive, but his advice may save you money on your tax bill and hopefully will avoid complications when the trust is activated.
1. Consult a specialist lawyer, well versed in inheritance tax planning. Ask your solicitor to recommend a specialist.
2. Ensure the trustees you appoint are willing to act and can be relied on to carry out your wishes.
3. Family members or close friends can act as trustees if they have the time and ability.
4. Some trusts can be run by you personally, during your lifetime, if they are for the benefit of under-age beneficiaries, such as grandchildren.
5. Professional trustees may take large fees out of the trust money, impairing its

199

investment performance. If you appoint a family solicitor, ensure you can make replacements if necessary.

6. Ensure you can appoint or dismiss trustees, if they are not doing the job as you wished.

7. Restrict the number of trustees to two or three – too many trustees create complications and disagreements.

8. Avoid using 'majority rules' for decision-making. They can create administrative difficulties.

9. Check all the rules and provisions listed in your trust before you sign. Once it takes effect if can be problematic, even impossible to change.

10. Lay down the investment policy your trustees are to follow, so that there is no confusion and less cause for subsequent disputes.

11. Financial adviser Towry Law has produced a free guide to tax saving trusts designed for investors who want to use a trust for tax or financial planning. Tel: 0345 868 244.

Update your Will

Once your will is made, take the following actions:

1. Keep it in a safe place.

2. Notify the guardians, executors and trustees you appointed so they know where it is.

3. File a copy with your bank or solicitor.

4. Write a letter outlining important aspects of your financial affairs including:
   i) Names, addresses and telephone numbers of your: a) boss b) bank c) solicitor d) business partners e) agent f) stockbroker g) financial adviser h) auctioneer – if you have antiques that might need to be sold.
   ii) Details of funeral arrangements.
   iii) The place where important keys or policy documents are kept.
   iv) The up-to-date picture of your investment family, including details of your: a) bank accounts b) national savings accounts c) other accounts d) documents relating to unit or investment trusts e) documents relating to all life policies, savings policies and pension funds f) details about your share portfolio, if any, including share certificates or nominee accounts.

5. Change your will as circumstances change, including:
   i) On divorce.
   ii) On a forthcoming wedding.
   iii) If you come into a large legacy.

6. Update your will whenever necessary (or at least once every ten years) i.e.
   i) Before you go on holiday.
   ii) Before you go into hospital for an operation.
   iii) When a guardian, executor or trustee moves, dies or decides he/she is no longer willing to act on your behalf.

iv) If a beneficiary to your estate dies before you.

Lifetime Gifts Exempt from Tax – Applicable before 5 April 1999

Each year everyone is allowed an annual exemption of £3,000 against capital gifts. If you do not take advantage of this annual exemption, it remains available to carry forward but this applies for the next twelve months only.

The following additional items are exempt from tax:

1. Small gifts to any one person per year, up to the value of £250.
2. Expenditure out of income:
   i) It must be regular.
   ii) It must leave you with enough income 'after tax' to maintain your normal standard of living e.g. monthly payments to an adult child who is not working or monthly premiums to a life or savings policy written in trust, but only if it falls within the normal expenditure rules. Otherwise it will be treated as a gift.
3. Gifts on marriage:
   i) £5,000 from a parent.
   ii) £2,500 from a grandparent.
   iii) £1,000 from anyone else.
4. Gifts to charities are unlimited.
5. Gifts to political parties with two current sitting Members of Parliament are unlimited.
6. Gifts for the public's benefit or for national purposes are unlimited.

Keep lists of all the lifetime gifts you make and leave these with your financial documents as they will be needed by the executor of your estate.

Ways to Avoid or Reduce Inheritance Tax

1. Write an effective will.
2. Equalise your assets.
3. Use trusts to take life policies and pension funds out of the estate of the policyholder.
4. Gift possessions up to the value of the nil-rate band to your children or kin, other than your spouse.
5. Make use of lifetime gifts.
6. Take out whole-of-life assurance policies that pay out on the second death. Write these in trust for your beneficiaries so they do not form part of your estate, or that of your spouse.

Final Thought!
Avoid inheritance tax by donating your assets to your favourite charity!

*'Retiring from dentistry at sixty was the best career move
I ever made.'*

My friend from college days, reflecting recently on his retirement

Glossary of Terms

Active fund manager: one who runs an actively managed fund and who aims to out-perform the market.

Actuary: the professional who calculates annuity rates.

Additional voluntary contributions (AVCs): additional payments paid into company pension schemes by members.

Administrator: a personal representative appointed to administer the estate of a deceased person.

Advance corporation tax: tax paid on dividends by a company to the Inland Revenue on behalf of the shareholder.

Analysts: professionals who work for the big brokerage and merchant banking houses whose job it is to analyse and report on national economies, individual companies and various sectors of a stock market.

Annuity: a form of income, guaranteed and fixed for life, which is bought through insurance companies with an accumulated pension fund.

Annuity rate: the rate applying when an annuity is purchased.

Annual bonus: a lump sum added to a policy every year it is in force, which cannot be taken away once it has been allocated.

Assets: physical and intangible goods (like goodwill) that a person or a company owns.

Auditor: an outside accountant employed to make routine checks on a business to ensure the company's accounts are being kept properly.

Balance sheet: the statement of the capital position of a company at any one time. It shows what it owns (assets) and what it owes (its liabilities).

Bear and **bull markets:** a bear market is one where prices are falling, usually across the whole market for a prolonged period of weeks, months or even years. A bull market is one with a rising trend. Investors who think the market is about to fall are bearish while those who think the market will rise are bullish.

Bearer bonds: a bond or share whose ownership is not registered. Therefore possession is considered to be proof of ownership.

Beneficiary: a person who inherits a bequest or gift made under a will.

Bequest: a gift to a beneficiary made under a will.

Blue chip: shares in a very large, well established and highly regarded company. It is named after the highest value chip in poker.

Bonds: a bond is a certificate of debt issued by companies and governments to raise cash. It usually pays interest and can be traded in a market. A bond is longer term than a bill. It is a fixed interest loan which guarantees to pay the capital at an agreed future date. UK Government bonds are known as gilts or gilt-edged securities because in the nineteenth century, when Britain was the centre of a thriving wealthy empire, they were considered 'as good as gold'. There are several time periods for UK gilts: short (under five years to maturity), mediums (between five and fifteen years) and longs (which mature after fifteen years).

Bonus: additional sums of money added at regular intervals, usually of one year, to a savings policy. Once added, the annual bonus cannot be taken away.

Brokers: professionals who buy and sell on behalf of their clients. They are sometimes called intermediaries.

Capital: an amount of money, a lump sum, that can be invested in assets or is available to invest.

Capital gains (or growth): the increase in the capital value of investments.

Capital Gains Tax: this is a complicated form of government taxation, payable on profits above a set level, from the sale of assets or investments, particularly shares.

Capital secure: a term used to denote capital which is safeguarded from the volatility that affects equity-based investments.

Capital transfers: assets passed on to someone other than a spouse which are subject to inheritance tax.

Cash flow: the amount of money that flows into and out of a business. The difference between the two is the important number. Cash positive – more money flows in than out. Cash negative – more money flows out than in.

Collective funds: any scheme where investors pool their resources to spread their investment risks. Popular forms of collective funds include unit and investment trusts in Britain and mutual funds in America.

Commutation of a pension: a government concession to take a certain tax-free lump sum out of an accumulated pension fund.

Compound growth: method of growth in which the interest is added back to the capital at each stage to increase the total.

Consols: non-redeemable, i.e. open-ended, gilt-edged stock. It has no maturity date.

Corporate bond: a fixed interest loan raised by a company which guarantees to repay the capital on an agreed future date.

Credit: credit is given by banks when they advance loans to their customers, and businesses when they allow their customers to take goods and defer payment for them.

Creditors: companies or individuals to whom you owe money.

Defined benefits: see **Final Salary Pension** schemes.

Defined contribution scheme: or money purchase scheme, the contributions go into a pot whose growth depends upon the investment performance of the fund; the fund is then used to purchase an annuity.

Deflation: the opposite of inflation; when general prices in the economy are falling.

Depreciation: the loss in value of an asset with time or through usage.

Direct pension provider: a company offering pension information directly over the telephone to enable you to set up your plan without using an intermediary.

Dividend: this is the proportion of a company's profits or earnings which is paid out to its shareholders as a distribution twice yearly, as an interim and a final dividend.

Dividend yield: the ratio between the dividend and the price actually paid for the share.

Economic cycle: this is a round of economic events that proceed in an irregular succession.

Endowment policy: a life insurance and savings policy which pays a specified amount of money on an agreed date (**the maturity date**) or on the death of the person insured, whichever is the sooner.

Endowment mortgage: a mortgage linked to an endowment policy where the policy matures at the end of the mortgage term. It is designed to be large enough to completely pay off the mortgage.

Equalisation of assets: a process by which spouses can share out their assets equally, to avoid paying large amounts of inheritance tax.

Equity: commonly used to mean the **ordinary shares** of a company. They are freely traded stocks and shares in publicly quoted companies that do not carry a fixed rate of interest; instead they entitle their holders to a share in the growth of the company through an annual dividend payment. The equity holders are the company's owners.

Estate: the name given to one's assets, i.e. all property, valuables and household effects, owned at the time of death.

Execution–only services: even if you have done the research and know what you want to buy, you still have to use a financial intermediary, but the purchase should be cheaper because the adviser does less work.

Executor: a person appointed to administer someone's estate after their death. It is usual for the person making a will to nominate two executors to carry out this duty.

Family income benefit: term assurance over a fixed period that pays out a regular income on death until the term expires.

Final Salary Pension schemes: also called **defined benefits**. Here the level of the benefits is guaranteed, regardless of the performance of the funds.

Fixed interest investment: pays a certain amount of interest until maturity.

Flotation: a new issue of shares available to the public that occurs when a private company comes to the market and sells a percentage of its shares to whoever wants to buy them.

Free-standing AVCs: are sold by insurance companies other than the company running the main pension scheme. They carry higher costs than internally-run AVCs.

FTSE 100 index: monitors the performance of the top 100 publicly quoted companies by market capitalisation (market value) on the UK stock market. It is weighted to take account of the largest and smallest sized companies within the hundred and is updated throughout the day. The initials stand for Financial Times Stock Exchange; a joint venture between the Financial Times newspaper and the London Stock Exchange.

FTSE 250: this index works in a similar way. It monitors the performance of 250 medium-sized companies that together comprise this index.

FTSE 350: this index covers the performance of the FTSE 100 and FTSE 250 shares. All three indices are updated continuously throughout the working day.

FTSE Small Cap: an index that covers a range of the small companies traded on the UK stock market.

FTSE All–Share index: covers about 830 shares on the UK market. It is updated at the start of every working day.

Funded pensions: are investment linked.

Gearing: the relationship between the size of the borrower's initial debt and the lender's initial share of an asset on which a loan is outstanding. High gearing means high borrowing relative to a person's contribution to the value of the asset.

Gilt-edged bonds: British government loans which carry a fixed interest.

Gilt-edged investment funds: a managed fund that only invests in gilt-edged stocks.

Gross: the interest or dividends for investors, which is paid before deduction of income tax.

Gross Domestic Product (GDP): the amount of goods and services produced by a country in one year.

Guardian: someone appointed to look after a minor under the age of eighteen.

Home income plan: an insurance-based product which provides income for elderly couples by utilising some of the equity tied up in their property.

Illiquid assets: assets or securities which are not easily transferable into cash.

Immediate care annuity: an annuity which is specifically designed to provide a regular income to pay for long-term care.

Impaired life annuity: an annuity with a higher than normal income for people whose life expectancy is diminished.

Income: money you earn or receive from a regular and reliable source.

Income fund: a unit trust that concentrates on companies which pay out relatively large dividends to provide an income.

Independent Financial adviser: one who is not tied to any particular company and who is legally obliged to give 'best advice' when making recommendations.

Index: a selected list of publicly quoted shares which represent all others of that type.

Indexation: system by which the value of securities and/or interest payments are linked to inflation, particularly index-linked gilts, annuities or National Savings products.

Individual savings account: (Isa) a new tax-exempt savings scheme due to be introduced in April 1999.

Inflation: a percentage measure of the amount by which the prices of goods and services rise in the economy, over a period of time, usually one year.

Inheritance tax: payable on death if your estate is above a statutory sum.

Institutions: usually financial institutions, the pensions and insurance companies in the UK. They handle huge sums of money on behalf of their clients, the policy holders and investors.

Integrated company pension scheme: a company pension scheme which factors in the state pension. It doesn't grow as much as a final salary company scheme.

Interest: a regular payment made usually twice yearly to savers who keep their money in deposit accounts with building societies or banks or who buy government or corporate bonds.

Interest only mortgage: the amount of the loan stays the same throughout the duration of the mortgage with payments of interest due plus payments into a savings plan. The intention is that the savings plan will grow in size sufficiently to repay the entire mortgage at the end of the period.

Intestacy laws: laws that come into effect to deal with a person who dies intestate.

Intestate: dying without making a valid will.

Investing: putting money into real financial assets with the hope of increasing the size of the original **investment** through future growth at the same time as receiving a regular and rising income.

Investment bonds: an equity-based investment issued by an insurance company.

Investment trust: a company which is quoted on the stock exchange and exists to invest in the equity of other companies. It is used by large institutions and also small investors to gain a wide spread of investments.

Isa: individual savings account with tax advantages, due to replace Peps (see page 209) and Tessas (see page 211).

Joint mortgage protection policy: a life assurance policy on both signatories to a mortgage designed to be paid out on the first death so as to fully repay the debt during the term.

Key features document: companies are required by law to provide prospective policyholders with a document explaining the key features of the policy before they sign the policy contract.

Legacy: a gift made under a will.

Liabilities: an amount of money owed to other people, a debt.

Liquid: a market for a financial commodity where there are many buyers and sellers so that it is easy to deal. Investors who hold cash are said to be **liquid**, as cash is the easiest commodity to use for buying any other asset.

Managed fund: broadly based investment fund run by a professional manager in a pension or insurance company or in an investment group.

Market capitalisation: a company's total value, that is, the number of its shares in issue multiplied by the share price at any one time.

Money purchase pension scheme: the individual contributes to the pension plan with or without additional contributions from the employer. The size of the final fund depends upon the performance of the funds. These schemes are also called **defined contribution schemes**.

Mortgage protection policy: life assurance policy which pays out on the death of the mortgage holder.

Mutual: a form of company structure where the members (usually borrowers, savers or policy holders) own all the assets of the company. It applies to building societies and some insurance companies, such as Scottish Widows and Equitable Life.

Mutual funds: the American version of British unit trusts.

National Savings: low-risk savings schemes run by the UK government.

Negative equity: the difference between the initial price paid for a property and its current value if the latter is lower.

Net worth: the value of your assets after deducting the full extent of all your debts (liabilities).

Nikkei index: bench mark index for the Japanese stock market.

Nil-rate band: the statutory limit below which no inheritance tax is payable.

Nominal value: the numerical value of an item, ignoring the impact of inflation.

Non-redeemable gilts: gilts without a maturity date.

Open market option: a scheme for an annuitant to purchase his annuity in the open market, not just from the company with which he built up his pension fund.

Ordinary shares: the commonest form of shares in a company; the holders own the company and receive dividends in accordance with its profitability.

Ordinary shareholders' funds: the money belonging to the ordinary shareholders in a publicly quoted company.

Paid up: a policy is made paid up when the policyholder decides to cease paying further premiums but leaves the accumulated fund in his policy to continue growing. This is a better option than surrendering the policy early because the policyholder cannot afford to continue paying the premiums. Surrender values may be low but if the paid up fund stays with the company to maturity, it will continue to grow and surrender penalties will be avoided.

Pension: a savings scheme whereby the contributions create a fund which from a specified date will return an income to the saver. Although contributions are generally tax exempt, tax will have to be paid on the eventual income derived from the fund.

Pep: Personal equity plan, a government sponsored scheme for investing up to £9,000 each year with income and capital gains free of tax. The £9,000 is split into £6,000 for a general Pep, which can be invested in mainly UK-based units or investment trusts or directly into shares, and £3,000 which must be invested in a single company Pep in which you can hold the shares of only one UK company at a time. New Peps were phased out in April 1999.

Personal pension: one in which there is a direct contract between the saver and the pension company.

Probate: the process of proving a will.

Profits: the amount of cash left in a business after deducting all the expenses from the revenues earned.

Premium: prices of the asset such as an investment trust, are selling at a level above its intrinsic value.

Permanent Health Insurance policy: pays out a regular income replacement if the policyholder is unable to work through ill-health.

Publicly quoted companies: companies that are listed on a national stock market.

Purchase life annuity: can be purchased by anyone with disposable cash, not simply by those buying pensions annuities.

Purchasing power: the amount of goods and services you can buy with your money at any time.

Real . . . : after taking account of inflation.

Real assets: assets which hold or increase their value over time, in spite of inflation.

Real financial assets: assets in financial investments that tend to hold or even increase their value over time, in spite of inflation.

Real growth: Growth after deducting for inflation.

Real rate of return: the capital growth plus income earned on an asset after deducting for inflation.

Recession: a downturn in activity across the economy which lasts for at least six months.

Repayment mortgage: the capital owing and the interest on it are paid off throughout the period of the loan. Therefore, at the end of the term, the entire debt will have been repaid.

Reserves: money put aside out of the profits of a company to build up the internal resources the company holds for future use, including expansion.

Retail prices index: the official measure of inflation in the economy. It is calculated by weighting the cost of goods and services to approximate to a typical family's spending patterns.

Retirement annuity plans: an early form of pension superseded in 1988 by personal pension plans.

Risk: this word has various interpretations. Broadly, it is the amount of money which an investor stands to lose from any investment.

Saving: putting aside a sum of money for future use.

Second mortgage: a legal contract with the same or a different mortgage provider to obtain further cash on a property. Usually carries a higher rate of interest. Positive equity needs to be still locked up in the property to be able to obtain a second mortgage.

Securities: tradable financial products, such as shares or bonds.

State earnings–related pension scheme (Serps): a state pension in addition to the basic state pension, plus widow's benefits and invalidity benefits, based on earnings.

Self invested personal pension (Sipp): a pension for the self-employed or for certain employees who make their own investment decisions within the plan.

Shares: part ownership of a business or company.

Sheltered accommodation: a group of warden-controlled properties for elderly or disadvantaged people.

Single premium pension: a pension policy made with a single lump sum.

Stockbroker: see also **Broker**; stockbrokers are professionals who buy and sell shares on behalf of their clients. Private individuals and institutions are not allowed to deal in shares directly with the market makers, who are the people that set the prices. Stockbrokers act as intermediaries between buyers and sellers.

Stock market: the market for equities, or shares, in public companies. In London called the **Stock Exchange**. A buyer is actually purchasing a share in the ownership of a company.

Sum assured: the amount of money insured under a life policy.

Superannuation: a government run pension scheme for state employees, such as teachers, nurses, civil servants, MPs. etc.

Surrender: when an insurance policy is handed back to the company in return for a sum of money.

Surrender value: a policy is given a value by the insurance company which assumes that the policy will run to maturity. The surrender value will be lower because before paying out, the company deducts all the costs that would have accrued if the policy had run to maturity.

Takeover: arrangement whereby the managers of a company offer to buy out the shareholders of another company.

Terminal bonus: a final sum of money added to a policy on maturity as part of the total payout. It is not guaranteed and therefore is variable.

Term assurance: life assurance which only lasts for a fixed period of time.

Tessa: Tax exempt special savings account, a government sponsored scheme for investing up to a total of £9,000 over a period of five years with interest paid free of tax.

Tied agent: a financial adviser who works for a single company and is legally bound to offer advice regarding only that company's products. He cannot therefore offer impartial advice over the whole field of financial products.

Total Return: the addition of the capital growth plus the dividend income received on an investment in real financial assets.

Tracker fund: a fund designed to follow some stockmarket index by investing in a range of shares which represent that index.

Trust: a legal document or part of a will stipulating how the estate or part of it should be administered.

Trustee: a person appointed to administer a trust.

UK growth and income trusts: forms of unit trust which invest in companies quoted on the London Stock Exchange which will give investors exposure to either a high rate of growth or a high annual dividend.

Unearned income: income derived from assets, not work.

Unfunded pension: today's workers pay the state pensions of today's pensioners through their taxes.

Unit–linked annuities: an annuity that is linked to units in a pension fund, so that the pension payments rise or fall with the value of the fund.

Unit trusts: a form of investment where investors' money is pooled in order to purchase a spread of shares to spread the risk. This enables each investor to have exposure to a larger range of companies than individual resources alone might allow.

United–linked policy: an insurance or pension policy in which the benefits depend on the performance of units in a fund invested in shares, property or fixed interest investments.

Volatility: a measure of the frequency with which share prices move up or down.

Value–added tax (VAT): a form of indirect taxation borne by traders and consumers. It is levied on goods and services. If a business has more than a certain level of annual turnover it has to be **registered for VAT** with the Customs and Excise.

Variable rates of interest: the rates of interest vary, according to the general levels of interest applying in the economy.

War loan: a non-redeemable gilt-edged stock. It has no maturity date.

Wasting assets: assets whose value declines over time, and with use.

Whole-of-life assurance: life assurance that continues throughout your life, as long as you continue paying the premiums.

Will: a formal legal statement of a person's wishes as to the disposal of their assets after their death; literally a 'willing' of assets.

With-profits annuity: an annuity linked to stock market performance so the resultant income is not guaranteed as it fluctuates with the markets.

With-profits policy: a life insurance or pension policy with additional amounts added at regular intervals to the sums insured. The additions take the form of bonuses, annual and terminal.

Yield: the annual rate of return on a share or a bond which the investor would earn from that security at the current market price.

Suggested Reading

The first group of books provide a gentle introduction to the broad topics of finance in general and investing in particular. It covers a wide range of views and investment approaches. The novice investor can tackle any or all of these as an introduction. They are listed in alphabetical order for easy access, but there is no preferred reading order.

The Beardstown Ladies, *The Beardstown Ladies Common-Sense Investment Guide,* Hyperion, 1994.

Blakey, George, *The Post-War History of the London Stock Exchange 1945–1992*, Mercury, 1993.

Drury, Tony, *Investment Clubs, the low-risk way to stockmarket profits,* Rushmere Wynne, 1995.

Lefevre, Edwin, *Reminiscences of a Stock Operator,* John Wiley & Sons, 1993.

Rogers, Jim, *Investment Biker, Around the World With Jim Rogers,* John Wiley & Sons, 1995.

Schwager, Jack, *Market Wizards,* Harper & Row, 1990.

The Money Maze (Orion Business, 1998) was my previous book and is intended for those who claim to be 'hopeless with money'. It leads you clearly and simply through the maze of money management, enabling you to learn the skills necessary to give you confidence in handling your money problems.

The Edge of Chaos (John Wiley & Sons, 1997) is my guide to the history of the greatest stockmarket crashes. It draws together in one account the concepts of the new science of chaos, and how investors can benefit from an increased knowledge of its application to the stock markets.

★ ★ ★ ★

Every investor needs one 'guide book' which explains all the jargon of investing in simple terms. This book serves as an ideal reference for all the complicated terms investing contains. It can be acquired after some of the introductory books have been read.

There are two excellent primers I use and highly recommend:

Gray, Bernard, *Investors Chronicle Beginners Guide to Investment*, Business Books Ltd., London 1991.

Slater, Jim, *Investment Made Easy*, Orion Business, 1994.

My book *The Armchair Investor* is a step-by-step, hands-on guide to the basic essentials that everyone needs to successfully invest in the stock market, and it will help you to become your own best financial adviser. It is published by Orion Business.

★   ★   ★   ★

The list below includes another wide range of books for people who have already acquired some knowledge or have direct investment experience. Most of these books deal in much greater depth with various aspects of investing, especially the stock-picking routines, managing a portfolio and learning about the markets in general.

Hagstrom, Robert Jnr., *The Warren Buffett Way*, John Wiley and Sons, 1994.

Linton, David, *Profit From Your PC, How to use a personal computer to buy and sell shares*, Rushmere Wynne, 1995, and an updated version, *More Profit from your PC*, 1996.

Lynch, Peter, *One Up On Wall Street*, Simon and Schuster, 1989.

Lynch, Peter, *Beating the Street*, Simon and Schuster, 1993.

O'Neil, William, *How To Make Money In Stocks, A Winning System in Good Times or Bad*, McGraw-Hill Inc., 1988.

Schwartz, David, *Schwartz Stock Market Handbook*, Burleigh Publishing Co., 1996.

Slater, Jim, *The Zulu Principle, Making Extraordinary Profits from Ordinary Shares*, Orion Business, 1992.

Slater, Jim, *Pep Up Your Wealth, How to Save Tax and Make Your Money Grow*, Orion Business, 1994.

Vintcent, Charles, *The Investor's Guide, Be Your Own Stockbroker, The Secrets of Managing Your Own Investments*, Pitman Publishing, 1995.

Weinstein, Stan, *Stan Weinstein's Secrets for Profiting in Bull and Bear Markets*, Dow Jones-Irwin, 1988.

NEWSLETTERS AND JOURNALS

Analyst, 5–9 Sun Street, London EC2B 2GU.

The Estimate Directory, Edinburgh Financial Publishing Ltd., 16 Randolph Crescent, Edinburgh EH3 7TT.

Equity Focus, Reuters Ltd, 85 Fleet Street, London EC4P 4AJ.

Financial Times, Number One Southwark Bridge, London SE1 9HL.

The Inside Track, 16 Randolph Crescent, Edinburgh EH3 7TT.

Investors Chronicle, Greystoke Place, Fetter Lane, London EC4 1ND.

Money Observer, Garrard House, 2/6 Homesdale Road, Bromley BR2 9WL or *Money Observer,* FREEPOST NB 2019, Bromley, BR2 9BR.

Company REFS, (Company Really Essential Financial Statistics), Hemmington Scott Publishing Ltd, City Innovation Centre, 26031 Whiskin Street, London EC1R 0BP.

Quantum Leap, Stockmarket Letter, and Chart Breakout, both by Quentin Lumsden, PO Box 1638, London W8 4QR.

Sharewatch, Equitylink Ltd, 75 High Street, Chislehurst, Kent BR7 5AG.

Techinvest, 31 Upper Mount Street, Dublin 2, Ireland.

SYSTEMS

I cannot advise you on hardware as there is such a choice. I suggest you seek advice from your software supplier. There are a number of software packages and systems now available, which provide a variety of share price information, portfolio management or technical analysis. The ones I have experience of using are

FT Cityline, 4th Floor, Number One Southwark Bridge, London SE1 9HL. Tel: 0171 873 4378.

Market Eye, ICV Ltd, 23 College Hill, Cannon Street, London EC4R 2RA.

Synergy Software, Britannic House, 20 Dunstable Road, Luton LU1 1ED.

Updata Software, Updata House, Old York Road, London SW18 1TG.

WEB PAGES TO TRY

Financial Times http://www.FT.com

Hemington Scott (excellent free information from publishers of REFS) http://www.hemscott.com

Electronic Share Information http://www.esi.co.uk

Updata http://www.updata.co.uk

Finally, look out for the Mrs Cohen web site at http://www.mrscohen.com

Index